Zhuri's Fight

Zay Cummings
Book cover art by: Osman Kamason and Ibeamaka Ubiomo

All rights reserved by Zay Cummings. This book or any portion thereof may not be reproduced or used in any manner whatsoever without the expressed written permission of the publisher except for the use of brief quotations in a book review.

ISBN: 978-0-578-94100-4

Distributed by Power Of Purpose Publishing

Www.PopPublishing.com

Atlanta, Ga. 30326

All rights owned and reserved by Zay Cummings

DEDICATION

For my parents, Alimamy and Kadijatu Kamara whose true grit of sacrifice, courage and character buoyed five children into adulthood and made them all think they are capable of doing great things.

For my late teacher, Mr David Biala Douganson whose passion for teaching and love of writing infected me like an active virus. I had no choice , but to succumb.

For my absolutely magnificent children, Kai, Tunji, Benjamin and Ella. Oh, how much I love you all. You inspire me to be better and do better every day of my life. My love for you is so deep.

For my bonus daughter, Jada, whose presence in my life has only made it sweeter. You brought clarity and so much light. I love you.

For the late Senegalese Author and feminist, Mariama Ba whose influence still resonates far beyond the grave. You, Madame, remain my hero.

TABLE OF CONTENTS

AUGUST 02, 1979	3
YOUNG LOVES	19
ST EDWARD'S	34
THE RETURN OF OLIVER	39
VISA INTERVIEW	50
WEDDING	53
COMING TO AMERICA	61
HOUSE WIFE	69
PREGNANT	77
MOTHER	85
POSTPARTUM BLUES	95
MOTHER-IN-LAW	100
SHAREEF AND SAAMI	110
SURPRISE FORTIETH BIRTHDAY PARTY	116
INFIDELITY	125
FREETOWN	135
TEN YEAR ANNIVERSARY	143
LEAVING HUMBOLDT	153
BLINDSIDED	158
DON'T KILL MY MOM	167
AMERICAN EMBASSY	176
GLIMMER OF HOPE	184
POLICE REPORT	195
NO WORD	206
ESCAPE	209
PROFESSOR NAMBUYA	223
KEZA	231
ESCAPE	235

PREFACE

With a four-year-old whose feet resembled the remnants of a rodent's supper, to a five-year-old who was feeble and emaciated from the early symptoms of malaria, to a petrified ten-year-old who was emotionally and psychologically wrecked by the trauma of domestic abuse they had all witnessed, I had all three clinging to me for dear life. We had all escaped from the immediate physical grip of their father, but we were still stranded in neighboring Guinea, not very far from Sierra Leone where we had escaped from. Penniless and with very little grasp of the language in Guinea, we were panic-stricken, frightened to death that he might come after us. We imagined the worst possibilities: what if someone had told him of our whereabouts? What if he crosses the border himself and unleashes his paid informants to look around for us? Should I stay indoors or go outside to look for medication for my five-year-old son, Shareef, whose fever had become unrelenting? He was restless, his eyes sunken and could barely speak audibly. I was filled with fear and regret. He was laying his head on my body as I stroked it rhythmically. I could feel the heat emanating from his body. If only I had listened to my ten year old son, Sankara. Sany, as we called him for short, had hated the idea of leaving his home in Tennessee. He had been depressed and had cried many times, begging me not to take him away from his friends. At that moment, I felt like I had failed him. And so, even though I was terrified, completely petrified of being discovered, I knew I had to venture out. My son's life depended on it. Him dying would be the worst outcome, a nightmare I would never forgive myself for. So even though I was shaking like I was having a seizure, my heart in my mouth, my blood running cold, I ventured out to seek help.

It was towards evening time. I kept my head bowed, trying not to make eye contact. I asked one of the young men in the compound we were staying in to take us to the house of an old friend of my father's who might be able to help us. As we got out into the streets, I realized how easily my husband could have discovered us in Guinea. A fashionable woman in western clothes with three American boys, who were dressed in denim shorts, t-shirts and sneakers, were a very stark difference from what the indigenes were wearing. It was during Ramadan when the Muslim Country is even more pious. The women wore loose gowns or robes and conservative clothing in every color, intricately embroidered with the finest threads. The men wore loose gowns over long, loose pants with tie strings along with skull caps. We stuck out like Shaquille O'Neal in a little people convention. My heart was beating intensely fast. The rhythm was like the one heard in movies prior to the preview of a horrific scene. It was the most loud and rapid sound I had ever experienced.

The smells of different foods pervaded the air as we walked. Aromas from the different spices and sauces which were prepared to eat with rice or millet could be smelled in the distance. The scent was of maafe, thiacri, huntu, bouille, yetisse, les feuilles de manioc, salade, all to be washed down with their local tamarind and hibiscus drinks. But, we weren't hungry for food. We were hungry for our freedom, for life as we knew it in America. We put everything on the line and were laser focused on regaining our freedom.

We made it to Monsieur Barry's house. He lived inside a gated compound with his wife, Neneh Umu, and teenaged children. His house easily reflected his middle class financial status. It was newly built; a generator on the outside, two cars in the driveway, cable TV and refrigerator. He was told he had some guests. I could see the confusion on his face. He wasn't expecting anyone and we didn't look familiar. His wife was sitting beside him and his children were watching MTV music videos. They all looked up with friendly but confused faces, maybe wondering if we were in the right place. I introduced myself as Zhuri, Monsieur Swarray's daughter. I heard the shrill of excitement from the whole household. They had heard many stories about me from my father but have never met me. And to meet me this way! They were yet to discover what had brought me from America, Sierra Leone, and into their house in Guinea in the dead of night, unannounced.

AUGUST 02, 1979

My mother and father met after both had left toxic relationships. Both came into their new relationship with a child, my dad with a one year old son, Rashad, and my mom with a two year old daughter, Somaya. They got married within three months of meeting, and a year later my brother Ahzan was born. My dad yearned for a little girl of his own. My sister, Somaya, also wanted to have another girl to play with, so when my mom got pregnant again everyone was rooting for a girl. My mom used to tell me that Somaya would say, "Mommy, please give birth to a little girl. Rashad has Ahzan to play with, but me, I have no one, please have a little girl." And so my mom delivered. On August 02, 1979, everyone's wish was granted. I, Zhuri Fatmata Swarray, came into the world. My mom said it was a rainy and stormy day with lightning and thunder, but towards the time I was born, the sun had broken through and there was a rainbow on the top of the hilly mountains outside Lumley Hospital in Freetown. My mother took it as a sign that I may face some storms in life, but would always be able to weather them and break through with gorgeous, brilliant, and bright colors like the rainbow. To her, the rainbow was a sign of hope. I was her hope. As expected, Dad and Somaya were overjoyed. Dad told me that he was cash strapped at the time, but would sing me songs and rock me to sleep. I still remember him singing, "Una, call Zhuri, una tell Zhuri, me money don o, Zhuri." That song translates to: "Call Zhuri, tell Zhuri, I have no money left."

I grew up in a compound with seven little houses all joined together. We lived in the biggest apartment with two bedrooms and a living room. The rest of the apartments had one bedroom, one living room, and two studio apartments. The compound was made up of seven different families, from different tribes; some Mende, some Temne, Loko, Limba and some Mandingo, all of whom got along very well. The families did almost everything together. Most of us went to similar primary schools and played games after school. Everyone gathered together to watch TV on the weekends either in our small two bedroom apartment or the corridor leading to the outside that we turned into a makeshift cinema. We shared our food and looked after each other. It was not uncommon for any of the mothers to announce that she was going to the market and expected the other adults to look after her kids while she was gone. We were all especially fond of Mr. Bangs who would play indigenous African music and lots of Bob Marley. Mr. Bangs just loved African music. He didn't care what language they were sung in, or whether he understood the lyrics or not. He loved the melody and loved that it was indigenous. He loved Bob Marley because he was intelligent and one of the few artists that took pride in his blackness and origin being somewhere in Africa. Mr. Festus was the Pharmacist who lived in one of the one bedroom apartments with his family of 6. He was the one everyone turned to when there was some kind of illness or a sore. Sisi Jeneba was a nurse with four children living in one of the studio apartments with her husband. She always had bandaids and mauve medicine for cuts and bruises. Sisi Aisha sold delicious mangoes and parched groundnuts at the Lebanese International School, and Sisi Yemi sold crisp fried plantain chips at the same school. Mr. Munu worked for the electric company, National Power Authority (NPA) and was at most times with electrical cords without the wires on the inside. He usually gave those out to other parents, unsolicited, in lieu of the normal canes or whips that were used to beat their children with.

I remember my dad being very loving, yet stern and overly protective of me. He loved to carry me on his back even though I was getting very big for piggy back rides. He didn't care when other parents in the neighborhood would say, "Mr. Swarray, Zhuri is too big to carry on your back. She is going to sprain your back. Let her walk. She is a big girl now." My dad was mostly unbothered. It was as if he wanted a little girl of his own so much that after he got one, he wasn't going to shy away from expressing his love and absolute adoration for her.
****

My earliest, vivid childhood memory goes back to when I was five years old. I remember my mom got me dressed in a brown uniform, white socks, and thoroughly polished black shoes for the first day of school. I remember going with my friend Lynette, who lived in another compound opposite ours. My dad was in the middle of us and held our little hands as he walked us to school. We got to our new school, June Holst Roness Municipal School, and the head-mistress asked us to put our right hands over our heads to touch our left ear. If we did, it meant we were age-appropriate and ready for class one. Lynette and I easily passed the test and we were approved to start school. Had we not been able to touch our ears comfortably, our parents would have been asked to wait another year before we could be eligible for enrollment. Lynette and I got put into different classes. I was put in the prestigious class 1A which was reserved for first round picks. It was for the students who had stood out in their first interviews and had impressed the head-mistress. Lynette, who was a bit shy and not very forthcoming, didn't do so well in her interview, so she was put in class 1B. Class 1B was for the students who needed a little more help from the teachers.

I was a very mouthy and opinionated child, and when the head-mistress started my interview, I took over the conversation. I answered questions intelligently and went on to talk about things I wasn't even asked about. I was asked how many siblings I had. It would have just sufficed to say, I have three other siblings, but I replied, "I have one sister and two brothers. My sister's name is Somaya and my brothers' names are Rashad and Ahzan. Rashad likes to eat a lot and Ahzan does not like being at home. My parents are always trying to find out where he went. And Somaya, she..." "O.K Zhuri, I think we get your point," the head-mistress interjected. "You are ready for school. Your new teacher is Miss Isatu Kanu. There is your classroom," she said, pointing to a room with the instription 1A on the front. I went to my class and Miss Kanu welcomed us. There were about 25 pupils in her class. She gave us our syllabus and book list, and told us she would see us the next day. On our way home, my dad stopped at Globe Cinema and bought us ice cream from the vendors who sold them in boxes pulling their carts along the streets. It was a great first day of school, and I loved every moment of it.

I did quite well in my primary school education; I was always amongst the top ten. I had a few friends who really liked me and I was respected by my peers. In my neighborhood, I was revered. The young girls looked up to me, not that they had much of a choice because their parents were always telling them, "why can't you be like Zhuri? She is studious and does so well in school." However, I was intimidating to a lot of boys around my age. They would not approach me, but admired me from afar. I had this air about me which may have been misconstrued as being aloof. One day while I walked past a group of boys in my area, I could hear their rowdy conversations from a distance, but as I got closer to them, they all got quiet, avoiding eye contact. As soon as I passed them the brouhaha ensued.

    I was raised a Jehovah's Witness and took my religion very seriously. This made me different from the other girls, even though I never felt like I was better than anyone else. I was taught at Kingdom Hall that true Christians were no part of this world, which meant we were to carry ourselves distinctively different from everyone else. The goal was to live according to the standards set forth in God's word the Bible, and not man-made laws or standards. I went to Bible Study every Tuesday. I was at the Theocratic Ministry School on Thursdays, and was out at field service preaching from door to door on Saturdays. Growing up a JW, short for Jehovah's Witness, was very fun for me. It taught me how to be well vast in Bible knowledge so I could defend what I was learning about Jehovah God to others. I could quote several scriptures easily to defend my faith in whatever topic I was asked about. It taught me how to dress well because I was a representative of the most high Jehovah, so when I was out, I dressed as one who wanted Jehovah to be proud of her. I was taught not to use bad words or swear or smoke cigarettes. I learned how to approach people and start a conversation about Jehovah. I loved the JW missionaries who came from all over the world to help with the preaching work. It was quite amusing to watch them struggle to learn krio so they could preach to the locals. Their accents were so thick and sounded very funny. I loved the picnics at the beach that were organized every last Saturday of the month. I loved that we helped other Witnesses who were going through tough times by taking them food, or volunteering to help with housework for the old and disabled JWs. We all would go to clean up the Kingdom Hall, which was always a thrill for me and felt good because I was making Jehovah happy. Being a JW was what made me stand out like a sore thumb outside of our compound. I understood why the neighborhood kids would have thought I was aloof; I was not like them and I had no desire to be.

I wasn't allowed to date anyone who didn't share my faith, not even the boys in my neighborhood. My dad and brothers tolerated no nonsense when it came to me. Nobody was good enough for me in their eyes. I remember how my dad had threatened to have one of my brother's friends, Kemo, thrown in jail because he had stupidly simulated kissing me one evening. My dad had angrily gone to his parents house and threatened his parents that if he saw him anywhere near me, they would have to go bail him from jail. My brothers were hung up on beating Kemo into a pulp should he happen to show up anytime soon. My dad also did not let me participate in many of the customs other girls my age participated in. He never allowed me to undergo bondo, female genital cutting. When I was thirteen, I did not understand why my dad would not want me to undergo this customary practice. I always envied my peers, the girls who joined the secret bondo society. I had no idea what happened during their time in the sacred bushes, but something about them after they returned made me intensely jealous. They became different, more mature certainly, but also very timid and secretive, withholding something.They changed from the girls who blabbed to me about everything to being guarded and deliberate in their actions. Even at a young age, I was never one to delve into other people's business, but it felt really weird that I could not be a part of this culture and traditional process without being told why.

I particularly remember Fatima's initiation, a girl the same age as me. She had become a wild, playful and precocious girl, whose hair was always wild and unkempt, and came out walking like a lady. She looked dainty like a gazelle, elegant and sleek. Her hair had been pressed with a hot comb and curled so tightly. Her beautiful, dark skin was glistening. Her nails were painted bright red, her face all made up with red lipstick accentuating her full lips. She carried a small hand bag and was smiling coyly as she swayed her hips to the beat of the drums celebrating the end of her initiation. She was now a 'shayma,' one who had gone through the rite of passage from girlhood to womanhood. I never understood why my dad would be against this. I was envious of these girls, but they never said what happened to them during the initiationceremony. I grew up a stone's throw from the sacred bondo bush and was literally neighbors with Mamie Nandewa who operated the bondo bush. I heard the traditional songs being chanted late into the night.

The first part of the initiation process involved girls, mostly in their early teens, painted with white chalk or clay from top to bottom, scantily clad, sometimes only a piece of cloth strategically placed to cover the pubic area. Most of the girls had their firm, perky, developing breasts exposed. They chanted traditional songs, clapped their hands and swayed their hips, dancing behind the masked bondo debul who led the way. The whole neighborhood would run up to the narrow dusty roads to catch a glimpse of these girls. Some of us called out their names and waved to them. They never waved back, but would break a smile to acknowledge us. They would later return to the bondo bush and stay there until the next public phase of their initiation. Sometimes the initiation process took just two weeks, other times it took a whole month. Dad's sister, Aunty Marie, would tell me that when the girls returned home to their families after their initiation they would be fully women, ready for marriage and taking care of their own families.

"You would remain worthless," she said. "No man in his right mind would want a woman who has not gone to the bondo society."

"Why?" I asked.

"That is for women to know and not children."

Aunty Marie stressed that the bondo society taught her how to cook well, dress immaculately, and take care of her household.

"Your father is ruining your chances of ever becoming that woman."

I was so confused. Dad had always told me that he loved me and wanted the best for me. How come he was standing in the way of me becoming a full-fledged woman? My Aunty wouldn't give me the answer, and dad sure wasn't going to tolerate me questioning him. He gave directives, end of story. "I pay the bills and feed you. Anyone who doesn't like it here can move out and find a place of their own. I promise I won't go and tell you what to do in your own house."

The end of the initiation ceremony was my favorite part. The girls came out into the public all dolled up, looking like pageant contestants. They had on Revlon foundation, and the eyeshadow they wore matched the colors of their beautiful dresses. Their hair was professionally done into all kinds of styles; silky, straight, and curly. Their skin glistened with all the scented, oily lotions they slathered on them. They wore long, beautiful, flowing dresses, some gara, some chiffon, and carried matching handbags. In Dad's Temne dialect, we referred to them as 'Shayma,' meaning the 'beautiful bondo graduates.' Everyone treated them like celebrities on that day until the next initiates stole their shine.

My older sister, Somaya, was no longer living with us because her father's family wanted her to be initiated into the bondo society to the disapproval of my father. My maternal grandma, Mamie Wenday, was all in and she was too strong a force for my mother to refuse. She came into our house and got Somaya, all while scolding my mom and telling her that her new marital status and education had changed her. She took Somaya and slammed the door shut behind her. My dad was as adamant as my grandma. He yelled after her, "You can do whatever you want with Somaya, you helped raise her, but it will never be Zhuri. Over my dead body! In fact, starting from today, Zhuri will never go to stay for holidays with any of you people."

I had all but given up knowing what actually went on in the bondo bushes when I found out by accident. I remember that day vividly. My six year-old cousin Nafissa was staying with us for summer vacation. I was happy when she came around since I treated her like a doll. I would wash her, dress her, comb her hair, and take her everywhere with me. One evening, I took off Nafissa's clothes to bathe her. I started scrubbing her body with soap and sapo, which is a wash cloth. She was fine until I ran the sapo between her thighs.

She let out a painful sigh. "Do not scrub here too hard," she said. I poured some water on her, rinsed the soap, and looked at where she was hurting. It looked different from mine. She didn't seem to have the clitoris I had between my labia.

"What's wrong?" I asked, nudging my chin in the direction of her vagina area.

"Na me bondo," she said, with nonchalance. She had just come to our house a week after her initiation. I wondered why she had told me she was feeling a burning sensation when she peed. Now I realize she was still sore. Her big eyes got red and pregnant with tears.

"I'm sorry, Nafissa. I will be more careful next time." I poured some more water on her body until the scrubbing bubbles were gone and patted her dry with a towel. I took her to our bedroom, and tenderly rubbed oil on her body and dressed her up. When I took my own bath shortly after, my hand strayed down between my legs, examining myself. I felt a soft, supple bud. It was my clitoris there, no scar. I kept rubbing on it in disbelief! It really is there. I noticed as I rubbed on it, that it felt good. In fact, it felt really good. When I stopped, I didn't feel anything anymore. I had stumbled on what happened in the bondo bushes and was grateful that my dad didn't want me to get cut, especially this part of me that felt so good to the touch.

My primary school, June Holst Roness Municipal School, was a single story brown building with yellow trimming. It had 14 classrooms, plus a headmistress' office. There was a big open field outside right next door to the Ascention Town Cemetery. The field was unpaved and very dusty. This was where we played and also bought and ate lunch. We were oblivious to the fact that we were even next to a cemetery. We just played catch, a little bit of soccer, and skipped rope until we heard the school bell and abandoned everything and returned to class. Our classrooms had wooden tables, chairs, and a blackboard in front of the class where the teachers would stand to teach. A big wooden table and chair was centered in front of the class, just behind the blackboard. This was where the teacher sat when she wasn't teaching. She would use that time to grade papers or listen to us after asking a question.

My dad must have thought I was smart and ambitious. He paid for me to have after-school lessons/tutoring. He was my biggest supporter. He told me I could do anything, and that I could become anything I wanted. He told me stories about women like Ella Koblo Gulama, Hannah Benka-Coker, and Constance Cummings-John who did exceptional things in the country. Madam Ella Koblo Gulama was a Paramount Chief and later became the first elected female member of parliament in Sierra Leone and the first female Cabinet Minister. She was utterly glamorous and would show up at meetings and seminars in the most stylish ensemble. She paired her African garbs with a mix of European accessories. It also wasn't uncommon for her to show up wearing European clothes with animal-skin handbags and oxford shoes. She was a fashionista and style icon even before these terms were coined. She made sure her presence in the places she went to was undeniable. Hannah Benka-Coker was an educator and one of the founders of the Freetown Secondary School For Girls who stressed the importance of educating young girls. Constance Cummings-John was the first woman in Africa to join a municipal council and was the first female Mayor of Freetown. These women were independent and did not depend on men to survive.

Dad made sure I knew the stories of these powerful women by heart, a constant reminder that everything was possible. He gave me Le 150 to buy my school lunch every day, but at the same time, my brothers would go to school without lunch money sometimes. He sternly told me never to accept money or gifts from men as, "..they always want something in return when they give you things. If you want anything, come to me and ask me for it." So, that's what I did. I loved to hear my dad say, "That's my girl!" I was addicted to that affirmation. I was a goody-two shoes in our compound because of it. I never took risks like the other girls my age, who would jump the fences and gates to go out after their parents went to sleep. Sometimes they were lucky to not get caught, and other times they would get caught and would be publicly caned and all in the neighborhood would hear their cries. My dad, after hearing about the shenanigans of these girls, would say to me, "That's my girl!" It meant, 'she's not like the rest of them. She's obedient and studious. She is mine.' Those three words had the power to make me break into the biggest smile, my chest puffed up with pride, and made me mentally resolve to conduct myself in more ways pleasing to my dad.

I wanted to attend St. Joseph's Secondary School, the very best high school for girls at the time. That school had been the alma mater of many high profile women in public offices. No one else in my neighborhood was going to that school. Most were going to grade 3 schools, failing schools. I had no role model in my area, nobody who had gone to Convent, as St. Joseph's Secondary School was called. I passed by Convent every day to go to my primary school, and every day I prayed to God to make me go to that school. When it came time for me to take the Selective Entrance examination into secondary school, my first and only choice of secondary school was Convent. The teachers at my grade 3 primary school were not so encouraging. One of them asked my dad to choose a 'safe' school. "Mr. Swarray, why don't you choose…" and would go on to mention three secondary schools that were underperforming.

"It's safer that way. You don't have to worry about much when the results come. One of them is sure to accept her," said one of the school counselors.

"There is no other school but Convent. Is there anything I need to sign before I leave?" my dad inquired.

"Yes sir, over here. Don't feel bad, Sir. Zhuri is clever, a good student, but Convent, that school only accepts schwen schwen girls. They usually don't look for girls from this school," the counselor tried to reason with my dad. "Over here, Sir, just one signature and you can leave, sir." My dad promptly signed the form with Convent as my only choice and walked away.

I studied hard everyday. I read revision books and practiced mock examinations with old selective entrance exams question papers. Those were very helpful as they showed the type of questions that would be asked, and you could also time yourself to see how fast you finished. When I finally took the real exam, I was very comfortable and felt that I performed well. It didn't help with my nervousness though. I had to wait for a couple of months for the results to come out. When the results finally came out, I had passed my selective entrance examination which meant I could now go to high school! However, I still had to wait three weeks until Convent reviewed the results of all the students that applied to them and sent word to different schools to inform them of the students accepted into their school. When my school finally heard from Convent, there were only three names of students accepted from my primary school. My dad took me to find out the results. As soon as the school counselor saw us, he said, "Mr. Swarray, you were right. Zhuri made it, Convent accepted her. See!" he said, pointing to my name on the list. "It's just the three of them: Zhuri, Daniella and Binta. Good job, Zhuri!" I was elated to discover I was one of them. I made the final cut! My dad hugged me tightly as he said, "That's my girl!" I melted into his arms.

Our walk home was as if we were walking on the clouds. It was the walk of happiness, the walk of relief, the walk of pride. When we made it home and announced it to the people in our compound, they were excited and happy. They hugged and congratulated me. My mother was beside herself. She told me she would cook my favorite food that day and I could have the biggest piece of chicken which was usually reserved for my dad. I told her I wanted some jollof rice with the biggest chicken leg. "Our labor is not in vain. Thank you, Jehovah!" she said aloud, lifting her hands towards the heavens. Word of my acceptance to Convent quickly spread in my whole neighborhood as it was such a big deal. I got congratulated by people I didn't even know. "Thank you so much," I would reply graciously to perfect strangers who would congratulate me as they passed me by. I was super excited to be wearing my convent uniform, and was looking forward to making new friends. I became restless. I wanted the summer vacation to be over already. I was ready to start secondary school.

My dad found a seamstress named Mrs. Momorie whose daughter already attended Convent, and she was going to be sewing my school uniforms. I went to her house for measurements, and together with my dad, they decided the length and width. Afterwards, my dad took me to town to buy my new black shoes and white socks, and a book bag. We went to the bookstore and got the books from the booklist Convent had sent us. I was so excited! Just one more week left and I would be a Conventonian. I wouldn't be walking past the school I was always praying to go to, I would be walking through the gates. Miss Florence Dilsworth, whom I had always prayed for God to touch her heart so she could accept me into her school, was now my Principal.

I was up early on Monday morning. There was one toilet and one washroom for the entire compound, and about 40 people used that washroom every day. I was first up this time. I went to the tap outside our compound to get some water to bathe. The entire neighborhood used that tap. Our house was the closest to the tap, so on most occasions we didn't have to wait too long in line because we got there first. I filled up my bucket, put it on my head, and balanced it as I walked and took it into the public washroom. Then I got my soap and sapo and went inside. I took a nice clean bath and went back into our apartment to get dressed for school. I put on my new school uniform, which was pink and blue, brushed my hair which had been braided intricately and neatly by one of my cousins, carried my backpack, and said goodbye to my parents, siblings, and the rest of the people in the compound. As I walked past everyone, I could see the pride and admiration in their eyes. One of their own was going to the best girls' school in the country. I couldn't believe it myself. It was going to be real when I actually made it to Convent and they gave me a class and a seat.

Indeed, my name was called. I was put in Form 1J and I was happy! I later found out that Form 1J had most of the girls from public schools, the ones who had the minimum grade of what Convent was looking for. Convent only accepted students who scored 250 points and above on their selective entrance examination. Those who scored below were rejected and had to go to grade B and C schools. I had barely made it. I scored 251 points and was now in Form 1J with the other girls who had made about the same grade. Those who had actually excelled with scores of 280 and 290 were in Form 1E, those who made around 275 were in Form 1L, those with 270 were in Form 1I, those who made 260 were in Form 1T, and me and all of those who made around 250 were placed in Form 1J. It was a blow for me; of course I wanted to be in Form 1E, but I didn't make the grade to make it to that class, so I tried to get over it as quickly as I could. I was in Convent after all, the best girls' school in the country, and no matter if I was in Form 1J or Form 1E, I was still in Form 1 in the best secondary school in the country. I was going to work hard and do the best I could.

I made friends quickly. The girls on the right and left of me were Jane Kelly and Marie Kamara. I became very close to these girls and did everything with them. We ate lunch together and did our homework together. We also shared the same hairdresser and would sometimes come to school with similar hairstyles. I just loved our class teacher, Miss Coker. I loved her because she was different from the rest of the teachers. I understood what it was like to be different. Miss Coker was not like the other teachers who seemed loud, bossy, and with something to prove. She seemed really self-assured, calm and restrained. She wasn't a woman of many words. She only spoke when it was necessary. Besides being our class teacher, she was also our music teacher; the only music teacher in our school. She was very neat, strict, and stern. She went to our class everyday for roll calls, would leave afterwards, and we saw her for music twice a week. My classmates were very scared of her because she seldom smiled and she spoke perfect English. She had an aloofness about her that made us intimidated by her sheer presence. Whenever we went to the music room to take her class, we all went straight to our chairs and kept quiet. When she would look at us through her glasses and notice we hadn't opened the windows in the room after we came in, she would ask every time, "Are you allergic to fresh air?" My friends and I would chuckle under our breaths because we had no idea what 'allergic' meant. After music class, we would walk outside and joke to each other, "Are you allergic to fresh air?" and just laugh and laugh.

    I was always bragging about my school, but the only thing I did not like about my school were the cliques. There was a lot of class and status segregation. The girls whose parents were ministers in the government or CEOs of major companies kept to themselves and would barely mouth a 'hello' when we crossed each other in the hallways. During lunch, those who had lots of money bought soft drinks and sandwiches from Miss Hassanatu, and those of us who were not so rich joined the line for Sisi Diro's fry-fry and abohboh with ginger beer or Kool-Aid tied in plastic bags. The rich girls changed shoes and bookbags a couple times a week. They talked about spending time at Aqua Sports Club over the weekend, or the birthday parties they went to. Some vacationed abroad. Their lives sounded very exciting.

As for me, my dad forbade me from leaving my house without permission. I couldn't even go to the fullah shop about 300ft from my house. My dad would ask me to send my brothers to go get anything I wanted out of our compound. I didn't like it one bit, but my dad didn't care about my feelings. He just wanted to protect me. He told me not to laugh too much when my brothers' friends visited. He would say, "You love to laugh too much, don't laugh or smile at your brothers' friends. If you do, they will think you like them." So, in school, when my other friends were talking about their boyfriends, I couldn't relate or add to the conversation. I had many crushes though. My dad couldn't stop what I was feeling. I hid it to myself, but I had huge crushes on two of my brother Rashad's friends, Ayo and Sullay. I liked Ayo because he was so intelligent in school, extremely brilliant. He was always first in his class and during prize-giving ceremonies, he would win all the awards and prizes easily. His intelligence was very attractive to me. When he came to our apartment, which happened to be everyday, he would play with me, crack jokes, and eat my food. I loved it! I secretly wanted him to be my boyfriend, but he never asked me out. He was just fond of me and looked at me as Rashad's baby sister. Sullay was tall, dark skinned, and easy on the eyes. He dressed very well and called me 'counselor' because I was appointed a Pupil Counselor at Convent. He would joke with me, "Zhu-Zhu! I have a massive problem, I need your counseling expertise." I would smile so widely. I would look at him with admiration and love in my eyes, but then shyly walk away. One day as I was walking to school, I saw Sullay on the other side of the street walking to the Technical Institute where he was studying building construction with my brother Rashad. He was wearing long, blue jeans and a long sleeved denim shirt with a folder in his hand. I did not call him, I just stood there and looked at him until he turned the corner and disappeared.

Of all my brother Ahzan's friends, I had a crush on Ben. He was cute, shy, and somewhat quiet. Ben liked me too! We knew we loved each other because Ben would visit my house under the guise of visiting Ahzan, but he would spend all his time with me. He brought me little presents every time, which he hid in his baggy jeans. Some days it was chocolates, other days it was a novel, and other days it was a trinket. There was nothing we could do about our feelings, but seeing Ben became exciting because of his clandestine little gifts he brought with him. We were very careful because my brother Ahzan would kill Ben if he found out that he even looked at me in a romantic way. Ben and I would talk and tell each other our feelings, but we were smart to just let the feelings be. One day while Ben was visiting, a photographer came to drop off some photos for my dad. Before he left, Ben asked him to take our picture. We took the picture and from that day on it was our mission to hide that photo from the light of day. It was a very brave act for us to have done. If my brothers or dad would've ever found that picture, it would have meant serious trouble for the both of us.

It was around this same time when I was 13 years old that I met Oliver Jones for the first time. I had heard quite a lot about him through my dad. My dad, who was a big proponent for education, used to tell me glowing stories about Ollie and his academic prowess. Dad told me that when Oliver sat his GCE O' level exams, he came 1st in the whole of West Africa. After two years when he took the GCE A' level exams, he came 1st in the whole of West Africa again. My dad knew his mom. They were from the same village in Rokupr. Dad had made me visit his mother at her office a few times for inspiration. She was one of the few women in my country who were highly educated and independent. I remember every time we visited her, we had to wait in the waiting room after making our announcement and then her secretary would tell us a few minutes later, "Miss Vincent can now see you." My dad would speak temne, their tribal language, with her and they would laugh and laugh reminiscing about the past. When we said our goodbyes, Miss Vincent would encourage me to keep working hard in school and tell me education would give me everything I wanted.

That day, Ollie was visiting his mother from England and had stopped by our house. My dad finally introduced me to him and told him how well I was doing in school. He was 23 years old and I was 13. He congratulated me on my hard work in school, had me sit close to him, and when it was time for him to leave our house, he asked me to go drop him off. "Young gial, go drop me off the road nor." His krio was perfect, like he wasn't living in England full time. I was so flattered and coyly replied 'ok', obliging him.

I skipped ahead of him as I led the way up the hill away from our apartment. At the top of the hill, we said our goodbyes. He told me he would see me again on Sunday; apparently my dad had told him we would visit them after Kingdom Hall. We said goodbye and I hurried back home. I was so happy to have finally met and interacted with him. He was very tall, had full lips, and the deepest dimples on his cheeks. He was so handsome and funny to me, with a very loud, infectious laugh. He had told a lot of funny stories about immigrant life in England. I couldn't wait for Sunday to come so that I could see Ollie again. I wore my best outfit to the Kingdom Hall that Sunday, and after the service, my whole family headed for Miss Vincent's house at Spur Road. Once we got there, it was business as usual. She gave us soft drinks and long conversations with my dad ensued. Ollie was there as well and thanked us for coming to see him. Before we left, he asked to take pictures. We all got together in two rows, the shorter ones in front and taller ones in the back. He positioned himself right behind me on the second row. He stood there with his hands on my shoulders and *click!* The pictures were taken. I was so happy that Ollie was fond of me and so happy that he had his hands on my shoulders while the pictures were taken. However, I knew he had a girlfriend in London. The girlfriend's picture was framed in his mother's living room. I also knew I was too young for him, but I still had a crush on him and his fondness for me just made me love him even more. Ollie promised to send us copies of the pictures after he developed them in England. This would be the first of many encounters with Ollie. I was already smitten, and couldn't wait for what the future held for the both of us.

YOUNG LOVES

In Form 3J, I was introduced to my first boyfriend by my close friend, Aziza. Aziza was my neighbor. We became fast friends because her cousin, Sadia, kept taking her to a tailor that worked opposite our apartment. I found out Aziza went to Convent too, and was one year behind me in school. We became fast friends and literally visited each other's houses back and forth every single day. We hung out so often that our families got very close. My dad would visit her aunt Isha who was raising her and her little brother, Navid. Aziza and I did so much together, we were inseparable.

It was through Aziza that I met Alpha. He was funny and made me laugh a lot. He later told Aziza that he wanted me to be his girlfriend. I had never had a boyfriend before, and Alpha kept on pursuing me. He sent a letter with his younger sister, Indira, who was a freshman at Convent. He laid the compliments so thick it melted my heart. Alpha didn't live close to my neighborhood so one day, after lying about our whereabouts, Aziza and I went to visit her cousin, Alpha. We met Tamba there, too. It was no surprise. Alpha and Tamba were inseparable. I agreed to go with Aziza to see Alpha for the first time at his house as his girlfriend. When we got there, Alpha took me by the hand and led me into his bedroom. He gave me my first kiss, but it was gross. I had never been kissed like that before. I was 13 years old and Alpha was 12, but he seemed to know more than me in that department.

I was completely embarrassed and terrified after the kiss. Embarrassed because I had never kissed a boy before, and terrified because he put his tongue in my mouth and sucked on mine. It was so quick, unexpected, and had the weirdest feeling. I thought I was pregnant after the kiss. In Sierra Leone at that time, parents didn't tell you about sex, and they were very tight-lipped about the specifics. All they said was if a boy touches you, you will get pregnant, drop out of school, and become the embarrassment of your family. I didn't want to be that, so my first kiss was also my last kiss with Alpha. I never visited him again. I was afraid that he might want to go further than kissing the next time. I still wasn't over the fact that he had surprised me with his tongue in my mouth without asking me first. After that day, I told Aziza I didn't want to have a boyfriend for a while. I asked her to tell Alpha for me because I didn't have the courage to tell him myself, nor did I want to see him again. All of a sudden, the boy I thought was cute and funny was no longer doing it for me.

A couple of years later, on another outing with Aziza after school at King Harman Road, just behind Lebanese International School, I met one of Aziza's male friends, Lenny. We had gone to practice for our upcoming annual school sports. We chose that spot because the road was paved and smoother over there, the best running surface we could find close to our area. I met Lenny up close since he was there running laps. I had seen him around the President's Lodge area coming and going, but we never talked. He lived in an uppity house by the junction, a yellow and beige three-story building. It was opposite from the former President Shaka Steven's house and was gated. The people who rented the lower level were diplomats. They had servants who tended to the garden and guarded the gates. They also had multiple cars on the inside. Lenny lived with his older brother, Ken, and their dad, and Ken was friends with my older brothers. In fact, they played football in the fenced compound in their backyard. Ken would come around my apartment sometimes to visit with my brothers. However, I had never met his younger brother Lenny, even though I saw him around. I always thought he was quite handsome. He had such big, piercing eyes and his smile was quite charming. His style of dress was different because most of his clothes came from overseas. He always wore a metal bracelet on his left wrist. When he walked, it looked like he was galloping like a gazelle. He was just different from the rest of the boys in my area. He looked sophisticated, and his big, full lips were so desirable to me. My attraction to Lenny, besides the fact that he was good looking, was because he was different. He spoke well and was very witty. He looked quite polished and had a distinct aura about him. He was his own man.

Although friendly with the other kids around him, he carried himself in a debonair fashion; stylish, charming, with just enough confidence to melt my heart. Lenny was friends with Aziza, and they could literally see each other from their houses. They started talking while we practiced. For a moment, I felt like the third wheel. They were laughing at their own jokes and inside stories. I tried to busy myself by starting my laps ahead of them. This made them notice me again, and Lenny started jogging and caught up to me. It was quite easy for him to do with his long legs. "For a newbie, you are very brave to go ahead of us," he said, starting a conversation with me.

I wanted to answer, but I was too shy to say anything, so I just smiled and stayed in pace with him. I was happy that he was right there by my side and even as Aziza jogged past us, he didn't try to catch up to her. He just kept his pace with mine and we heard each other's breathing as we ran. By the end of our workout session, Lenny said, "It was nice to meet you today, Zhuri. I hope you come out here more often. Aziza, please let me know the next time you two have your session."

"Okay," I replied with a smile. I was blushing on the inside and didn't want too many words to betray me.

A day or two after our meeting, Lenny told Aziza that he wanted me to be his girlfriend. I was so happy on the inside, even though I feigned nonchalance on the outside. I told Aziza to tell him I would think about it. Two days later, one of Lenny's contemporaries, Amadu, stopped me on the street and gave me a letter he said was from Lenny. I took the letter from him and hurried home to read it. Lenny wrote exactly what he had told Aziza to tell me, that he thought I was beautiful and wanted to be my boyfriend. "No date, but love," it said on the corner where the date should be. My hands were shaking as I tried to hold on to the letter. I was filled with so much excitement!

"Dear beautiful Zhuri, I don't know if Aziza already told you this, but I would love to be your boyfriend. I always see you as you cross the road in your Convent uniform. I love the way you walk. You are very pretty. The way you style your hair with the coronet on the top looks good on you. Please write back to me and let me know if your answer is yes or no. I love you so much Zhuri, with lots of love, Lenny".

I couldn't believe my luck! The boy I fancied, fancied me too. I read the letter over and over just to make sure I wasn't dreaming. I put the letter on my chest which was beating so fast. I laid on my bed and immediately started fantasizing about kissing his big, full lips, with his face so close to mine that we could smell each other's breath, him looking at me with those eyes of his. I was so flattered that he had eyes only for me. However, I did not reply to Lenny's love letter right away despite my excitement. I wanted to play hard to get and let him wait a while. A week later, as I was walking home from school, I met Lenny at President's Lodge and he came over to me. I was so shy, I felt my heart would betray me. I did not know how to act. I felt so transparent, like he could just see through me. He asked me if Aziza told me anything. I was so embarrassed, I replied, "maybe." There and then he said, "I want you to be my girlfriend." I immediately melted. I was blushing all over with embarrassment. I couldn't look at him and say *no*. He was so dreamy to me, so I replied with, "Okay." His eyes lit up, and there was a spring in his step as he walked with me along the road. I was 15 years old and Lenny was a very tall 14 year old. And so, that's how my first real love life started. Lenny was the first boy I actually fell in love with.

    I was literally feeling all tingly on the inside. My heart paced so fast with thoughts of him and in anticipation of seeing him again. I knew I was in love with him because he was the first boy I was willing to take the ultimate risk for. Lenny didn't live more than ten minutes away from my house which made it inevitable of us getting caught. I didn't want us to get caught ever, but for the first time, my desire to be with him was much stronger than the fear of being caught. Even if I was caught, I was determined to take the punishment of getting beat and being humiliated from it. But even with that scary thought, it just emboldened my desire to see him. I was so in love with him that my JW beliefs and convictions started taking a back seat. I pushed the idea that I wasn't supposed to date someone outside of my faith far away from me. I reasoned that we were all God's children and even though Lenny wasn't a JW, he was still a Christian and believed in God. It was my preference whom I wanted to be with as long as we didn't commit a sin, like fornication. I was determined that it was going to be two teenagers who were crazy in love, but would date without sinning. His friends and brother were happy for us as a couple. They would greet us on the road with kindness and affection and lots of jokes. As for Lenny, we wrote love letters back and forth to each other and would deliver the letters to ourselves every time we saw each other, which was almost every day.

Our relationship was sweet and innocent and clandestine. Lenny was so cool, unassuming, and always a gentleman. We kissed so much, and that's all we did basically. We wrote romantic letters, which pretty much expressed the emotions and feelings we felt in our last meeting.

"...when you came in with that red mini skirt and tube top yesterday, I couldn't believe my eyes. You looked like you just walked out of the WordUp magazine on my nightstand. My love for you just grows and grows and I really feel like I cannot go a day now without seeing you."

We always read our letters after we had left each other. I would read those sweet words and place the letter on my chest. The feeling was exhilarating. I wanted more and more of this feeling. Lenny and I held hands when it was possible, kissed many times, and looked forward to doing it all over again. We would make arrangements to see each other again at the end of every visit. Sometimes Lenny couldn't wait till my next visit, so he would call my house. If I answered the phone, he would ask me to come over to his house quickly. If someone else answered the phone, he would simply say, "I'm sorry, wrong number." Sometimes when my dad would say, "that was a wrong number," I would get the clue that it was Lenny and found a way to go to his house quickly. Most of the time, we made arrangements to see each other a few hours before school ended and no one else was at home. We were hiding the relationship from my brothers and my parents, so Lenny and I would leave our respective schools a couple of times a week after lunch and meet at his house. It was there that we would talk about our hopes and dreams. Lenny wanted to be a lawyer. As for me, I didn't have a clear indication of what I wanted to be just yet. I was in limbo because my dad had told me the possibilities were limitless. I wanted to be a supermodel like Naomi Campbell and Iman, then I wanted to be a writer, then a public speaker, a psychologist, I couldn't decide just yet. Lenny would interrupt me and say, "you're already my supermodel." We also talked about our home life a little bit. I didn't have to emphasize to

Lenny how strict my father was, he already had a reputation for it in the neighborhood. Lenny told me his mother worked for the U.N. and his dad had his own bakery. We would play truth or dare and laugh hard upon hearing our truths and dares. We would hold each other, and kiss some more. And boy, did I love kissing him. His breath smelled like fresh baked bread and his tongue tasted like fresh, sweet dough. I longed for more as soon as we separated. The way he would pull me close to him, wrap his arms around my waist, and press his lips on top of mine with his tongue entering my mouth to search for mine, the feeling was exhilarating, unlike the way I had felt with Alpha. It was the kind of high I had never felt before and never knew I wanted. Lenny never asked me for sex. I had a reputation of being a decent church girl, and I think Lenny was scared that he would lose me if he ever asked me that. I also think he had never had sex and had no clue what to do. Also, the high we got from our slow, wet, sensual kissing and caressing was so tantalizing and intoxicating, we didn't feel anything else could top it. We were content just being close and being with each other.

One day I wore a one-piece bathing suit that looked like a blouse and shorts. When I got to his room, I asked him if he wanted to see what I looked like in a bathing suit. He quickly and happily responded, "Are you kidding me? Yes!" I took off my shorts, exposing my slender legs and barely there cleavage in my black and white polka dot bathing suit. I could see his eyes pop out of their sockets. "You really are beautiful," he said, and proceeded to run his hands against my smooth, brown skin. He felt my small, perky breasts just beginning to come in. I inhaled and exhaled and put my shorts back on and he held me close, squeezed me tightly and kissed me so long that we both ran out of breath.

On one fateful day, about four months after we started dating, I went to a JW convention and they preached about how having boyfriends when you were not ready for marriage was against God's law. They talked about all the 'unholy' practices that come with having relationships that led to sin. I sat there and felt so guilty. They were preaching against everything I was doing with Lenny; sneaking around, kissing, caressing, hiding from our parents, etc. I was torn and saddened. They said that if someone really loves God she wouldn't do such things, which made me feel conflicted and confused. I loved God so much, in fact, that's why I was at the convention because I loved God, but I loved Lenny also. They continued to preach that if you really loved God and you were doing those things, you should choose God and what God requires of you and refrain from the bad things. I loved Lenny so much, but I had to choose God over him. I was sad when I got home that day because I had resolved in my mind that I was going to break up with Lenny. I was going to break up with the love of my life, a sweet boy who had done nothing to me, except give me butterflies and excitement and love. I sat down and wrote Lenny a letter and gave him a flimsy excuse about why I was dumping him. My heart was breaking. I held the letter and walked by Lodge where I knew I would find a couple of his friends. I found Andrew, another friend of his, and handed him the letter to give to Lenny. He gladly took it from me and asked how I was doing. I faked a bland smile and replied that I was fine. After I turned my back to leave, I felt like I was dying inside. I had dumped the one person who made me happy every day, who made me look forward to the next day, who made my heart do somersaults, whose kisses were sweeter than honey. I justified that whole thing to myself that at least I was choosing God over him.

The next day, I saw Andrew and he immediately said to me, "Zhuri, what kind of letter did you give me to deliver to Lenny? I thought it was a love letter, otherwise I wouldn't have delivered it." I smiled dryly and walked past Andrew. Lenny and I were broken up for about two weeks or so. One day, I was missing him so much, I found the courage to go past his house. I always passed his house to go to my friend, Lynette's house, so on this day, I left my house telling my mom I was going to see Lynette, hoping I would see Lenny as I walked by. Indeed, Lenny and his friends were in front of his house. They called out my name and asked if I was just going to pass and not greet them, so I smiled and crossed over. I met Lenny face to face and he took my hand and led me upstairs to his bedroom for a private conversation. "I am so sorry," I began. "I want to be your girlfriend again." He yanked me toward him and we kissed and kissed. Our kiss was so fierce from how much we missed each other, and had it not started getting dark and time for my parents to notice I had been gone for quite a while, we would have had a marathon of a kiss. However, my relationship with Lenny wasn't the same after the break up. He didn't know if he could trust our intense love and passion anymore. He wasn't sure if it would all go away on just a whim. He had been the laughing stock of his friends who made fun of him for getting dumped and for never asking me for sex. He told me they called him, "Bol head," a guy who wasn't savvy enough.

A month or so after our reunion, Lenny told me that he would be going to London to live permanently and his brother would be joining him a couple of months later. I was shocked and saddened by the news of course, but even sadder that I made him the butt of his friend's jokes. Three weeks later, I went to Lenny's house to say goodbye and that was the last time I saw him as my boyfriend. We held on to each other tightly, kissed tenderly, our hearts heavy and aching. He told me he loved me and we shared our last kiss, sweet and lingering. I savored how his tongue tasted like bread from the Red Lion Bakery. He walked me to a safe distance towards my apartment and said goodbye, telling me he would write to me when he got to London.

Two months later, out of the blue, I received a letter from London that Lenny wrote to me. I was so happy to receive it and it was about three pages long. He wrote about his new life in London, the miserable weather, and how much he missed me and his friends. He also talked about his new school and new neighborhood. He said he missed our rendezvous and would do anything for a kiss from me. I held the letter close to my chest, sighing long and deep, and hiding it with caution. Later that week, I asked the photographer close to my house to take a picture of me. It was a close up picture of me with long, curly braids wearing a studded pink top. I smiled the way he had always wanted me to smile, and the picture came out beautiful. It showed my trademark smile and my top was low enough to show the silhouette of my small, yet perky and firm breasts. I wanted him to remember me as beautiful as he left me. I posted a copy of it to Lenny along with my reply.

By my fifth and final year at Convent, I had adjusted to the status quo and was having a great time. I was now friends with some of the big guns; daughters of government ministers and diplomats, but I still hung out with my regular friends. My closest friends at this time were Farida and Adisa. We hung out many times at our unfinished school hall during P.E and talked about boyfriends and shared secrets. Whenever a boyfriend gave any of us gifts, we would immediately tell each other that we would tell our parents that one of us gave the other the gift. So, if Farida's boyfriend gave her a necklace, she would tell me in advance that she was going to tell her parents that I gave her the necklace. We kept each other's secrets fiercely. If Farida's mom or dad ever asked me or mentioned it, I would confirm without any hesitation or awkwardness that it was from me. Farida had a boyfriend who lived in the same neighborhood as her named Amadu. He was very articulate and wrote Farida the most beautiful love letters. Every morning at school, Adisa and I couldn't wait for her to come in with a new letter from Amadu for us to read. We would swoon at his brilliance. The way he would express himself so poetically, his use of colloquialism and palance. His diction was impeccable. One could tell he was in university already. I thought Farida was very lucky to have him. His letters never failed to excite and entertain us. Dating at that time was pretty innocent, you kissed a lot and wrote gazillion letters to your love interest. We had pet names for Farida and Amadu, calling them Faridu. As long as couples were in love, they were fine with the pet names, no matter how cheesy they sounded.

Adisa's boyfriend at the time was Kekuda and of course, we called them Kekisa. She came to school with updates about the goings on in their relationship, but it was nothing as exciting as Farida's. But soon, it was time for us to get serious. We were getting closer to taking our GCE 'O' level exams and that was no joke. Farida's father was a professor at the University of Sierra Leone, so I always thought Farida had an advantage over us as far as getting schooled by a professor. But, she worked as hard as the rest of us. I was very good with languages and the arts, so I was pretty confident I would do well in those areas, but math and science weren't my forte and I was struggling miserably. My dad hired one of my teachers from school to teach me biology at home. I loved my teacher, Mr. Lamin, as he was a really good teacher. He quickly became a part of my family. He taught me every chapter of the biology textbook, but skipped 'Reproduction.' I kept hounding him to teach Reproduction, but he never did. He told me to read the textbook on my own and learn what I could from reading it. Mr. Lamin's reluctance to teach reproduction came from our culture's reluctance to talk about sex. It was a taboo and awkward topic, therefore it was left alone. I wanted so badly to cover this topic because my parents and anybody else I knew would not talk to me about sex. I had just had my period and told my parents about it, and all I got was a pack of feminine pads and a stern counsel that if I got close to any boy or allowed them to touch me, I would become pregnant. I was the last of my friends in school to have a period, and I would say I just had mine the week before. I would talk about the bloating and stomach cramps that came with it, everything I have heard them say before. But, it was not until I was 16 that I had my very first period.

Although I was 16 at the time, I was completely innocent about sex and my body. I had no idea how sex happened or what part of my body the penis enters. I had examined my body and seen the vaginal opening, but that's where I peed from. I thought that was the sole purpose of the opening of my vagina, for me to urinate and have my period. I would innocently and confusedly search for another opening, maybe a bit larger to see where the penis went. I never found another one besides the anus. I was baffled. I thought something was wrong with me. I thought I did not have the opening in my body to receive a penis. I also checked out my growing breasts and I did not see any holes on the nipples for milk to pass through to feed a child. My nipples were closed shut. What is it with my reproductive organs? I couldn't find the opening to receive a penis and now I couldn't find holes in my nipples for milk to pass through. Was I barren? Would I ever be able to conceive a child? The worst part about all this confusion was that I did not have a single person to go ask about my concerns. If I asked my parents, it would be the same as making a death wish. They would think I was now interested in having sex, hence the curiousity. If I asked an aunt or an uncle, they would tell my parents to pay close attention to me because I am now bold enough to start questioning them about sex. So, there was no one else to turn to. I couldn't talk to my peers about it because they were in the same predicament as me. It was a dilemma.

When it came close to taking the exams, they announced where we would go to take each exam. I would take my exams at FSSG, Freetown Secondary School for Girls, another girls' high school across the street from Convent. I studied very hard, however I decided not to go take my maths exam without telling anyone. I was really horrible at math and I didn't want to humiliate myself and waste two hours watching my friends doing their best and turning in their work. So, I skipped my math exam without telling anyone. I studied for the rest and was confident I was doing well. One day, after my English exam as I was walking home, a girl called out to me.

"Hey! What's your name? My name is Salem. I just love how you walk." I smiled and told her my name. She told me where she lived and I told her I lived around the corner not too far from the same area. Salem was very talkative and definitely not shy.

"How come I have never seen you before?" she probed.

"I don't know, but I've seen you around." I replied.

"Tell me where you live, I will come visit you."

"Ok. Let me know when and I will take you."

The next day, I saw Salem again and after our exams we walked home together. Salem was who I had been missing all my life. She was being raised so differently from me. Her mom had travelled extensively, therefore she was more exposed and tolerated things that my parents would kill me for. Salem was liberated. Her mother tolerated things like openly dating, talking back, receiving boyfriends at home, and she could come and go as she pleased, leaving her house without supervision. The very first time I visited Salem, her boyfriend was at her house hanging out in the kitchen with her mom. How could this be real? Her mother not only allowed her to date, but the boyfriend could come to their house and she was friendly with him too? It took me the whole day to get over my shock. Salem kept telling me that it was the norm for her. She explained that her mom was just making sure the boyfriend was good for her, so she hung out with him for a bit. My mouth was wide open as she explained her lifestyle to me. She told me about her vacations to London and her obsession with Janet Jackson. She would sing and perform her songs at variety shows. She was really good at impersonating Janet, her dance, her clothes, and her style. Every time she performed at variety shows, the audience would break into thunderous applause.

That summer, after our exams were over, Salem and I became fast friends. We went everywhere together. We hooked up in the afternoons and just hung out all day with my brother Ahzan. Dad did not allow me to go if Azhan did not come. We had the best time together. We went to the park and hung out with Azhan's friends. We rented movies, went to the supermarket and bought ice-cream and foreign magazines, like *Ebony* and *Hello* magazines. Our families got close and she came to my house whenever she liked. We were at each other's houses almost every day. I had never had a friend who felt so passionately about me as I did her. She respected and loved me, even admired me sometimes. Salem was just what I needed at that point in my life. She told me about boys she had dated, about not being in love with her current boyfriend, and the boy she really loved who was too shy and timid to reciprocate her love. Her boyfriend Dez was crazy about her, but she only cared about Neelam. She told me how much she fantasized about kissing Neel, but he was always too shy and timid to even ask her for a kiss. He never even looked her in her eyes, let alone held her hand or kissed her. We talked about everything. I wasn't afraid to be myself or ask anything or just tell her what was on my mind. She wasn't judgmental and she listened to understand, then she would relate and we would make light of everything and just laugh. I felt so close to her, like a sister. She was not embarrassed to talk about taboo topics. I told her stories about my past loves, Alpha and Lenny. She found my stories so innocent and sweet, but told me I was so lucky to have shared passionate kisses with Lenny as much as we did. She said she wished Neelam had done those things to her.

One day, I left my slime book at her house. A slime book is like a diary where you air out your innermost thoughts and fantasies. The difference is, you don't mind your best and closest friends reading it. Usually, close friends exchange slime books. Many times, you learn a lot more about your friend after reading their slime book. When I saw Salem the next day, she said, "Zhuri, you write as beautiful as you look.

Your slime book was a joy to read. I laughed throughout. It was so intriguing. I also wrote some things in there for you to read." I was surprised that Salem felt this way about me. I always felt she was the pretty one, the smart one, the liberated one. When I took my slime book home with me, she had written several letters to me, all about how happy she was to have met me, how grateful she was for our friendship. It was the first time I felt equal to a friend. I didn't have to do anything to earn her friendship, I just had to be myself. With some of my other friends, I had to feign interest in what they loved and thought were cool. If they thought going to the Aqua sports club was the thing to do, I had to be ready to hear all about it and act like I loved it, or pretend to be just as excited! With Salem, I didn't even have to say a word. She liked me because I walked a certain way and the more she got to know me, the more she liked me. Finally I felt like I found my kindred spirit. The feelings were mutual. I felt incredibly lucky to have her in my life. She opened my eyes to so many things, like not being ashamed to talk about boys, her unrequited love with Neelam, and letting me know that it was okay to be different from the norm. I felt comfortable asking her questions because I knew I wouldn't get in trouble for my curiosity or be laughed at for my ignorance. She simply just thought very highly of me. "You're so beautiful, never forget that," she would say. "You're so articulate, so brilliant. I am so happy we are friends." I was always taken aback by Salem's praise of me, even though she does it so often. I had never gotten compliments of that nature from another girl. I would hear it from men, but never another girl who would just go on and on about it. I felt just as lucky and happy to have Salem as my friend. She came into my life and shook things up a little, actually a whole lot.

Then one day, out of the blue, Salem told me she would be leaving Freetown to go do a course in Nigeria. It was a big blow for me, making me sad beyond words. My first thought was how could she do this to me? Salem had never even talked about Nigeria, and now all of a sudden she was moving there? I was crushed and heartbroken. The day she left for Nigeria, I was beside myself. I cried so hard, I was inconsolable. My dad reassured me that she would come back after her course or maybe I would go visit her in Nigeria. I was not buying it. I cried until I had no more tears left to shed.

After Salem left, I felt empty. I didn't know what to do with myself. I made sure I still visited her mom, Aunty Tina. She would give me letters Salem wrote to me. I would reply immediately, telling her how much I missed her and for her to hurry back. As the months flew by however, it was time to worry about my GCE 'O' level results. I had to pass to further my education. Sixth form was the next prestigious step; it was pre-university. Again, I never had anybody in my family or neighborhood go to sixth form, so it was a big deal. I waited anxiously for the results to come, and I didn't have to go to school to find out. As soon as the results came out, Mr. Lamin checked and called home to tell my parents the results. I had performed exactly as I expected. Of course, there was no grade for me for mathematics because I didn't show up to take it. I had failed my science subjects including biology which Mr. Lamin taught me, but I passed with flying colors on everything else. I passed French, English, History, and Literature. I was immensely pleased with myself. I had performed exactly as I had wanted and now these results reflected my hard work. My dad was on the telephone bragging to his friends that I had passed my exams and heading to 6th form.Now, I had to apply for a space in the art schools with my results.

I applied to St. Edward's, a public Catholic secondary school, and was accepted. Even though St. Edwards was designed to be an all-male school, female students were permitted to enroll as A Level candidates. I couldn't believe I had made it to sixth form. Not a girl from my neighborhood where our parents came from humble backgrounds, had made it. My dad worked as a manager for an insurance company, but most of the other dads were clerks, janitors, and tailors, while the mothers were petty traders who sold food items on the street corners or at the famous Congo market. My mom, who was a clerk at the Ministry of Agriculture in Brookfields, was so proud of me. She told me she had always wanted to go to 6th form herself, but she was the oldest of eight children and furthering her education beyond high school was selfish. She didn't expect her struggling parents to keep on paying her school fees while there were seven more children after her to pay for. She had to find a job after high school to help out. She said I was living her dream and she couldn't be happier. She would tell everyone who cared to listen that I was going to be in 6th form.

As for me, I was happy because I had made them proud. It seemed that had become my thing. Most things were never about me, it was either about making Jehovah happy or making my parents proud. Going to 6th form had been a dream and now all of a sudden, it was my reality and it was an incredible feeling. My dad once again took me to Mrs. Momorie to have my uniforms made. I was so little, so skinny, but I was in pre-university already and I couldn't contain myself. My dad called me into the living room and sternly warned me, "I don't want to see any boys in my house, do you understand me? I never want to see you with any boy. That is not why I am sending you to school. If I catch you with any boy, the thing I will do to you, you don't even want to know."

"Yes, Dad," I said, exiting the room and walking into my bedroom. I sat on my bed and let out a deep sigh. It seemed like my dad's grip on me was getting tighter and tighter. I felt there was no way of getting my dad to change. I wanted to go back to the living room and ask him why he couldn't be like Salem's mother. Salem's mother trusted her, gave her liberties, yet she was still a good girl. I was a good girl, why couldn't he just trust my judgment? Of course, I didn't have the nerve to question my Dad's authority. I just wallowed in self-pity for a bit and got excited again about going to sixth form. Despite Dad's fears and threats, I was looking forward to going to school with boys. I had been so overprotected all my life. I was stoked that finally I was going to be around boys for most of my day.

ST EDWARD'S

My first day at St. Edwards was good. I saw a few familiar faces, one of which was Kwame. He had been friends with my older brothers for years and used to visit our house frequently. We were in the same class now. Kwame was very sure of himself, highly intelligent, and cocky too! When he discussed topics and issues with his other classmates, he was very staunch in his opinions and would refuse to budge or be swayed, no matter if he got new information or enlightenment. He always had to have the last word in and would casually refer to other people as "stupid" who would not agree with him. He used superfluous vocabulary and would use his hands to say a whole lot of malarkey, but because he used big and unfamiliar words, he had convinced himself and those who are not too vast in the english language that he sounded deep. He instantly appointed himself the overseer of me. He became very protective. He was quick to let everyone know that he knew my father and brothers. He would tell me that if I encouraged any boy to get too close to me he would tell my dad. I did not like that at all. I wanted to have a little bit of freedom at St. Edward's, not to be hounded by my brothers' friend. I already had an overprotective father and overbearing brothers, the last thing I wanted was an overbearing friend. But I loved Kwame because he was fun to be around. He loved to debate about everything. He found a suitable match in Qadir. Qadir was in the same class with us, having come from Bo school. He was handsome, unassuming, brilliant and loved to debate as well, only he did it in a more civilized, quieter tone. He was controlled and more composed. He would debate with Kwame about everything. I had a crush on Qadir. We had become fast friends and I was very happy about that because Qadir was very selective when it came to the people he chose to hang out with. He only had a chosen few and the rest of the class, he just said hi and bye to. Qadir told me I was different from the rest of the other girls. It wasn't the first time I have heard that. He said I had good home training and wasn't trying to fit in. I was tired of trying to fit in at that point. I knew myself better and liked myself more. I didn't even care about having a female friend. I decided to let my spirit move me and naturally gravitate towards who I was vibing with mentally and spiritually, someone who got me, celebrated me and who I didn't have to perform for. Qadir and I would talk about different things like the movies we liked and the books we were reading at the time. Qadir's favorite movie was 'My Cousin Vinny'. He liked that I had seen the movie as well, so we would discuss the hilarious scenes and laugh. Coincidentally, we were always on the same side on the issues. I also met Yaegar and Nash. They were from Bo school as well. We became close friends, especially with Yaegar. He was a born-again Christian, recently converted from Islam, and we would have very spirited, fierydebates. He wanted to know why JWs didn't believe in the trinity, or why JWs believed Jesus was the son of God and not God himself. I would quote many scriptures from the bible, like John 14:28 where Jesus said: "The father is greater than I am", also the scripture at Luke 22:42 where Jesus prayed; "..Father, if you want to, remove this cup from me. Nevertheless, let not my will but yours take place". "Surely, Jesus wasn't praying to himself, he was praying to the Almighty Jehovah God." Yaeger would come back with; " what about the scripture at John 10:30 where it says, "I and the father are one"?

"Oh, Yaegar, in the right context, it means he and the father are "one" in complete agreement, in one accord as to their values, intentions and standards. His statement, "let not my will, but yours take place" would be meaningless if Jesus and his father were really just one person". We would go back and forth with our arguments and quoting of scriptures, but, there was never any love lost. Yaeger taught me one could disagree with someone without being disagreeable, rude or spiteful.After the first few weeks of school, our class size more than doubled. This was the time when the teachers took bribes and brought in other students that really didn't make the grade to enter the first weeks, but could do so when things were more settled.

For my english literature class, a man of medium height and build entered the classroom. He looked very slick in his business casual attire. He introduced himself as Mr. Douganson. I perked up in my seat, having heard about him vaguely. He had a reputation for being strict and impassioned about teaching. He was a no-nonsense teacher, firm and very thorough. He set the rules right away. "My period is 45 minutes long and I intend to use all 45 minutes of it. Get your books out and get ready to take great notes. I only want to hear my own voice throughout this class unless I call on you to ask or answer a question. If you're inclined to be recalcitrant, pack your things, get up and leave now."

Even though Mr. Douganson was authoritative, it was very easy to see that he knew his stuff and was quite impassioned by the subject matter. He knew the textbook like the back of his hand, and he taught with so much passion and conviction. He never came down to our level, he was always raising the bar and challenging us to rise to his level. He also used big and unfamiliar vocabulary. "Young man! You're at the precipice of being booted out of my class if I hear you speak without my sanction. Such behavior is obdurate. I suggest your silent acquiescence or else!!!" He did not care whether we understood the meanings of the words he used. He wanted us to broaden our vocabulary, to look up words, and learn to use them the proper way. We sat and listened to him dissect books like *Coriolanus*, *A Man For All Seasons*, and *Native Son*. When he read parts of these books aloud, he enunciated every syllable, paused at every comma, and was animated with his hands and voice. It was impossible not to be moved by his sheer presence, gravitas and authority of the subject matter. He quickly became my favorite teacher, even though some of the boys thought him to be too rigid and maybe even cocky. I hated lawlessness and Mr. Douganson brought decorum and control. He believed in us and wasn't afraid to push us or hurt our feelings in the process. He was such a great story-teller. He made the books come alive to us by the way he taught them to us and he also arranged for us to watch the movie adaptations of these books. I still remember him teaching us about Sir Thomas Moore in *A Man For All Seasons*. "...he is a man with an adamantine sense of himself. He is veracious, unyielding and would not break his integrity even if it meant he had to lose his life." I couldn't help but think Mr Douganson was trying to inculcate those qualities in us. He knew our society was rife with corruption. He also knew we were going to be the future leaders of our country. This was his opportunity to shape the future and he took full advantage of it. I looked forward to my classes with Mr. Douganson. I cared about learning and he was the most passionate and thorough teacher I had ever had. He was unapologetically tough when he graded our tests and exams. He didn't give high marks to students. He wanted to be convinced by our answers, and he insisted we quoted sources and paragraphs to support our responses. One had to intensively and extensively study because his texts, quizzes, and exams were no joke.

Mr. Douganson was also the teacher presiding over the Literary and Debating Society, also called L&DS. This prestigious society, open only to upper and lower sixth formers, was formed to nurture students to be fluent and persuasive orators. It was beautiful to watch shy, nervous, and inexperienced students blossom into commanding orators. Every Friday afternoon we assembled at the school hall for the weekly L&DS meeting. It would open with a prayer, then the student secretary would read the minutes of the last meeting, the floor was then open for debating the topic of the week and lastly, the section called Bulletin ensued. During bulletin, jibes were made about unsuspecting students; those who tried to talk to a girl but failed to impress her, someone who got dumped, someone who couldn't construct a simple correct English sentence, someone who didn't dress well, or someone who had worn the same pair of shoes for the whole term. No one was safe. It was always very funny until you became the butt of a joke that was randomly told. Some of my female classmates were sensitive and would cry if they were made fun of, but the boys mostly took it in stride. I remember one of the girls, Kumi, was very beautiful and well endowed with a big, round butt. The joke about her at L&DS was, "Kumi is carrying a bundle behind her back but she calls it a butt." The whole hall roared with laughter but Kumi was red-faced. I noticed a tiny tear roll down her face, and she tried to get up and leave but her friend next to her told her to just sit through it and let it pass. The same had happened to my good friend Olu the week before. They had blasted him during the bulletin even though he was the President of the student association. "Ay bo, Prezo go butt aid to Zhuri. Nor hope nor dae for we de lowly civilians now." The crowd roared with laughter. I was shocked. It was true that my friend Olu wanted more than a friendship with me, but I hadn't divulged that information to anyone and was therefore at a loss on how they found out. I later discovered that one of his many friends he had confided in leaked the information.

It wasn't all about debates and memorizing quotes in our English Literature class, Mr. Douganson also organized excursions to the beach and other fun places. This was the only time dad permitted me to attend a school function with boys around. He had great confidence in Mr. Douganson as a teacher and a chaperone. "As long as Mr Douganson is going to be there, you can go. Make sure you come back at a respectable time."

THE RETURN OF OLIVER

I had gotten so immersed in my sixth form routine and studying for my 'A' Levels that I had very little time for anything else. The academically elite in my class were very competitive and it took blood, sweat, and tears to stand out. Then one day after coming from school tired, out of the blue my Dad asked me to take a large brown envelope to Miss Vincent's house. He told me she was expecting it and had requested that I take it. This seemed quite strange to me, as my Dad almost never lets me go out by myself. I was going to take a taxi, then walk up the hill to Miss Vincent's house in Wilberforce, surely this was a task for one of the boys. However, I did not argue, but did as I was told. When I got to Miss Vincent's house, she welcomed me and offered me a coke. I drank it quickly and told her I had to leave. She escorted me to her front door and told me to say thanks to my dad for the envelope, then put some money in my hands for my taxi fare back to my house. All of this going to Miss Vincent by myself felt strange, but I just shrugged it off. Maybe I was being tested to see if I could handle a little freedom and responsibilities before I could be trusted with even more.

One Sunday afternoon, about two months after I delivered the brown envelope at her house, Dad told me that Miss Vincent would be paying me a visit by early evening. "Visit me, Why?" I could not figure out why Miss Vincent would want to visit me. I was an almost 19 yr old sixth former at the cusp of her 'A' Level examination, what do I possibly have in common with Miss Vincent, possibly in her early 60s, to prompt her to visit me? My dad kept telling me, "Make sure you look very neat, brush your hair, wear a longer skirt, make yourself look pretty and elegant." These directives from Dad puzzled me. Why must I do all of these things to receive an old lady? The answer to my question came an hour later. Miss Vincent came to our house, and all of my family greeted her with respect and warm regard. After 10 minutes of chit chatting, Dad told me he was going to excuse us. "Let me leave you two to talk. Call me after you are done talking."

Miss Vincent inquired about school and asked what my next move was after my 'A' Levels. I told her I was thinking about going to Fourah Bay College. Commonly known as FBC, Fourah Bay College is the oldest university in West Africa. It was an elite university in its prime and became a magnet for many West Africans seeking higher education. It's student body included Ivorians, Ghanaians, Nigerians, and many other West Africans.

"How ambitious! That's very nice, Zhuri. I am so proud of you, but now I must tell you about the purpose of my visit. I will go straight to the point. My Oliver has asked for your hand in marriage," she declared.

I heard myself asking, "What?', but only in my head. My eyes got really big and shiny, and both of my hands went formy open mouth. I couldn't breathe.

She went on to ask, "So, what should I tell him?" I couldn't reply. I was filled with so much shock and awe. I had seen Ollie three years prior when he returned to bury his father who passed away. He had invited me to the funeral, with me being about 16 years old at the time. He kept me company at his family home after the burial, but we were constantly interrupted by visiting family members. When it came time for me to leave, he arranged for a driver to take me home. But what I remember takingmy breath away was the kiss he gave me on my cheeks as he opened the car door for me. It was just a peck on the cheek, but it was a wet one. I got in the car and touched my cheek, still wet from his kiss.

I didn't want it to dry up, and to add insult to injury he bade me farewell by saying as he slid a piece of paper into my hands, "Have a good night, Sweetheart. This is my address in America, write to me and send me a picture."

"Of course I will! Right away!" I told him. He waved goodbye and watched until the BMW drove out of sight.

I kept replaying the scene in my head. First, he got me a driver, gave me a wet kiss on the cheek, then he called me Sweetheart? When I laid in bed that night, I kept fantasizing about us being in a relationship. I knew I had fallen madly in love with him, but I also understood I was ten years his junior. Ten years I didn't care about. What did it matter? What mattered was that I loved him and he loved me too. I fantasized about kissing him deeply with tongue, about laying in bed with him making love. My imagination took me to fantastic places. However, reality hit me when I didn't get a reply from him after I sent him a letter. "Oh well, he must think I'm too young for him. But I'm not. I can love him in all the ways that he wants. If only he realized I am more mature for my age," I thought to myself.

I had put all of that behind me and now, three years later his mother was at my house on a Sunday evening in my living room with a marriage proposal? *He hadn't forgotten about me after all*, I thought. Has he felt what I was feeling, if so, why didn't he communicate for three years?

"I know this is shocking for you, my dear. You don't have to give an answer right away! Think carefully about it and give me an answer by next weekend," his mother said.

"Yes, yes and yes!!!" I was screaming in my head, but like they say about the duck, "above the surface, look calm and unruffled, below the surface paddle like hell." I feigned calmness and sophistication outwardly, even though I wanted to scream for the whole world to know that I am about to be Mrs. Zhuri Jones!

"Thank you for coming Ma, and for the proposal. Indeed I am very shocked. I will give you my answer by the weekend Ma. Thank you" I replied, all the while shy and timid. I got up and went to my dad's room to tell him what had transpired and to also let him know Miss Vincent was in the living room waiting. I went to my bedroom stupefied. Was this real? Was I imagining things? I could hear dad and Miss Vincent talking and laughing in the living room, so I knew I wasn't dreaming. But how was this all possible? Can one actually will their dreams into reality?

After Miss Vincent left that evening, dad told me he was going to install my own personal telephone in my room.

"Oliver wants to start calling you, I figure you're going to need some privacy," he said, and I couldn't believe it. This was the same man who had made my life miserable insisting I don't go near boys and now he was going to install a phone in my room so I could have some privacy to talk to a man?

"I know what you're thinking, Zhuri. I am in full support of you dating Oliver. For one, he is thousands of miles away and cannot possibly tampa with you and two, he has good intentions. He wants to marry you, not dilly-dally with you aimlessly like these young boys like to do these days. He is good for you, Zhuri. He has promised me he will make sure you continue your education. He is a doctor, he values education and is still very ambitious. He will make sure you match him. Also, he will be unlike the school boys here, who just want to sleep with innocent girls. He was raised overseas. He has lived in many countries, from England to Japan to America, and many other countries in between. I see you reading those romance novels, he will be like one of them. He will bring you flowers, take you on dates, buy you cards, just spoil you. That's what they do in those countries. You're going to experience something special and different than what your friends have experienced. See, this is why I have been telling you to be a good girl. It does pay off, Zhuri. Now look, the most eligible bachelor of them all comes back for the good girl." Those were great perks for sure, but until dad brought them up, I was only happy that Ollie loved me and had chosen me. My fantasies were about to be realized and I was beyond stoked. Even though our parents have been doing something in the background, It didn't feel like a set up to me at all because Ollie and I had been fond of each other first, we had spent that time together at his father's funeral, he had given me his address and phone number, I had written him a letter, and he had asked about me to his Mom and asked for my hand in marriage. So, we had been the ones who had put our feet to the steering wheel, now, after a slow burn, we were taking off from where we left off. And all those feelings were coming right back and taking me to cloud 9 all over again.

    The next day, I received a call from Ollie. "Hi Zhu-Zhu! Hello my Sweetheart, how are you, how is school going?" I heard him say on the other side of the phone.

    "Oh, hi Ollie," I greeted him between giggles. "I am fine, thank you. What about you? What a beautiful surprise to hear from you."

    "Surprised that I am calling you or surprised at my proposal albeit the fact that I had to do it through my mother?"

"Actually, both," I said, giggling again. "I thought I was the only one who felt that way. I wondered why you never replied to my letter."

"I see you still like to laugh a lot, Zhu. To be perfectly honest, I knew I loved you, but I also knew you deserve the better Ollie, the one that is settled and more composed. I did not want to hurt a good girl like you. When I received your letter, I read it and thought to myself, what a clever girl. I put your letter and picture in my drawer and told myself I will party and run around a bit, but when I'm ready to settle down, I will go get my Zhu-Zhu."

"Aww, that's sweet."

"I brought the idea up to my mom and she talked to your dad about it, but they both decided not to tell you about it for fear you will stop studying for your 'A' levels. They felt the excitement would be a distraction for you. But, I told them I couldn't proceed further until they let you in on it. You might have a boyfriend and might not even want me. So, talking about boyfriends, do you have one?"

"Boyfriend? I already have a fiance, who needs a boyfriend?"

"Ha! That's a good one, Zhu! I promise I'll get you a ring soon. Do you know your ring size?"

"No, I do not. I will find out and let you know soon." I couldn't believe that Oliver Jones was actually asking me for my ring size with the intention to marry me. Even my fantasies didn't take me this far. I was hoping for a love connection with him at some point, but I never allowed myself to go as far as the point of marriage. But there he is on the other side of the phone asking for my ring size. I was screaming on the inside, but I managed to stay composed. I decided I would pinch myself later after I hung up.

"Aww man! My calling card is telling me I only have three minutes left to talk. Let's keep talking anyway. I will have to get a more expensive card with more minutes. But if you ever need to reach me, please call me, collect. I will pick up and call you right back."

"I know collect calls are expensive. I will never need to call you via collect as long as you call at the times you say you will."

"Most definitely. You can count on that. So, you seriously do not have a boyfriend?"

"No, Ollie. I have been concentrating on my studies. Besides, you know the type of dad I have. He is not one to tolerate it..." Ollie's minutes were running out, there was no time to talk about my brief relationships with Lenny and Alpha.

"I know, I know. I'm sorry about that. He should let you live a little. Don't worry Zhu, not too long now, you will be far, far away from him and you will make decisions on your own and be in charge of your own household."

"I cannot wait, Ollie!" Then the phone was cut off, his minutes used up. I touched my cheeks, looking at myself in the mirror. This was my reality? None of this was some kind of fantasy anymore? Ollie had just called me. He had confirmed the proposal, he had asked for my ring size. He was taking me far away to go live with him. Somehow, my reality was better than my fantasies.

It turned out that our parents were right about me getting distracted by the excitement of an impending nuptial to my longtime crush, Ollie. I had to keep it a secret from my friends. I wrote to Salem to share the news with her. I had to tell someone or I would burst. 'A' level stopped being a priority, I longed for the next phone call from Ollie. He would give me a day and time he would be calling and I would sit by the phone in anticipation. As soon as the phone rang, I would pick up on the first ring.

"Hi Sweetheart, sorry I'm five minutes late to call. I got paged just before I was about to call you, so I had to call the hospital back."

"No worries, Ollie. I knew you would call sooner or later. How are you, how is work?"

"Good, good, no complaints. Check this out, Zhu, I was thinking that instead of us getting married in June next year after your 'A' levels exam, we should just go ahead and get married in December or January. The reason being I will have two weeks of vacation time in late December/early January and also because you don't need the 'A' levels to attend college in the U.S. All you need is your high school diploma which you already have anyway. 'A' levels are useless in this country.

"Oh wow! You mean I don't have to vigorously study anymore? And I get to be your wife sooner? Let's do it, Ollie! Let's do it! But wait, what are we going to tell our parents?" I wondered whether my dad would be turned off by me cancelling my 'A' levels. My dad was all about the importance of education and I wondered if there would ever be a good enough reason for me to put off taking my exams.

"Don't worry about our parents, Sweetheart. We are making decisions about our lives now. This has nothing to do with them. We will inform them after we agree on things and not a moment sooner."

"Goodness gracious, this is all so strange to me, Ollie. I've never made my own decisions before. Not what shoes I wear, who sews my school uniform, what time I get home, nothing."

"Well, get used to it, Zhu. You're an adult now and almost a wife. My wife! We will be making a lot of decisions together."

We told our parents about our decision a week later. Surprisingly, they

were quite supportive. They understood that my 'A' levels were not a necessity in the U.S. I also knew I didn't need it to start university, so I was fine with the cancellation. I was just extremely stoked that I was about to be free! I didn't even know what freedom would feel like, but I could bet anything it would be better than being constantly told what to do, where to go, being threatened or at the worst, getting punished. It was going to be strange discovering who I was without parental pressures and expectations. I felt like I had been molded into the daughter of my parents' dream at this point. One who was "different", with good home training, who didn't talk back or challenged them, one who was making them proud by passing her exams and going to grade A schools, one who accepted their religion. Now, I was going to start living for myself. How will that even feel? Do I even know the real Zhuri, or is the real Zhuri about to emerge far, far away from them?

We now embarked on planning our wedding. Ollie sent money to my parents to help with some of the expenses. When it came to what I would wear, I had an idea. I wanted my wedding dress to look like that of my favorite singer, Whitney Houston. Her dress was ivory, long, elaborately beaded, sequined and form-fitting, with a sheer neckline and long sleeves.

Dad immediately shut down my choice. "No, that would not be appropriate. You are too skinny. That type of dress will accentuate your skinniness. You need a wedding dress that is big and puffy. It will hide how slim you are."

I did not like the idea of a big and puffy dress, but dad had made his decision and that was that. My mom did not argue with my dad or even interfere. She didn't come up with any ideas for my wedding dress either. I was taken to a seamstress on the weekend and she showed us a wedding catalog on her desk, to which dad pointed to a dress he liked and I got measured for it. I tried not to resist because I saw the light at the end of the tunnel. I would just have to put up with this a little while longer before I got to be with my Ollie in America and make my own decisions.

Ollie announced that he would be coming to Freetown one week before our wedding. I would have to go pick him up at the airport because he was exclusively my guest this time around. We would not share the same house, but I would have to go welcome him home as my fiance. After Ollie bought his ticket, he told me the date and time of his arrival. I must have been walking on clouds the whole time; I couldn't wait or stop smiling. I kept thinking about what hairstyle to wear to the airport. Should I perm my hair or just braid it? Should I wear jeans or leggings? I wanted to impress him so badly. I had never picked up anyone from the airport before, this was going to be my first time. Dad had me take my cousin Ahmad with me. I stood on the arrivals balcony at the Lungi International airport waiting for Ollie to get out of his flight that had just landed. I saw many de-plane, but Ollie was nowhere in sight. I was nervous and anxious. Did Ollie miss his flight? Was this whole thing a joke? I knew this was too good to be true, I thought. I bowed my head down in disappointment then Ahmad tapped my shoulder and said, "Zhuri, look!" pointing to the direction of the plane.

There he was, coming out of the plane and talking to the pilot. They stood for a while talking, then I saw them shake hands.

"Ollie! Ollie! Over here!" I shouted, waving to him from the balcony.

"My Zhu-Zhu! I'll get to you after I get through customs."

I ran downstairs waiting for him to get through customs. When he finally came through the door, I ran to him and hugged him so tightly. Then we faced each other and kissed on the lips.

"Hello Sweetheart, I am so happy to see you again. Finally!"

"Me too! Look! We made the taxi driver wait to take us back. Let's get your suitcases and leave. This is my cousin, Ahmad."

"Hello Ahmad, thank you, man, thank you," Ollie greeted Ahmad.

"Hello Ollie. I had to bring her. All we hear every day from her is Ollie, Ollie, Ollie. You should see how sad she looked when you didn't come out of the plane sooner."

"Oh really? Ha, ha, sorry to worry you sweetheart. I found out the pilot lived in the same neighborhood I used to live in England, so I engaged with him a little. But I'm here now. Are you ready to get married?"

"Is she ready? She is" Ahmad stated.

I pouted. "He asked me Ahmad, not you. Yes! I am ready to get married. Only to you".

Ahmad sat with the taxi driver in front, while Ollie and I sat in the back. Ollie would turn to me every so often and whisper, 'let's steal a kiss,' and I would oblige and kiss him on the lips. Before we got to his mother's house, Ollie asked the driver if he had a match. The driver gave him one and he proceeded to get a Newport cigarette box out of his pocket and lit one. I was shocked and scared. What else did I not know about Ollie that will be a deal breaker for me? I would have never in normal circumstances chosen a man who smoked cigarettes. My dad had literally spent my whole childrenhood talking about the evils of cigarette smoking, drinking and drugs. Surely, he must not know this side of Ollie as well.

"You smoke?" I asked him.

"Yeah, it is just a bad habit I picked up in college. I promise to quit soon. In fact, I have been trying to quit. I bought the nicoderm patch. It's not so easy. But I have a reason to quit now, you!"

"Please do. It is bad for you. I had no idea you smoked cigarettes."

"Uh oh, I hope it's not a deal breaker for you, Zhu. I will quit, I promise. You are my biggest motivation now."

"As long as you're going to quit, it's fine."

We drove to his mother's house with me leaning on him and him stealing kisses the whole way. It was very romantic to me. I loved kissing him. He would press his lips so softly against mine and make a smacking sound. When we got to his mother's house, his room was ready. He asked me to come with him to get some of the stuff he brought for me. "You can open the suitcases. Whatever you like, you can have." As I made my way to one of the suitcases, he held me by my waist and said, "A proper kiss?" I was going to say yes, but he was already kissing me, his tongue sliding in my mouth. I could vaguely taste tobacco and vodka. He sucked on my tongue long and hard and when we were done, he said I was yummy. I felt embarrassed. I had never had to stay and face a man after such deep kissing. With Lenny, I would have to leave after our steamy kisses. But here I am, still in the room after our first real kiss. I suppose this was how it was going to be from now on. To escape the awkwardness, I asked Ollie about the diary he said he was bringing for me. He had asked me what I wanted him to bring, and I didn't ask for anything else but a diary. He and the diary were more than enough. I hated asking people for things. This attitude is because my dad had told me many times not to ask men for things because they would take it to mean that I want them or simply because they would want something back in return. So, I wasn't good at asking for things or wanting something of value. The diary however was simple and inexpensive, but it was of great value to me because I loved to write my thoughts down, especially those things that were taboo to talk about with anyone else. I could tell it all to my diary instead.

In the evening Ollie got us a taxi to take me back home, since we were not going to spend the night together until our wedding day. "Welcome, welcome, welcome!" Dad greeted Ollie when he walked through our gate. "We are glad to have you with us. You are now part of the family. How was your flight?"

"It was good, nothing out of the ordinary. I'm glad to be here myself. Time to take care of business. Thank you so much for giving your blessing."

"Well, I saw you grow up a little bit, even though you've spent most of your life overseas. I believe you will take good care of my daughter and help her succeed."

"We will be taking care of each other, Sir. You and Mrs Swarray have raised a great daughter. I am very grateful and look forward to all the great things she will add to my life."

VISA INTERVIEW

Our wedding was barely three days away, but what made me even more nervous was going to the American embassy to interview for a visa. It was very common to be rejected for an American visa, especially since I had no travel history, and also because there was not a lot tying me back to my country except my family. I did not have properties, children, or a job that I needed to come back to. My immediate family was about to be my extended family. I was going to be building a new family with my soon to be husband, Ollie. I kept praying to Jehovah to help me. The thought of getting married and being left behind gutted me. I was so eager to start my life with Ollie. The consul could reject a visa application for a reason as vague as, "I'm not convinced." It was totally up to their discretion and there was nothing one could do about it. Ollie could sense my nervousness as we stood in line waiting for my name to be called.

Sooner rather than later, I heard my name. "Zhuri Swarray!"

"Right here!" I answered, walking up with my brown envelope containing my documents.

"So, Miss Swarray, what is the purpose of your visit to America?" the consul asked, a paper and pen in her handready to write down my reponses.

"Well, erm, actually, my fiance lives and works over there right now. I will be joining him after our wedding."

"When is your wedding?"

"On the 5th of January, Ma'am. Only 3 days from now."

"What is your fiance's status in America? What's his nationality? Does he have permanent residency? What does he do there?"

Ollie, seeing that I was getting bombarded with questions and knowing that I don't have some specific information, rose up with his British passport in hand and stood beside me by the window.

"I am British. I am currently doing my residency and working at the Cleveland Clinic after graduating medical school in Cambridge."

The consul immediately gravitated towards Ollie's accent as he did not sound African. He had a British passport and was name-dropping Ivy league schools.

"Mr. Jones, why don't you both go live in England after your wedding? Why America?"

"Oh, I haven't abandoned England at all. But for now, I am in America. It is where I am doing my specialty and working simultaneously. The next step is to go practice in an under-served, rural area where most Americans don't wanna serve while I wait for my green card. I look forward to giving back that way. My wife will be of enormous support to me and a very necessary addition since I will not know anybody else."

"That's quite altruistic, Mr Jones. I wish you the best. Both of you!"

Both of you? Did she just say, "both of you?" Does that mean my application has been approved?

"I see you have a J1 visa right now, Mr Jones. I cannot issue her a J2 visa until you both are legally married. I will keep your application active until you return with your marriage certificate by Friday next week?"

"Most definitely! We will be back on Friday. Thank you so much!"

"No, thank you and congratulations on your upcoming nuptials."

That's it? I got the visa? I didn't even speak to the consul for a complete five minutes. She totally ignored me after Ollie stood by me and started answering her questions. I did not care; I just got approved to go to America with my Ollie. I wasn't going to be left behind after all. I was going to be a full-fledged wife. My new life was about to start. I couldn't wait to go home and tell everyone.

A huge trepidation was off my mind now. I got the visa in the bag. Now all my nervousness and unrelenting agitation was about my wedding night. I was more in distress than excitement. Of course I loved Ollie and wanted to sleep with him, but I was embarrassed about being completely naked. I had never been completely naked with a man before. I was nervous about not knowing what to do. My absolute concern was not being able to please him sexually. I didn't want him to see me as a prude. But it will be evident soon that I was indeed a prude.

I had never had sex. When we used to watch movies with our parents, if a sex scene came on, they would either change the channel or ask us to leave the room immediately. Would my imagination of what I had read and think sex is going to be enough? I didn't want my first duty as a wife to be disappointing. Was I going to enjoy sex? I knew I would be embarrassed to be completely naked. I have never been completely naked for anyone before. Thoughts of my wedding night began to be nerve wracking instead of exciting. The unknown can be pretty scary.

After sharing the good news about my visa, I went to my room and buried myself in my favourite Mills and Boon novel, *Passionate Obsession* by Christine Greig. Like most Mills and Boon novels, *Passionate Obsession* was filled with romance, intrigue, passion, and a tantalizing description of sexual escapades. I imagined this would be how our first night as husband and wife will be. I wanted to prepare myself.

WEDDING

I wasvery excited the night before our wedding. Word had spread far and wide that I was getting married to a doctor from America I had never met. I invited a handful of my classmates. Some people were happy for me, some were shocked, and some were jealous. I had not made a single decision about my wedding, not what I was going to wear, not how my hair was going to be styled, makeup, the reception or party dresses, nothing. The only thing I had a say in was loving Ollie and being ecstatic to start my life with him. No one had to convince me of that. He was my crush and now my crush was going to be my husband the very next day!

When I woke up in the morning, I was whisked away to a hairdresser where I got my hair styled. When I returned home, my Aunt Fatima who was visiting from America applied my makeup. She also gave me one of the dresses in her suitcase to wear for the wedding party in the evening. It was a long, beige, sparkly, sequin, low cut dress with a long slit on the side. I liked it a lot. Ollie and I were to get married at the Civil Court at Walpole St. I got dressed in the puffy wedding dress chosen for me and my oldest brother, Rashad, walked me down the aisle to meet Ollie who was sweating profusely. The weather always took a toll on him every time he returned to Sierra Leone. It was always very hot for him and he always had a handkerchief with him. He would wipe his brow and neck and put it back in his pocket until the next sweaty moment.

Ollie took me from my brother and we both sat in front of the registrar who reminded us why we were there. He also read our vows to us and asked us to repeat them. He pronounced us husband and wife and told Ollie he could kiss me. Ollie obliged, to the cheer and laughter of the surrounding witnesses which included our parents, a few relatives, and a few of my schoolmates. It all felt very strange to me. The same people who would have beaten you black and blue for sneaking around with a boy, are now all cheering and clapping by the show of public affection right in their faces. The hair stylist gave me some finger waves that would stay in place because of the hair gel. My fashion fair foundation gave my face a very smooth look. Ollie kept whispering in my ear that I looked beautiful. I felt more beautiful because of how absolutely sweet and complimentary he was of me; "your teeth are sparkling white against your brown skin. Your skin feels so soft. You look so beautiful my angel, so beautiful. I'm a lucky man". I kept saying thank you and blushing. I thought he looked quite handsome too in his grey suit. I couldn't believe he had come so far away to marry me. He was six foot three inches tall. His sheer presence made me feel so protected. His hands were so much bigger than mine. When we held hands, mine got lost in his. I loved how he had to bend over to kiss his five feet four inches bride. He smiled really great, there wasn't any tobacco scent lingering in his breath. He used his middle finger to scratch my palm as he held hands with me. It was his way of communicating with me without anyone noticing. It was his way of saying, I'm right here with you, I'm in this with you.

After the ceremony at the registry, we had to visit the home of our respective parents to drink 'col water.' Drinking cold water prepared and served by one of the parents on each side is part of the marriage rites in Sierra Leone. One of the parents blesses the water and tells both partieswhat it represents. Our first stop was my house. My mother was already back from our registry wedding and was standing at the front door of our house with a glass of col water in her hand. As we stopped in front of her, she blessed us and then said: "Drink this col water. This is so that you two will always remember to cool down your tempers when things are not going well. Do not deal with each other with hot tempers. Do not be quick to be irate. Both of you must strive to be cool, calm, refreshing, just like this cold water." She then put the glass on my lips for me to take a sip and then did the same with Ollie. We had no time to rest as we had to make the same trip to Ollie's mother's house which was about 25 minutes away. Her house was also where the wedding reception was being held. By the time we arrived at her house, it was packed with people waiting for us. We were greeted with cheers, songs, music, and dancing. His mother offered us some col water and gave the same speech as my mom.

Later, we got seated at the head of a dazzling table set up. The rectangular table was covered with cashmere tablecloth. There were flower trimmings all around the table, with colorful balloons decorated on the four corners of the table. Our three-tiered wedding cake was mounted in the middle of the table. Prayer was offered by a pastor from my mother-in-law's church, and speeches and toasts were made to Ollie and I from several family members. Soon after, everything became a blur to me, including whether I ate or drank, because I was so exhausted. However, I remember Ollie constantly reminding me to smile for the photographers. "Don't forget to smile, darling. I know you're exhausted. It's been a long day, but these pictures will last forever."

"I'm smiling, Ollie, see! Say cheese!"

"That's my wife!"

"Your what? I didn't hear you."

"Oh, you heard me alright, Zhu-Zhu. Get used to being called that, my wife and also Mrs. Jones."

"You mean Mrs. Zhuri Fatmata Jones?" I asked him, cheesing so hard and so widely.

"Yes, that's exactly what I mean, Mrs. Zhuri F. Jones. I love the sound of that." He then leaned in for a quick kiss, and the photographer caught that sweet moment. Festivities continued till 2am. Then it was time for us to go to our bedroom. I went and took a quick shower because I felt very sweaty and sticky. I put on my nightgown and waited for Ollie to join me after his shower. He made it to bed and held me really tightly. He started kissing me and when it began to get passionate, he asked me if I wanted to have sex.

"Sweetheart, do you want us to consummate our marriage tonight or are you too tired?"

"I am okay, whatever you want to do is fine with me," I answered. I wasn't expecting to be asked. I expected him to just make love to me like they did in the Mills and Boon novels.

"Now, this is new for you, baby. I want to make sure you're comfortable, that's all."

"Oh, I am very comfortable," I assured him. "As long as I'm with you, I am fine."

"That is great!" Ollie resumed kissing me, touching me in places I had never been touched before. He then cupped my small, perky breasts and started kissing them, all the while whispering in my ears if I was okay. He took off all my clothes piece by piece and then got on top of me while kissing and caressing me. I felt his hard erect penis making its way towards my vagina. After some intense pressure trying to penetrate me, I felt a sharp pain and moaned.

"This will only hurt a little, but it will be over soon, sweetheart, I promise," he tried to reassure me. He kept trying several times and when he finally entered me, I let out a loud sigh. He covered my mouth and reminded me that his mother was in the next room. "Shhhh, not so loud, sweetheart. I'm so sorry you're in pain. Not a pleasant night for you. It gets better, I promise. What can I get you, a coke, a fanta, sprite, anything? Oh snap! There's blood all over the bed, these sheets need to be changed. I will be right back, sweetheart."

Ollie came back with a Fanta for me to drink and also some new sheets. He put the soiled ones next to the foot of the bed on the floor. He made the bed and asked me to lay back down, and then offered me a wet towel to wipe the blood between my legs.

"Just lay down, I will wipe it for you. Now Zhu, I want you to know that this is not what sex will always be like. Look at me, don't be embarrassed, be proud. Look at me." His hand grasped my face and held my chin up. "There will come a time really soon when you will enjoy all this. I promise you. Very soon, you will be looking forward to being intimate with me in this way. There will come a time soon when it will not hurt. It will feel really good. Do you hear me? It will begin to feel really, really good. Do you trust me?" He asked me looking straight into my eyes.

"Yes, I trust you. I just wasn't expecting it to hurt so badly."

"I am sorry, Zhu, we have to cross this road to get to the other side. There's lots of pleasure, innumerable orgasms waiting for you on the other side. But come on closer, I will just hold you in my arms till you fall asleep."

I rolled over to him and he held me against his hairy chest, I could hear his heart beating fast, his chest heaving up and down rhythmically.

I was still in pain, I felt sore and tender, but I was happy to be suffering this pain with Ollie by my side. I felt very protected in his big, strong arms. I felt happy that he chose me and that I chose him. It didn't go unnoticed to me that Ollie was really comfortable taking off all his clothes and walking around naked. I, on the other hand, kept pulling the cover over my body. I had never in my life seen a man walk around naked in front of me, without a care in the world. He looked even taller naked. I was embarrassed to stare at him. I was too shy to even make eye contact. This was all so new for me. It felt uncomfortable to some extent.As much as I loved Ollie with all my heart, he was still a stranger. It was amazing that someone so much bigger than me can get on top of me and I would hardly tell the difference. It was as if we were equals in bed. All of a sudden, sex was just about the hype. I haven't been as pleased as I had hoped to be. I thought it would be a heavenly feeling inadequate to put in words. But here I was, sore, hurting and bleeding.I fell asleep in his arms and didn't wake up till 10 am the next day. He had woken up earlier and had tea with his mother. He had also handed over to his mother the bloody sheets. When I joined them in the veranda after my morning bath, his mother gave me the biggest smile I had ever seen from her.

"Good morning Mrs. Jones. How are you feeling this morning? Do you need anything; food, tea, pain medication?" she asked with a wink and a smile. I felt so embarrassed. She knew about last night, my first night with my husband.

"No, Ma. I am fine, thank you," I said as I turned around and started walking away.

"No need to be embarrassed, Zhuri. I am proud of you. You have been a good girl. You have kept yourself for your husband and have never been touched before. I am so proud of you. I will be going to see your parents this evening to tell them the good news and of course to add to your bride price."

My parents! Did she just say my parents? It's not enough that she knows I had sex but now my parents are going to know too? I let out a long sigh and returned to our bedroom. Ollie came after me asking, "Sweetheart, are you ok?"

"Ollie, I don't know how I feel about everyone knowing I had sex last night, especially my parents."

"C'mon Zhu-Zhu, you're a married woman now. That's what married people do. Get used to it. Trust that your parents expect you to have sex, especially last night."

"Expecting that we had sex is one thing, but going to be told we did have sex is an entirely different thing. I'm-"

"Zhu! Stop it! You knew this day would come. Why have you kept yourself a virgin until this time? Why have you not given yourself away to the boys you went to school with? It must be because you wanted to bring honor to your family. Now, how are they supposed to know you kept yourself chaste and honorable and untouched without being told? You had sex, Zhu, but guess what, no one can do anything to you because you're a married woman and you're mine."

"Well, I don't know if I want to see them this evening. It all feels so weird," I retorted.

"Me and my wife are going to see my proud in-laws this evening and my wife will be just fine."

"Urgh! Ollie! Excuse me if my brain can't make this sudden shift from being conditioned that sex was vile, problematic, dirty, unwholesome, a taboo, to all of a sudden being something I am about to be hailed for participating in. A participation that is pleasing to everyone else because they deemed it the right time for me to do it. This has nothing to do with me and what I want, how I want it, and when I want it. It has everything to do with them. It's what makes them feel good. To hell with my feelings, huh?"

"Zhu-Zhu, are you seriously trying to tell me you didn't know this day would come? Look, sweetheart, it's part of our culture. It will be over soon. We'll go over this evening and see them and get it over with." He laid on the bed with me and kissed my forehead and held me close to him. "Listen, Zhu-Zhu, I know some of our culture and practices suck, especially for women. Trust me, I know. But I will be there with you. I will protect you. I will make sure they do not go on and on about the issue. I will quickly try my best to change the subject. I realize now how awkward this will be for you. Give me a chance to be there for you for the first time, ok, darling?"

"Ok. Thanks Ollie".

That evening when we visited my parents, I could barely make eye contact with them. I felt so exposed, so embarrassed. They, on the other hand, were beaming with pride, telling me how proud I had made them. They told me word had spread throughout the neighborhood because they had celebrated by cheering and dancing after my mother-in-law came and told them I was disvirgined by my husband.

How does one go from absolute chastity to being renowned for one's first sexual act? How is that not odd? Why does the value of the woman appreciate by waiting for a man who did not wait for her to be his first? Why does a woman's value depreciate after she willingly participates in sexual activity with a man of her choosing? Does our worth lie between our thighs? Why is virginity used to determine our worth? Why is a man's virginity worthless and yet a woman's is so prized? Why doesn't anyone bat an eyelid when a man isn't a virgin, yet a woman loses respect and value when she chooses to sleep with a man? I kept pondering these questions in my head as I got ready for bed at night. Ollie came to bed with just his boxers, but I was fully dressed. "What's all this?" he asked, pointing to my clothes.

"What do you mean?" I asked.

"All these clothes on you, sweetheart. You're overdressed for bed. This is only your second night after our wedding."

"I was hoping to just cuddle with you and go to bed since I am still hurting down there."

"We have to do it again tonight, sweetheart. That's the only way it will get better. If you stop doing it, the next time you do it again it will hurt like new."

"But I'm still-"

"It's okay, Zhu-Zhu," he interrupted, "we have to keep doing it. The more we do it, the less it keeps hurting. Your body is going to get used to receiving me and my size and it will adjust. Don't worry, I will be gentle, I promise."

He unzipped my clothes and gently pulled my panty, kissing me all over. I was just beginning to enjoy the foreplay when I felt some pressure and a sharp pain. I took a deep breath and sighed quietly as I felt him enter me. As he stroked me he whispered in my ear, "See, it's not so bad this time. Everyday it will get better. I love you, Zhu-zhu, thank you for saving yourself for me."

"I love you too, Ollie. I cannot wait to start enjoying this with you and maybe even start initiating."

"That's what I'm talking about! That's my wife talking. It hurts me that it is painful for you and not me. I truly want you to experience your first orgasm, but until you physically heal soon from the soreness and slight virginal tear, it will hurt. However, you will heal sooner rather than later. Trust me."

"You know all too well about all this, how many women have you..."

"See! No, never go there, Baby! This is supposed to be our honeymoon. We are not talking about other women. I am concentrating solely on my wife". He kissed me long and hard until I started gasping for air. He climaxed and then held me close to him and fell fast asleep. As he slept, I wondered to myself whether I'd ever get the feeling he seems to be getting. The way he looked like he was going into a trance before he orgasms, the way he would say; "yes, baby, yes, baby, yes baby" before he orgasmed, the way he ran out of breath afterwards and would just fall asleep. Surely this can't just be about him alone. At some point I have to feel this way too.

COMING TO AMERICA

By the time we knew it, a week had flown by and it was time to go to America with Ollie. I was overjoyed about having Ollie all to myself and also about going to America, the land of opportunity. I had been Mrs Jones for one week and it had been a whirlwind experience. I have been disvirgined, I was no longer living with my parents or consulting with them. I had gone to bed with a man constantly by my side and with trepidation about being touched every time. I loved being with him, but the sex part was still painful, so every time he would touch me, I knew it would end with sex. He had told me stories about his life in America, we had visited many relatives and I was feeling more like his wife because everyone was addressing me as "Mrs Jones" including Ollie himself. I had begun thinking about my life with him in America. I would have my own apartment, cook my own meals, not have to ask for permission from my parents about anything anymore, andhave a self-contained house with all the modern amenities I could think of. My style of dressing would change. I would have to dress up for four seasons now, winter, summer, spring and fall. I would have my own car and anything else I wanted. For the first time, I felt really free.

Ollie took me to PZ, a shopping district in the eastern part of Freetown, to get a coat. He lived in Cleveland, Ohio in the US and it is extremely cold over there in January. My family came to see us off at the airport, and I bid farewell to them as I boarded the flight. I didn't have time to be sad about leaving. I was too excited about gaining my freedom. Also, I knew my parents were going to miss me for sure, but they were excited about the opportunities that awaited me in America. My dad was looking forward to me 'saving' the family from poverty. "Make sure you do not forget about us, don't forget about where you came from, how much we suffered and sacrificed to bring you up. Make sure you do not forget about your brothers. You are our hope. Don't you ever forget that." My dad said to me as he hugged me goodbye. My mom wiped a tear and said;" Jehovah will always be with you, my daughter, he will always protect you. Remember to always listen to your husband and obey him".

"I will never forget about any of you or our struggles. I will write as soon as I arrive. And anytime I have money, I will send it immediately". I hugged all of them and headed towards the plane.

We were flying with Air Afrique, transit in Senegal, and then to New York. I had never flown before. Ollie told me it would sometimes get bumpy up in the air. I was excited and nervous, but I had Ollie all to myself for the next 12 hours. I couldn't believe my life. After a long and tiring flight, we landed in New York. Everything looked so strange and different. There were bright lights everywhere, even from the air as we were descending. There was no sign of blackouts, The airport looked immaculately spotless, the young women who worked at the desks looked very sleek and beautiful, their hairstyles were just like I had seen them on Jet and Ebony magazines, directions were clearly posted everywhere. Once we got out of the airport, I could hardly understand the New York accent.

"Are they speaking English?" I asked Ollie.

"Haha! First of all, welcome to America, sweetheart. And yes, they're speaking English with slang and their own twang."

"I do not understand anything that man just said to us." I was referring to the TSA agent who processed our luggage.

"Not to worry, sweetie, with time you'll get used to it."

"I don't know, this is not the type of English I learned in Mr. Douganson's class."

"Ha! Definitely not. I would love to take you for a walk outside but it is 15 degrees outside. You will not make it".

"I haven't been outside yet, let me go and see."

"Ok, brave girl, let's go. We have two hours of down time before we catch the greyhound bus to Cleveland".

As soon as we made it outside, I rushed back in. "Oh Ollie! It is so cold. I cannot go outside. I don't know if I can go outside to catch the bus". I held myself shivering. I had never felt such cold temperature before. It felt like I was inside a refrigerator. I could never have prepared myself for such harsh, frigid temperatures. I had no concept of anything else other than the dry and rainy seasons we have in Sierra Leone. During the rainy season, when the sun is mostly overtaken by clouds, we complain about it being so cold. "So cold" weather in Sierra Leone is about 60 degrees.

"You'll be fine. You're just not dressed warm enough for the weather. I am going to leave you for a brief while. Make sure you keep an eye on our luggage at all times. Don't move from this area okay? I am going to go outside to get you a proper winter coat, gloves, tights, hat and boots. What's your shoe size, Zhu-Zhu?"

"8.5".

"Ok, see you soon, sweetheart. Don't move away from here!"

Ollie disappeared from sight and I was left with just our three suitcases. I looked around me in amazement at the technology and efficient way everything flowed. What fascinated me the most were the vending machines. I had never seen one before. But I noticed people would go to one, put some coins inside a slot, push some buttons and a drink or a snack would fall right at their feet. They would pick it up and enjoy their drink or snack. This was more fascinating to me than the conveyor belts at baggage claim which brought all the bags to the passengers after their flights. What had me transfixed before all of this was the escalator, the vertical transportation of moving stairs where you just stand and it takes you where you wanted to go, whether up or down. Everything looked so easy. The US seemed to have found a way to let machines do all the hard work for them, unlike the backbreaking work people did back home.

"Look at you, still right where I left you. That's my wife!" Ollie exclaimed as he appeared next to me.

"Ollie! You're back already. I was busy looking around trying to make sense of my environment."

"Don't worry. You have all the time in the world. Now, you see the women's restroom over there? Go put these on. It'll make you feel warmer and more comfortable and ready for the bus."

I went to the restroom and put on everything, feeling warmer already. I came back out and twirled around. "Look, Ollie, what do you think?"

"I think they fit you perfectly. Do you want anything to eat before we board the bus?"

I pointed to the vending machine. "Zhu-Zhu, not the vending machine. You need proper food. Something to carry you for a few hours at least. Come here, let me get you a burger or something. Have you ever had a burger before?"

"Not really. But can we get my drink from there?" I asked, pointing to the vending machine again.

"You want to see how it works, don't you?"

"Yes! Please, Ollie," I said, cheesingwidely.

"Okay, okay, I think I have a few quarters. Here! You need three of these. A quarter is 25 cents, the drinks are 75 cents, so you need 3 quarters. Now put all three quarters in." I did as I was told and could hear the quarters falling into the machine. It showed that it had received 75 cents. "Now, choose the drink you want, Zhu. Press the button underneath the drink." I pressed the button underneath the coke and it left the position it was and fell to the bottom of the machine and I put my hand in and picked it up.

"Whooa, this is so cool."

"Haha, you think so? Now let us go over to McDonalds and get you a big Mac and some french fries."

He ordered our food and we sat and enjoyed our first meal together in America. I looked straight at him as he looked at me between bites. We both knew what I was thinking; new lease on life, freedom, and a new beginning.

I fell asleep as soon as we started riding a few miles on the bus. I was so full and jetlagged that I leaned on Ollie and passed out. Ollie woke me up when we arrived in Cleveland. His friend, Khalil, was there to pick us up to give us a ride to Ollie's apartment where his car was parked. He introduced us and told me I could go to the back and make myself comfortable.

"Don't worry, Zhuri. You guys will be home in about twenty minutes. I know you're very tired".

"Thank you for coming to pick us up. Indeed, I am very tired. I cannot wait to get home."

Khalil and Ollie started catching up as I made myself comfortable. There was snow on the ground in Cleveland. When we got to the parking lot at Ollie's apartment, he took me to see his car covered in snow. It was my first time seeing snow and I couldn't help but touch it. It was white and mushy and cool to the touch. Finally I could see and touch what I have been seeing in books and movies all this while. As a person from the tropics, I was overwhelmed. I couldn't wait to tell my brothers when I got to call them. It was like the frost from the refrigerator all over the ground and I got to walk all over it!

"Okay, let's go in now. Thanks for the ride, man, I'll call you tomorrow," Ollie said to Khalil as he shook his hand.

I followed Ollie into the apartment complex, he took me to the elevator and pressed number 15, reminding me that we lived on the 15th floor. I thought that was pretty high, but he assured me I would get used to it.

When we arrived on the 15th floor, Ollie walked ahead of me carrying our luggages. He stopped at about the 7th door on the right hand side, and pointed out that our apartment was 1513. He repeated that I would be taking the elevator to the 15th floor and looking for door number 1513.

Ollie opened the door and said, "welcome home, darling," thengave me a smooch and showed me around the apartment. "This is a two-bedroom apartment. The master bedroom is our bedroom and the other room I turned into an office. I'll take you to the office last. But this is our bedroom, over here is our bathroom, it has a nice tub and shower, whichever you're in the mood for. Out here is our living room. The kitchen is over there. It has a cooktop stove, an oven, a microwave, and a blender. I will show you how to use all of them in the morning. There is this small dining room right outside the kitchen. It seats only four people. Out here is the patio, and over there is Lake Erie. We can see it right from our balcony. I pay a little bit more for this view, but it's worth it. Sometimes when it gets really, really cold, like below zero, the lake freezes. It is such a beautiful sight. Now, my home office. Come on, open the door."

I opened the door and the first thing I saw was the computer on top of the big table with the screensaver and the words: "Welcome home, Darling" on boomerang.

"Awwww, Ollie, this is so sweet. My dad was right about you, you are different. You are so romantic."

"Hahaha! Your dad was right? He told you I was romantic? Where did he get that from? Anyway, I'll let you take your shower first, then I'll take mine. It's almost 10 pm. Time for bed already."

I went to my suitcase and got my night clothes, then went to the bathroom. When I was finished, I dressed up in the bathroom and returned to our bedroom in my night dress.

"How did you get dressed? I thought your things were in the suitcase here."

"They were, but I took them with me to the bathroom to dress up when I finished showering."

"Oh no, Zhu! I was looking forward to seeing you naked. I was hoping to get turned on, so I could hurry up with my shower and be all over you."

"But I'm not used to-"

"Zhuri, stop it!" he shouted. "You're not used to this and you're not used to that, just stop it! You're a married woman now, for god's sake. Act like it."

It was the first time Ollie was mad at me. I didn't know what to do except to keep quiet. I noticed a tear roll down my eye and I caught it quickly. Ollie saw the tear, but walked past me and made his way to the shower. While he was in the shower, I got on the bed and laid on the furthest side of it and covered myself, turning my back away from Ollie's side and just laid still. I laid there wondering if what I had done was so bad? Did he expect me to be an exhibitionist? Was everything about marriage supposed to come to me immediately after I said, "I do?" Does he not understand that all of this was not only new to me, but had been taboo for me for so long?" The way he had shown such disregard even when he saw a tear roll down my eye, is he going to be like this sometimes? I have never been ignored when I was in distress before.

Ollie came out of the shower with a towel and went straight to our bedroom naked. He was wiping his body as he spoke to me.

"See, Zhu, this is what I was expecting. I want you to feel free to be completely naked and open with me. You have a beautiful body. Show it off. Look at that Coca-Cola bottle shape you have! Sheesh! Entice me, baby! Look over here, stop giving me your back. Be my seductress and I will always run home."

I turned towards Ollie and looked at him. He was a handsome man to look at. I made eye contact with him and we both smiled. He came towards me and started kissing me. He reached for the lamp next to the bed and turned it off, but there was a dim light coming through because of the street lights outside. It set the perfect mood, not completely dark, but not bright either.

He reached for my panty and pulled it down. He got me out of my night dress and told me, "Today is the day you enjoy sex. There is no mother sleeping next door, or your

family to go visit later on. It's just us. In our own home and our own bed. Today, I will make love to you like you deserve. I will pleasure you until you climax. Are you ready, sweetheart?"

"I don't know what climax is, but I am ready for us to make love. I have dreamed about this since I first met you."

"Don't worry, sweetheart, the climax is better experienced than explained. When you reach it, you will know and when I notice it, I will let you know".

I moved towards him as he began kissing me all over my forehead, my lips, my breasts, and even in places I didn't know could be kissed. He used his hands and fingers to caress me so tenderly in delicate spots. Once he noticed I responded well to something, he did more of it. It got so intense that I let out the words, "yes, yes, don't stop," and he continued until I couldn't take it anymore. "Oh! oh! Oooooohhhh, Ollie!"

"How did that feel?" he whispered in my ear.

I couldn't answer. I was panting so loudly andsweating profusely. I had just felt the most intense, yet also fleeting, intoxicatingly good feeling. I needed to recover.

"Did it feel good? Zhu, talk to me. I'm learning how to please you sexually. Did it feel good?"

"It felt great! Like nothing I ever felt before. It's weird because it felt so good, but it's all I needed at that moment. I don't need more than that."

"That's called an orgasm, Zhu. You just had your first orgasm. You just climaxed."

"Oh wow, so it's going to feel like this from now on?"

"Most times, sweetheart, if I had my way, every time. I am going to learn how to please you and you will learn how to please me too."

"Ok," I replied with a shy smile.

"Isn't married life beautiful?"

"Yes, it is, Ollie."

Ollie let me fall asleep without trying to satisfy himself that night. I think he was genuinely happy that I had enjoyed sex for the first time ever and wanted me to just soak in that feeling. His chest was my pillow. He rubbed my back and waist tenderly, up and down until I fell asleep. I smiled in my sleep. I had just had my first orgasm with the man I fell in love with, who was now my husband.

HOUSE WIFE

When I woke up the next morning, Ollie was still asleep. I kissed his lips with a "Good morning, Sweetheart."

"Good morning Zhu! I see someone slept well last night. Someone ruined me last night. I slept so late cause I needed my energy back," He teased.

"I was about to go take a shower but had to kiss you and say good morning first. I slept well because I'm still jet lagged."

"Are you sure that's where all the tiredness comes from? It had nothing to do with 'Oh, oh, oh, Oliie, don't stop!?"

"Now, stop it Ollie! That's it! I'm going to go take my shower. Someone's trying to give themselves a big head."

"I'm coming with you to the shower."

He followed me inside the shower and scrubbed my body. I did the same for him as well, but I could hardly get any water on me. Ollie was so tall the shower got to him first, he moved out of the way to make sure the shower got to me too. When I was all clean, I got out of the shower and left him to finish. He finished and we both got dressed for breakfast. He took me to the kitchen and showed me how everything worked, suggesting that we made some eggs and bacon.

"I want mine sunny side up," he said.

"What's that? I don't know how to do that." My mom had been the one making us breakfast in the mornings and most times, it wasn't anything fancy like eggs. It was mostly bread, a spread of butter and some hot tea. Other times, it was just some leftovers from the rice and plasas the day before. I had no way of knowing how to prepare my eggs sunny side up because we couldn't afford it.

"Don't worry, just do what you can. We'll figure that one out later."

While we were sitting in the dining room eating breakfast, he told me his regular schedule would resume the next day.

"It is going to be quite hectic, Zhu. I will have to do my residency and work at the hospital next door for extra cash. I will also be taking exams or studying for one. Most days I won't be back till 3am in the morning."

"What? You mean I will be in the house by myself all day till 3 in the morning? I am scared to be alone, Ollie. I don't know how things work. What if I need you?"

"I know everything looks overwhelming right now, but you're only 3 days in. You will learn everything soon enough. But in the meantime, you have options."

"What are my options?"

"You can go spend the day with Nyesha, Khalil's wife. She is a new mom. Her son is only a year old. You guys can hang out all day and you can return in the evening before it gets dark. Another option is the library next street down. You can go there, read, rent some movies, and return home to watch them. There is lots to do, Zhu-Zhu."

"How do I get to Nyesha's house? I can't drive."

"You don't need to drive, Zhu. You can catch a bus or two there. We'll call Nyesha soon and she'll tell you what buses to take."

I didn't like that Ollie was going to be gone a lot and for long hours, but I had to be realistic. He has to finish his residency. He also has to work to provide for us. It was time to grow up and become the housewife I was so looking forward to becoming. I was going to miss Ollie, but I could busy myself with other things and get ready to receive him at the end of his shifts.

Ollie called Nyesha and put me on the phone with her. Nyesha was also from Sierra Leone, and about 5 or 6 years older than me. Ollie used to spend his free time at their house before I arrived. She told me she would teach me how to make some of the foods Ollie loved to eat at their house.

"Tomorrow, when you get to the junction from your apartment, just take the number 6 bus. It will take you all the way to the Rock and Roll Hall of Fame museum on 9th street, then take the number 2 bus, which will bring you to Chester Avenue. Once you get down the bus, stay on your right, our house is third on the right. Make sure you get our house number from Ollie, if you get lost just call me. Get some quarters from Ollie for the bus and the pay phones," Nyesha said in detail.

Afterwards, Ollie took me to the top of the building where the laundry was. He showed me how to load the clothes into the washing machine and the amount of money I needed to put in the slot to get it going. We left and came back an hour later and he showed me how the dryer worked. That was pretty much the crash course I got for how things worked and what I needed to do to survive on my own. I had wanted all this freedom, but I never stopped to think that I had never lived by myself before. I always had people around me. I grew up in a compound with multiple families, so even when my immediate family wasn't around, there were many more people around. There was never a time when I found myself completely alone. I started thinking about all the horrible things that happened to people in American movies when they were home by themselves. It became clear that I would be spending most of my time at Nyesha's house.

Ollie left very early the next morning to go to work. When I got up to see him off, he just asked that I make him coffee, nothing else. He told me to have a good day and kissed me goodbye. I missed him as soon as he walked out the door and almost immediately, I became very frightened of being alone. I was very sensitive to every little sound I heard. I was scared someone else was in the house hiding somewhere and would come out to hurt me at any time. I became paranoid. I called Nyesha to find out if she was home. I had to get out of my house as soon as possible. I hurriedly took a shower, got dressed, and ventured out for the first time by myself to catch the bus.

There were about three other people waiting at the bus stop. No one spoke to the other; we just stood there waiting until we saw the bus five minutes later and got closer to the curb to get on it. I got in and looked up and down and decided to sit in the middle of the bus, by the window. It was so different from the poda-podas back in Freetown. There was no pushing and shoving, no squeezing, or crushing each other to get some space on a seat. I didn't expect it to not be so chaotic. When someone wanted to sit next to me, she actually asked, "Is it ok if I sit here?" I was stunned, so I just nodded my head. Being by the window gave me a beautiful view of Cleveland. We passed by fast food restaurants, public schools, libraries, churches, and parks. I tried not to get carried away and forget my stop. I got off at the Rock and Roll Hall of Fame museum and was lucky to see the number 2 bus going to Chester Avenue. I got on it and soon enough I made it to Nyesha's house. She was very happy to welcome me.

"And this is the new Mrs. Jones. Welcome! Look at you, you're just a tiny little thing! Come on over to the living room, the baby is over there watching *Barney*. Hey, Jamil! This is your Aunty Zhuri."

"Nice to meet you, Nyesha. And thank you for taking care of Ollie. He told me all about your cooking."

"Ollie is family now. He has been so lonely. He comes here, eats, takes off his necktie, lays on the couch and sleeps. I am glad he has you now. You are what was missing in his life."

"And he is what was missing in mine. Come here, Jamil," I stretched my arms to the baby. He came over to me briefly and went back in front of the TV to continue to watch his show. Nyesha and I started talking about life back home in Sierra Leone and about her marriage. Her husband and her just reconciled after a split and they were working on their marriage. Nyesha had most of the ingredients for the foods we ate in Sierra Leone, and decided to cook some while I was there. Before she began, she put Jamil in his bouncer and took him to the kitchen.

"Zhuri, we are going to cook potato leaves today," she announced.

"Really?" I asked with excitement and glee.

"Yes! Khalil and Ollie like it very spicy, so we're going to cook it that way."

"I haven't eaten Sierra Leonean food in so long. I'm so happy right now!"

I watched Nyesha cook the potato leaves soup while I cooked the rice and handled Jamil. After we were done, we ate from the same bowl like we usually did in Freetown. Nyesha loved to watch the comedy sitcom, *Martin*, so we had it on and laughed as we ate. After we were done, I got a bowl to put some of the potato leaf soup to take home to share with Ollie. I said goodbye to Nyesha and set out to take the bus back to our apartment. I was so glad that Nyesha was so friendly and hospitable. She really saved the day for me. I would have been miserable at the apartment by myself. Time seemed to have flown by fast when I was with her. I didn't feel homesick because speaking our native krio and eating Sierra Leonean food made me feel like I was back home in Freetown, if even for a few hours. I made it home by 7 p.m with Ollie nowhere in sight, still at work. Spending time at Nyesha's house was a godsend but returning to an empty house in the evening, every evening, was difficult. I became depressed. I would cry out of fear and desperation. I would tell Ollie how I was feeling and he would say, "Okay, call your family. Don't stay too long on the phone, but call them if that would help."

Calling my family was a quick fix. I couldn't talk to them as long as I wanted because the phone bill would be ridiculously high, but after I spoke to them I would fall back into my depression and crying spells. I was paralyzed with fear every time I was by myself in the apartment. All those American movies I used to watch which portrayed home invasions and murders were doing my head in. I wasn't rational enough to reassure myself they were just movies. I convinced myself they were art imitating life. I thought I stuck out like a sore thumb because of my accent and style of dress. I would be an easy target, I thought to myself. This led to constant anxiety and panic attacks. I found myself spiralling every time I heard an unexplained sound. Instead of my house being a haven of peace, it became like a haunted house to me, every sound was suspect, every flash of light was cause for concern.

"I just wish I had a baby. At least someone to keep me company when you're not here. I am tired of being all by myself all the time," I said to Ollie between tears when he returned home that night.

"Oh Zhu-Zhu, a baby won't fix your loneliness. It wouldn't fix anything. This is just a phase. Pretty soon, you'll learn how to drive, start university, meet some friends, and have a whole lot of homework and projects to do."

"But I cannot do all that now until I have all my documents in place. It's going to take months and months."

"Come here. Look at me. Now sweetheart, I know this is all new and overwhelming for you. You have a new marriage, new country, new role and no support system, but you were made for this. I don't want you sitting at home crying or missing me too much. You can come to work with me on weekends. You can stay in the doctor's room at the hospital, watch TV and sleep, and we can return home together after my shift."

I broke into a smile. "I would prefer that Ollie. I hate to be a distraction though."

"You're my wife, not a distraction. I have a feeling this arrangement won't last very long because those hospital beds are so small and uncomfortable, you'll be asking me to stay home." At that, we both laughed.

I looked forward to spending time with Ollie on weekends. His presence was comforting to me. We kept company in his doctor's room until he got paged. He would kiss me goodbye and go attend to his patients. He would also call me when he was taking too long.

"Just sleep if you have to or watch a movie. I have to do my rounds. Make yourself comfortable."

Except, I wasn't comfortable physically or mentally. Ollie was right about the beds being uncomfortable, but I just didn't like the idea of being with him at work because I was too depressed to stay home. We hardly had any time together before he was being paged left and right. Sometimes it seemed like he was the only doctor on call. I never imagined how disruptive the life of a doctor would be. Ollie was called all times of the day, everyday; in the middle of everything; a serious conversation, sex, exercise, and dinner. On our drive home early the next morning, I told Ollie, "I will be staying home by myself and trying to get used to it. I will read a lot. I will also go to the kingdom hall. Don't worry about me. I will be fine."

"What's with the sudden change of mind and rapid maturity?"

"I just want you to concentrate at work and I concern myself with home."

"Thank you, baby," he said as he reached for my hand and squeezed it.

When we got home, I asked Ollie to paste his schedule in the home office, so that I could have a visual of when he would be home. He immediately obliged. "I understand how that would be very calming for you to know ahead of time, so that you can mentally prepare."

"It will be very helpful. I have been thinking of so many ways to deal."

I busied myself with reading, learning new recipes, visiting nearby landmarks, and watching movies. Ollie became a guinea pig for all my new recipes. He never complained about any new recipe not tasting nice. He knew I was still adjusting to my new role and maybe he felt guilty for leaving me by myself 14 to 16 hours a day. Whenever he got home, I would jump on him. He would be really exhausted and would just sit on thefloor in the living room, get his tie, socks, and coat off and let out the biggest sigh.

"What can I get you? I cooked your favourite, wanpot couscous with shrimp and plantain on the side. I made it really spicy, just like you like it. Also, I have some veggies. Peas or corn? Do you want some fruit? I can peel some mangoes."

"Yes, I'll have all of that and you later on," he replied with a giggle. He got the TV remote and tuned to his favorite news show, *Hardball with Chris Matthews*. I disappeared into the kitchen and came back with a full tray. His couscous and plantains on a plate, corn and peas on a small saucer, and peeled, sliced mangoes in a small bowl. He ate in front of the TV and asked me how my day went.

"It went okay. I just missed you as usual, but I am adjusting. I take naps now sometimes without being scared. I am actually getting used to my own home. I am so glad I found the kingdom hall. That has helped me so much, Ollie. I have Sister Sonya picking me up to go to the meetings and field service. I am out of the house on Tuesdays, Thursdays and Sundays. When we do house to house preaching, it really makes me realize there's really nothing to be afraid of. Also, talking about it with Sister Sonya has actually helped me a lot. She told me there were many causes of sounds in a house. It could be that the fire alarm battery needs to be changed, also the wood framing, plumbing pipes, and other building materials all expand and contract at different times.The creaking sounds can be the result of temperature change and house settling. I didn't realize how sensitive I had been to every sound. Growing up in a compound with over forty people, the sounds I heard were mostly of people talking, crying, laughing, celebrating. It was all human sounds. House settling sounds out of the blue are new to me, but after two months of agonizing and finding ways to cope, things are actually falling into place little by little".

"I wish we had thought of this sooner. What a brilliant explanation by Sis Sonya. This is one of the reasons I love the Jehovah's Witnesses. You guys really do support each other".

"Yes, in every way! Things are finally looking up". I told him.

"I can see that. This is really tasty. Thank you sweetheart. I was thinking today that you should go to the DMV and get a state identification card while you wait for your documents to come. All you need for that is your visa. That way, you can rent books and movies from the library; also, you can use it as an identification at the bank. The DMV is not far from here. I can drop you off tomorrow at 11am, since I have to be at work at 12 noon. You can take a bus or taxi back home."

"That sounds like a good idea."

"Make sure you rent a lot of books and movies when you go to the library. I think you can rent up to 10 books at one time and up to 5 movies at one time as well."

"I will ask when I get there. I am about to be a kid in a candy store!"

PREGNANT

The next morning, Ollie dropped me off at the DMV. There was a long line and I must have been behind fifteen people. I stood in line with my purse containing some cash, lip gloss, and my passport. I also had my diary which Ollie gave to me in Freetown. Suddenly, I started feeling very dizzy. I felt my head spinning and too weak for my feet to hold me up. I couldn't go sit down or I'd lose my place in line. I stood there knowing I was going to lose my balance at any moment. I wondered why I was feeling so sick all of a sudden. I was not feeling this way the day before or even earlier in the morning.

"Don't worry, you will be just fine, your husband is on his way to get you," a lady said to me in a room I don't remember ever being in. Somehow, I found myself laying on a couch.

"Where am I? What happened to me?" I asked the lady.

"You are at the DMV, you passed out in line waiting for your turn to go to the desk. We searched your bag for an emergency contact and called your husband. He is on his way here. How are you feeling?"

"I was feeling very dizzy. My knees just felt weak and I don't remember anything else."

"Has this ever happened to you before? Do you have dizzy spells often?"

"Never! I don't know what's wrong with me."

Someone called the lady I was talking to on the phone and told her Ollie was in the building to pick me up. She instructed them to send him to her office. Soon there was a knock on the door and the lady answered for him to come in. Ollie entered the office with a worried look on his face.

The lady explained to him what happened, and Ollie let out a sigh "Thank you so much for taking care of my wife. Sweetheart, let me help you up. What happened? How are you feeling now?"

"I don't know exactly. I just remember feeling very dizzy after I stood in line. My head started spinning and I just passed out I guess."

"Okay, let me help you to the car outside." He carefully led me to the car and helped me in. As soon as I was settled, Ollie spoke up again. "Zhu-Zhu, I think you may be pregnant."

"Pregnant? No! I am not pregnant. How can I be pregnant?"

"Well, let me see, we've been having unprotected sex for about two months now, you have never felt this way before, and dizziness and neasea are symptoms of pregnancy."

"Okay, I know all that, but I am not pregnant."

"Well, we are about to find out soon enough. There is a Walgreens pharmacy coming up. I am going to stop there and buy a pregnancy test to take home."

"So, I felt nauseous and fainted and the first thing you think about is pregnancy?" I asked him with my arms crossed and suspicion on my face. "If I was in Freetown, these symptoms would sound like malaria. I would be asked if I had malaria, not if I was pregnant."

"Well, I'm the only one here who happens to be a doctor. I think I'll go with my expertise and gut instinct on this one, considering how much sex you've been having these couple of months."

"Considering how much sex I have been having? Last time I checked you were right there with me! Oh! I think I remember, you were there with me every time. Let us not pick and choose what we remember, Ollie."

"Haha! I think I just stepped on someone's toes. Someone feels attacked." Ollie replied, laughing loudly and pinching my arm.

He stopped by the Walgreens and left me in the car to rest. He came out about five minutes later with a pregnancy test in hand and we drove home. Once we got in our apartment, he told me to go to the bathroom and do the test.

"This is about to be very simple Zhu-Zhu. All I really want you to do in the bathroom is pee on the stick, leave it on the counter, and come outside and lay on the couch. I will go check it in five minutes."

I did as he said, and after a few minutes he went in after me. "It's not even a whole five minutes yet and the stick says it's positive. There are two lines, Zhu. It means we're pregnant. Congratulations!"

"I'm pregnant?" I didn't quite understand it. It was like an out of body experience for me. I had stayed a virgin because I didn't want to risk getting pregnant and dishonor my family and now I found out I'm pregnant and I can actually celebrate it? I thought pregnancy would be something so obviously different from what I experience everyday, like a different state of being, that I would have no choice but to know I am pregnant. But besides the previous dizziness and fainting, I felt normal. I ran and hugged him. "But I don't feel pregnant. My stomach is not big, my br-"

"Zhu-Zhu, you don't feel pregnant because you have never been pregnant before. You do not know how it feels to be pregnant. But you'll get the hang of it pretty soon. What you experienced this morning was morning sickness. I need to get you some things to help you with the morning sickness. Some ginger for the queasiness, crackers to help with your stomach, prenatal vitamins, also some orange juice, and I'll stop by the library to get a book called *What To Expect When You're Expecting*. It will tell you pretty much everything you need to know about being pregnant."

"Oh wow! I cannot believe it. We are going to have a baby?"

"Yes, Zhu, you are about to be a mommy. I am about to be a Daddy. I hope it's a boy."

"Oh no! Not a boy! I want a girl. I do not know anything about little boys. I want a girl. I know everything about girls. I can comb her hair, style it, make her look cute and beautiful. Definitely a girl." I said with much delight. It was natural that I wanted the baby to be a girl. I had experience playing with and nurturing many little girls back home. I feel like I would know exactly what to do.

"I'm putting my money on a boy. I will see you soon, Zhu, lemme go grab these items. Page me if you need anything. Now, just lay down and rest and take care of my little boy."

"You mean little girl."

"Haha, a healthy little boy. You'll get used to him like you've been getting used to everything else. I'll be right back."

After Ollie left, I kept replaying the results in my head over and over. I'm pregnant? I'm having a baby? I touched my stomach and rubbed it. A baby is growing inside of me? I was ecstatic. I am carrying me and Ollie's baby! I was so excited I wanted to share it with the world. Ollie came back an hour later with the book and some groceries. He was as excited as I was.

"I cannot believe I am going to be a father. I mean, I can believe I did that, but I didn't expect it to be so quick. I am really going to be someone's dad."

"I cannot wait to tell my family. They're going to be so happy!"

"I don't know about that, Zhu-Zhu. I promised your dad I would let you finish college first before we have babies."

"I can still go to college. I'm still going to go to college, but I'll just have a baby first."

"I don't think your Dad is going to be so happy about that." Ollie replied with a slight worried look on his face.

"Didn't you tell me it was our life now, our decisions? Why do you care how dad feels? I am so happy, I cannot wait to tell them!"

"Not so fast, Zhu! It only makes sense that I talk to him man to man. I will get a phone card this weekend and I will call and tell him. In the meantime, let me think about how I am going to break the news to him."

Ollie and I went to bed feeling so elated that night. We were going to be parents soon. He touched my stomach and rubbed on it. "Little Zhu-Zhu is about to be a mother. Mommy Zhu!"

I smiled widely as I curled up to him. "All my dreams have come true," I thought to myself. "Thank you Jehovah."

I started seeing a doctor at the Cleveland clinic. I would go once a month and she would run all the tests to make sure the baby was fine. I remember asking her why I was having excess saliva in my mouth. It was gross and I was so over it.

"It's just something that comes with some pregnancies. Not everyone has it, but some of my patients complain about it as well. It has something to do with the change of hormonal levels while you're pregnant. It may go away on its own before you give birth, but it will definitely go away after you give birth".

"It just grosses me out to no end," I complained. I have to carry containers to spit in discreetly everywhere, and sometimes I run over them at home and I spill it all on the carpet. I can't wait till it's over."

She laughed a little. "Yeah, some things you have to put up with until the pregnancy is over. Overall, everything is looking great. The baby has a strong heartbeat and is growing just fine. On your next visit we will find out the sex, if that's what you and your husband want."

"I cannot wait! I want a girl but my husband is rooting for a boy," I said.

"I'm sure you'll love whichever one you have. Finding out makes preparing for the baby a little easier and specific."

She gave me the information for my next appointment and I left. Ollie was always eager to find out how the appointment went. He had only gone to one appointment with me since we found out I was pregnant. He said my appointments clashed with his work schedule and he had to make money to provide for his family. "Besides, you can always tell me what happened at your appointment."

During the weekend, we called our families in Freetown to tell them about my pregnancy. To Ollie's delight, my father was ecstatic! He never said anything about me going to college before I got pregnant, he was just happy to know he was about to be a grandfather for the first time. As for the rest of my family, we could hear them in the background cheering. They were all very happy for us.

Ollie's mother, Miss Vincent, was also happy to hear about her first grandchild. She asked Ollie if she could speak with me, and asked me how I was feeling and if I needed anything.

"I get morning sickness, I spit a lot and eat a lot. I have been craving foods from Freetown, especially gari gron soup."

"Haha! Gari gron soup. You are too far away to have that made for you. What alternatives do you have over there to curb the cravings a little?"

"I have gari, lime and maggie. I just eat those everyday. I can also finish a gallon of orange juice a day."

"Whoa! That's a lot. Take care of yourself and the baby, Zhuri. I will be checking on you often."

"Thank you, mommy. Talk to you later".

Sometimes when I woke up to brush my teeth in the morning, the brushing action in my mouth was vomit inducing. So, I tried not to brush too hard. I found myself very tired and weak. My morning routine became waking up, showering, brushing my teeth, eating and going right back to bed. Five months along, my stomach was still small. My breasts were fuller and my nipples were darker and larger, with bump-like structures on my areola. There was also a black line running down my stomach to my pelvis. I drank a gallon of orange juice everyday like it was water. My appetite became ravenous as the baby grew. It seemed like I was never full. I got hungry thirty minutes after I ate a meal. I had gained about twenty pounds. I was very eager to let my doctor know about it on my next visit. However when I returned for my five month check up, I was so excited about finding out the sex of our baby that I forgot all about it. I laid on the bed in the examination room and the nurse was rubbing the aquasonic gel on my belly to do the ultrasound. I looked at the images but could only make out a head, legs, and hands; she could make out everything else. She was looking and measuring body parts to make sure the baby was growing properly. Later she asked, "Do you want to know the sex?"

"Of course! I've been waiting all this time."

"It's a boy!"

"What? A boy? Are you sure?" I asked her.

"Yes, I am very sure. It's a healthy baby boy. Everything looks exactly as they should and the baby is growing well."

I laid quietly and took in what she just told me. It was a boy and the boy was healthy. "I am glad the baby is healthy, thank God. I have to get used to the idea that it's a boy. My husband is going to be very happy."

I thought about the baby being a boy the whole day. I need to start thinking about names, haircuts, and shopping for blue items instead of pink. When I told Ollie the news, he was very happy as expected. That evening Ollie informed me that we would be moving to a rural area in Tennessee as a condition to get his green card. He had several offers from Texas, Michigan, and Colorado, but he chose Tennessee because they were hiring him immediately after residency and also because someone told him there was one Sierra Leonean in Humboldt where we would be moving to. He had communicated with the person who was also a doctor and he had offered to have him stay with his family until he found a place of his own.

"I will pay for you to go be with your relatives in Virginia until it's close to the time for you to give birth. I don't want these new people taking care of me and you at the same time since I don't know them . Once I find a place for us to stay, I will bring you over."

"I don't mind going over to my Aunty Fatima in Virginia. She will take very good care of me, and my cousins will be home all the time. I will miss you too much though." I assured Ollie.

"Zhu-Zhu, this is just a temporary arrangement. By the time you start missing me too much, it will be time to come over."

"Or you can say you will miss me too, Ollie."

"It goes without saying, sweetheart. I will be missing both my girl and my boy. Come over here lemme play with your belly a little, maybe my lil man will start kicking." He held me close and rubbed my stomach. The baby didn't kick but it felt great, so much love from Ollie.

When I made it to Virginia, my Aunty Fatima picked me up at the airport and drove me directly to their local African market in Alexandria. She asked what I would like to eat and bought every ingredient for every little craving. By popular demand, my first meal was foofoo and sawa sawa.She cooked it with smoked fish and cow feet, making it taste so delicious. My Aunty catered to my every need. My last trimester with her and my cousins and uncle were the most fun. She catered to my every little craving and was sending me back to my husband fully stocked. Aunty Fatima cooked some food to take with me. I got to know my cousins Habibah, Hawa and Zainab. Habibah, who was 16 years old and the oldest, would tell me about the boy she had a crush on at school. I told her stories about Lenny and I back in Freetown. She thought my clandestine love story with Lenny was the most romantic she ever heard. I would resist and tell her that my love story with Ollie is the most romantic. We would argue back and forth and just laugh so hard. My cousin Hawa, 13 years old, was very shy. She seldom spoke and was always engrossed in a book. My little cousin, Zainab was only 5 years old and was mostly at the daycare. My Aunty Fatima's delicious cookingquickly made me gain weight by the end of my eighth month of pregnancy, and I was about to leave for Tennessee in a few days.

MOTHER

Ollie picked me up at the Memphis International airport. When he saw me walk towards him, he laughed. He walked towards me, hugged me tightly and said, "Zhu-Zhu, you're about to pop! Look at you, looking like a full-fledged woman. Look at your hips, your waist, your boobs. Zhu, you look fantastic! Everything is more than I left it."

"Well, I've been eating for two. Plus my Aunty Fatima kept feeding me. I had a beautiful stay, but I am glad to be back with you to start our family." I told him.

"That's right, baby! I have a surprise for you, Zhu! I bought a house, our new home."

"You did what? You bought a house without telling me?"

"I thought you'd be happy about it, Zhu." He said nervously.

"Happy about it? You completely left me out of the loop. In our culture they say, 'na uman get os.' 'The woman is the owner and heart of the home'. How am I supposed to be happy about it, Ollie? You robbed me of the excitement of looking at many different homes, you robbed me of the opportunity to settle on one with you. I had no input whatsoever, not about the location, the style, the color, the size, nothing at all. It's like you're going to install me and our child at this place of your choice."

"I was going to drive by it so you could see what it looks like. I actu- "

I cut him off. "I am too tired. I just want to go wherever you're staying with the Sierra Leonean family and get some rest."

"I'm sorry Zhu-Zhu, I didn't mean to upset you. I thought you'd be too heavy to want to go looking at different houses." He opened his car door by the curb of the airport and helped me get in the passenger seat. Then he went to the back and put my luggages in the boot.

"Just say you wanted to make the decision all by yourself. Looking at houses doesn't require me walking from one distance to another. I will be in a car, like I am now, and stopped at different locations, until we found something we BOTH loved. Now, I have no choice whatsoever!"

"Here we are, let me help you out of the car so you can look at our new house. This is it!"

I wasn't having any of it. "I am not getting out of the car, Ollie, you do not care about my feelings. I specifically told you I wanted to go rest where you're staying at the moment. Instead, you disregarded my wishes once again and did as you pleased. Just take me somewhere to rest. I need to put my feet up."

Ollie got back in the car and drove me to Dr Kaloko's house. We did not speak to each other the whole way there. However, once we pulled up and Dr. Kaloko and his wife Ramat came outside to welcome us, I broke out a smile.

"Welcome to our humble abode, Mrs. Jones. Please make yourself at home. If you need anything, don't hesitate to tell us." Dr Kaloko said.

"Thank you for your hospitality, and please, just call me Zhuri. Thank you for all your help with my husband. We are very grateful."

"Don't mention it, Zhuri. We're all one family. Just make yourself comfortable. Again, please don't hesitate to ask for anything that would make you comfortable."

"I will. Thank you both so much!"

Ollie took me to the guest bedroom where he was staying. As I expected, his stuff was all over the room. There was a pile of dirty work clothes on the floor, a few shirts from the drycleaners hung on a chair, a vague smell of tobacco, and the TV in his room was on and tuned to C-SPAN.

"Ollie! This place is so disorganized and untidy. And the smell of cigarettes! You were supposed to have quit by now. You cannot do it around me or the baby. This is disgusting!"

"Well, I'm so happy to have you back Zhu! I know things will change once you get back. About smoking, I'm trying Zhu, I really am. It's not easy to just give it up. I bought the Nicoderm patches and everything. It was just so hard without you here for a while and then the stress of a new job and a new place and starting all over again. The stress got to me." Ollie said, trying so hard to convince me.

"Ollie, you tell people to quit smoking everyday, regardless of any compelling excuses they may have because their health comes first. Health is the priority here. Our baby is the priority, I am the priority, you are the priority, so do whatever you have to do to not expose us to that nicotine."

I couldn't rest in a room that looked disheveled. I immediately got to work tidying the room. I asked Ramat for a change of bed sheets and for her to show me where the laundry room was. "You're not about to do all that Zhuri. I'll get the sheets, but tell Ollie to bring the dirty laundry out. There's soap and bleach and fabric softener, everything he needs for the laundry is there. Ah! These our men!"

I knew exactly what Ramat meant by 'these our men.' It is a loaded statement. It is a statement we all heard our mothers and Aunties made growing up. It meant their husbands always kept them in the societal role of what a woman was supposed to be. They were to be good wives, well behaved, good cooks, impeccable housekeepers, and tireless rearers of multiple children. They were to wake up first and go to bed last, they were supposed to do the laundry, iron the clothes, braid their daughters' hair, take care of a crying baby at night, have sex with them, and wake up the next day and do it all over again. The worst part was the mentality of the community about this issue. Even if a man was kind and considerate and loved his wife, because he had subscribed to this antiquated ideology of what the traditional role of the woman was, coupled with the fact that he doesn't want to be viewed as weak or accursed, he just watched his wife embody these roles without lifting a finger to help her. After all, it's a 'woman's job.' How backwards is that mentality where a kind, considerate, helpful and loving husband is viewed as weak or bewitched by the wife if he offers to help her out? People on the outside take offense to it. The friends of the husband, his extended family, and neighbors all take offense to the fact that a husband is unselfish, compassionate, and helpful to his wife. If a husband is seen helping his wife in a domesticated way, other men get uncomfortable, they beckon to each other, "Look, look, look! Look de big fool man! Ay, dis wan ya e uman don do am. Lagilaaaaa," an expression of disgust that your wife has bewitched you.

But this was not supposed to be our plight, I tried to convince myself. My husband was schooled in three continents: Africa, Europe, and America. Surely that should have impacted him in some way.

"My sister, these men don't make it easy for us. You're almost nine months pregnant, you're not supposed to do any of this. Just get the dirty clothes out of your room. I'll put them in the washing machine. I hear our men talking outside already, we're not going to wait on them."

I got all the dirty clothes outside to Ramat and told her to hold on until I brought the dirty sheets out as well. I replaced the dirty sheets with fresh, clean ones. I vacuumed the floor of our medium-sized bedroom, and sprayed some febreze air freshener all over the room. I then wiped the surfaces of the TV and nightstands. Now, I could take a shower and relax without all the clutter and disheveledness. While I was in the shower, I heard Ollie enter the room.

"Oh wow! My wife is back indeed. Thank you Zhu-Zhu! The room is so tidy," he shouted towards the bathroom.

"Well, I couldn't just come and lay down in all that mess. But you're welcome. Ollie, you have to remember this is someone's house. You can't just leave it anyhow. You don't know if they come in here when you are away at work. The least you can do is make sure the space they give to you is well taken care of and definitely NO tobacco inside their bedroom".

"You're making me feel bad, Zhu-Zhu". Ollie replied.

"Oh, well. It's not meant to make you feel bad. You were here by yourself. The least you could do was clean up after yourself". I continued.

"Ok, ok, enough already! It is clean now. I was not looking forward to having this kind of conversation with you. I was hoping we would be talking about the baby and how you're almost about to pop". He said digressing from my answer.

I got out of the shower, got the towel by the door and walked towards the bed as I patted myself dry. It was the first time he was seeing me naked in almost four months.

"Oh my God, Zhu-Zhu, you are, you are a woman, you are just beautiful. You are glowing. You have boobs, Zhu! Big boobs. Come here, let me put lotion on you. Lay down on the bed, I'll slather you up with lotion." He said to me, his eyes about to pop from their sockets. There was so much lust in his eyes.

As I obliged, Ollie slathered me with the lotion and massaged me gently. First it was a regular massage, then it became sensual and by the time I knew it, Ollie had sex on the brain.

"Let me lock the door quickly. Zhu, if you turn sideways, I'll be able to slide in nicely."

I obliged because I had missed my husband, I had missed our sexual activities and I wanted to feel close to him that way. I couldn't lay on my belly anymore. I could only lay on my back and my sides now.

"Oh wait! I'm not just sliding in Zhu. I want to cup these big beasts first. I want to do other things to make you feel good, then I'll slide in." He said.

It was the first time I smiled at him since I was mad at him about the house purchase behind my back. It was also the very first time I felt completely comfortable being naked with him. I wasn't self-conscious or shy. It felt very organic. I was very proud of my pregnant body, my new curves and bigger breasts. I made eye-contact with him as he started touching me sensually. I could tell from the way he looked at me that he too sensed the shift from the self-conscious girl to a confident woman. I didn't realize it was possible to have sex so late in my pregnancy, but here he was making love to me so sweetly and beautifully. I orgasmed and fell right asleep afterwards. He exhausted me.

Two days later, we had to move to our new house. There was actually nothing for us to move except our suitcases. Our new home was about twenty-five years old. It had an antiquated kitchen, the oven was antic, and the rest of the house was modern. There werethree levels; a finished basement, living room, dining room, and kitchen on the first floor, andthe four bedrooms on the second floor. There was a two car garage and a large patio open to a big backyard. It was a nice house, too old for my liking, but nice regardless. I would have never chosen it, as my style is more contemporary and sleek. I hated being disregarded and my input for something as significant as our first house not being inquired. Ollie already had a used couch in the living room, a queen bed in the master bedroom, and he bought a bassinet for the baby. He said he didn't have any more money after the downpayment for the house. We didn't have a refrigerator, so we didn't buy anything that would spoil. We ate what we needed for the day and replenished the next day.

At 5 a.m on a Monday morning a week after we moved, I left Ollie upstairs in bed because I was feeling restless. I was tossing and turning endlessly and didn't want to wake him up. I came downstairs and laid on the couch, but started feeling pains that would come and go every 15 minutes or so. I made nothing of it and thought it would pass away soon enough. However thirty minutes later I was still feeling pain, only it had gotten more frequent. It would come and go every five minutes. I decided to go wake up Ollie and tell him I was having abdominal pains.

"How long have you been feeling this way?" Ollie asked me.

"For close to an hour now. The pain doesn't stay, it comes and goes, but it's becoming stronger and closer now. Aaaaaaaaaaaa! I'm having another one now," I said as I winced andstarted breathing deeply.

"Come here, sit on the bed, lay down if you want to. You're in labor, Zhu. I'll put on some clothes so I can drive you to the hospital. Do you need anything?"

"No. I'm just ready to go to the hospital."

"We'll be on our way soon!"

When we got on the street it was snowing outside. Tennessee usually doesn't have snow, but it was snowing that December morning. Ollie told me to breathe in and out when I had pain.

"I can't drive fast on these snowy roads, but we'll get to the hospital soon enough, sweetheart. Just breathe okay?"

Upon arrival, the nurse on duty confirmed that I was in labor, but my cervix had only dilated 4 centimeters. She told Ollie to walk with me around the floors so I could dilate faster. We walked around the hospital, but I would stop every five minutes and cry in pain. I would squeeze his hand really tight and breathe in and out very fast. When the pain subsided I would walk with him some more. I was in labor for most of the day, close to twelve hours after we arrived, and finally the doctor told the nurses to get ready for delivery. He said I was 10 centimeters dilated. They propped me at the edge of the bed as the contractions were coming 2 minutes apart with a strong urge to push.

"Push! Push! Push!" Everyone was saying, but despite my efforts, the baby wasn't coming out. After 45 minutes, my doctor said, "Every time the contractions come and I reach for the baby, I can feel his hair but he coils back in. I think it's time to use the forceps." I didn't know what a forcep was, but anything that could get the baby out was good enough for me.

"Mrs. Jones, the forceps will go in and grip your baby's head softly and I will guide it out of the birth canal, okay?"

As soon as my next contraction came, Dr. Endelman got the forcep in and tried pulling the baby out. It was the worst pain I had ever experienced. It felt like someone had grabbed a hold of all of my internal organs and was yanking them out of me at once. I was screechingand then I could hear another voice yelling as well. It was the baby! It was out and crying loudly. I looked down and saw that he had a head full of hair, but the forceps made his head look a little longer than normal. The doctor laid him on my chest and handed a pair of scissors to his delightful father to cut the umbilical cord. He couldn't stop staring at the baby. I held the baby close, skin to skin. He was still crying as if he had felt pain coming through the birth canal.

"Don't worry," Dr. Edelman assured us, "the baby's head will go back to normal in a few days. Mr. Jones, you can go ahead and cut the umbilical cord."

Ollie cut the umbilical cord and the baby was wiped with a clean towel. He took the baby from my chest and held him close to his chest and whispered, "Welcome to the world, son." I was too exhausted to keep up with them after twelve excruciating hours of labor. I leaned back on the bed and fell asleep for three straight hours.

When the nurse woke me up later to take my vital signs, I saw Ollie lying on the chair with the baby still on his chest.

"Thank you, sweetheart. I know it was tough. Thank you for my son. Do you want to hold the baby? Do you want anything to eat?"

"Yes! I want to hold the baby. And yes, I'm hungry. I want real food." I replied. I wanted some steak and potatoes from Outback Steakhouse and not the regular hospital food.

I held our baby and couldn't stop admiring him. He was perfect. Ten fingers, ten toes, smooth skin, and smelled so heavenly. I kept sniffing him and rubbing his head. He was worth all the heartburns, unrelenting spitting, discomfort and twelve whole hours of labor.

Ollie came back an hour later with carryout steak and potatoes from Outback Steakhouse. I ate it like I hadn't eaten for days. "Soon the nurse will be coming to register the baby in the morning. We have to agree on a name now. It must be African and very strong. You're still going with your choice?"

"Yes! Sankara! That's a very strong African name and it is not common. Sankara was a great man, a great leader, a great African, exactly what I want my son to be."

I had made the case for the name Sankara before and Ollie knew how passionate I was about Thomas Sankara, the late Burkinabe revolutionary and former President of Burkina Faso. He was called the Upright Man because of his honesty, love for his people, defiant spirit, and his altruism. Unlike many African leaders he believed in servant leadership. He believed his job was to serve his people and not to enrich himself. Symbols of extravagance for government officials all disappeared under his leadership. He had innovative ideas for African self-reliance as opposed to incurring debt from foreign financial backers. 'He who feeds you, controls you,' he would say. He was also staunchly against imperialism and put programs in place to make his country self-sufficient. He wanted the local farmers to produce the food they ate and encouraged government officials as well as local citizens to wear their native clothes. He increased literacy rate by 60%, built about 350 schools, gave land to the poor, vaccinated 2.5 million children, planted 10 million trees, and he was a champion for women's rights. He outlawed female genital mutilation, the clandestine excision of the clitoris of girls, and forced marriages. He felt the revolution and women's rights go hand in hand. "The revolution and women's liberation go together. We do not talk of women's emancipation as an act of charity or out of a surge of human compassion. It is a basic necessity for the revolution to triumph. Women hold up the other half of the sky." Sankara had so many qualities I wanted my son to either possess or ones I can inculcate in him at an early age. Ollie eventually gave in. "Okay, Okay, woman! You have Sankara's whole biography in your head. There is no way I can make a comeback after that spiel. At least not with anyone I can think of at the moment. Sankara it is! Sany for short, right?"

"Right, Sany for short," I replied with a big relief.

"He gets my middle name, David. That's settled. Sankara David Jones."

After being with me and Sany the whole day, it was time for Ollie to return home since it was around 9 pm. He kissed my forehead. "Good night mommy and good night Sankara. I'll see you both in the morning."

"Good night honey, don't forget to buy the car seat before you come tomorrow. We need it to be discharged in two days."

I put Sankara on my chest. He loved our skin to skin bonding. The nurses would come to check our temperatures and give us medications. They took Sankara to run the basic screenings for newborns to check for phenylketonuria, cystic fibrosis, sickle cell disease, critical congenital heart disease, hearing loss, and others. I waited anxiously to get the results back.

The nurse didn't bring my Sany until around midnight. She told me everything was fine, which made me breathe a long sigh of relief.

"Mrs. Jones, try to sleep when the baby sleeps. We just bathed and fed him. He is sleeping now. Try not to hold him just yet until he wakes up. Go to sleep now, you need all the energy you can get. If you need anything, press the button and someone will come see you. Can I get you anything before I leave?"

"Yes, some ice and some orange juice. Thank you for everything."

"You're welcome. I'll be right back with your ice and orange juice."

I listened to what Nurse Amy told me and went to sleep after I had my orange juice and ice. Sankara didn't wake up until about four hours later. I picked him up and tried to breastfeed him. He wouldn't take my breast. He was really hungry and my milk hadn't quite come in yet, even though the nurses told me, him sucking on them would stimulate the milk to come, Sankara seemed impatient, so I bottle-fed him and put him on my shoulders to burp. Afterwards, I propped my bed up and had him sleep on my chest till the morning.

An official for the vital records office came to my room early in the morning to register the birth. She asked if we had chosen a name for the baby.

"Yes, Sankara David Jones," I replied.

"Sankara, that's a nice name, never heard it before. Can you spell it for the record please?"

"Yes, S-A-N-K-A-R-A."

"Thank you. The middle name is David and the last name is Jones?" she asked.

"Yes, Sankara David Jones."

She filled in the day and time of birthday, the weight, and height. She asked for my address and told me we will get a copy of his official birth certificate in the mail. She wished us well and bade us farewell.

POSTPARTUM BLUES

I was very happy to take Sankara home. He was healthy and thriving but he also cried a lot, which confused me. I did everything they told me to do; fed him, burped him, made sure he had a clean diaper. However, none of these things were sure to make Sankara quiet. Sometimes he would have crying spells and nothing I did made a difference. I would hardly have time for myself after I woke up. Sometimes I realized I hadn't showered or combed my hair in the early evenings. I was disheveled. Sany demanded constant care. I was either catering to him or washing his bottles, preparing a bottle, getting rid of soiled diapers, washing dirty linens and making sure he was still breathing. I experienced extreme feelings of anxiety and sadness. I felt guilty for feeling that way. Hadn't I looked forward to having my baby? Didn't I say I wanted a companion? Didn't I love my baby with everything I've got? If so, why was I feeling such sadness? I felt very empty, feelings of inadequacy swamped me. Life looked very bleak to me. Would I ever be able to enjoy a single day like I used to before or would everything seem gloomy from now on? I worried that my life was over. I was constantly exhausted, the thought of waking up the next day to the same routine frightened me. I cried everyday, for most part of the day. I decided to tell Ollie after he came home one evening and saw me crying bitterly with the baby on my shoulders.

"What's wrong? Why are you crying Zhu-Zhu? Ok, you keep quiet, and baby, you keep quiet as well," he said to both of us. We both continued crying. "Now Zhu-Zhu, the baby can feel your energy. If you are stressed out and panicky, the baby can sense that. He becomes nervous and reacts by crying. You have to calm down and be in control."

"I don't think I can do this by myself, Ollie. I need help. I need a nanny. I need someone who can help with the baby so I can rest, so I can take a nap, so I can shower and eat my meals. I haven't been able to do those basic things for a while now. I am exhausted and overwhelmed." I explained to him with tears rolling down my face.

"I will find out at work about help. But every woman does this Zhu, every woman. They take care of their child."

"I need help. You do not help me with the baby. No help whatsoever. When you get home from work, you ask to see the baby. If the baby is asleep, you wake him up and play with him for 30 minutes and you're done. You leave me with him and go to another room to sleep. Do not compare your 30 minutes with the baby to my 24 hours with him."

"Well, I have to go to work in the morning, so I need my rest," he replied in a snappy way.

"Even on days you don't have to go to work, you have never woken up at night to help me with Sankara so I can sleep. You just leave me with Sany even when you hear him crying late into the night, and instead, you'd get up and go to the opposite wing of the house. Sankara is our baby, not just my sole responsibility."

"I will ask about a nanny at work tomorrow. Now, let me hold Sankara, you go take a shower and get something to eat." He said.

I went upstairs to the bathroom and cried in the shower. I just stood there for about 10 minutes and just cried. I didn't expect taking care of a baby was going to be so exhausting. Back in Freetown, there were many people to help out. I remember when one of the kids in my compound was born and we would all tow a line to carry him after he was washed. "After you hold him, it's my turn next." One person would say. Then another would chime in, "No! It's my turn, I was here first". That was the life I was used to. Everyone was eager to pitch in, eager to help raise the baby. I had never imagined when I had mine, I would be by myself with him all of the time, without help for weeks and months at a time.

The next day, Ollie asked at work about a nanny, but we lived too far away from the people near his clinic who wanted to help. He worked about 40 minutes from our house. He called Dr. Kaloko to ask if he knew anyone or could recommend anybody.

"Why does she need a nanny? She doesn't work. She stays in the house all day. Her job is to take care of the baby, let her do just that," Dr Kaloko told him.

"Well, she's not necessarily adjusting to her new role quite smoothly. The other day I got home, both her and the baby were crying. She seemed overwhelmed. I think she might have postpartum blues. She-"

"Her mother gave birth to five children and took care of them all. She can take care of one child. Don't worry about a nanny, she will find her footing" Dr. Kaloko concluded.

When Ollie told me about his conversation with Dr. Kaloko, I was very livid. I didn't know where to begin. Should I start by debunking the fallacy that my own mother did not raise a single one of her children by herself? That many new mothers in Africa have their mothers or in-laws come to help after giving birth? Or that most live in communal apartments with thirty or forty people around readily available to help? Or that those who can afford it, almost always have 'house girls'? Doesn't the adage, "it takes a village to raise a child" come from Africa with the premise that everyone must pitch in to rear a successful child? If one member was struggling weren't other members, the extended family, friends, and neighbors, an entire community coming together to raise that child? Most importantly, doesn't he have empathy as a medical professional? Isn't he familiar with postpartum psychiatric illnesses? Why is he adamant that I do it all by myself even with the information that I was struggling miserably? Weren't there stories on the news about new mothers harming their children because of postpartum depression and psychosis? Wasn't there a story about Andrea Yates who confessed to drowning her five children circulating the news? Why was there this notion that women, black women in particular, must suffer first before they can experience joy or relief? Why can't a man alleviate suffering for his wife if he has the means to do so?

Postpartum depression comes with so much guilt for the mother. Even though it may seem like she regrets having her child or like she doesn't appear to love the fact that she just had a child, she indeed loves her child very much. So many mothers are overcome with guilt about being very despondent at the time they're supposed to feel the most euphoric. For as long as they could remember, societal norms about motherhood had been one described as the best thing that could ever happen to a woman. It was supposed to bring unmatched, unadulterated, life-affirming joy, exuberance, and unbreakable, nurturing bond between the mother and her child. Instead, as a new mother, there'sa feeling of disconnect from your own child. You don't feel enamored, you're feeling guilty about not bonding right away, dreading being left alone with your own baby. You feel terrible about not immediately feeling this gushing, all-encompassing love that you have been conditioned to believe happens straight away. The feelings of being inadequate, unworthy, fearful, judged and shamed by our own husbands and society eats you up. You feel guilty for wanting to take a break or asking for help. You feel guilty and ashamed for not cleaning the house properly as you once did, or that you cannot do laundry as often as you did before, and sometimes it is impossible to take showers and tend to yourself in a timely manner. All your time, energy and concentration goes to this little baby who must be fed, held, comforted, changed, rocked to sleep at it's own convenience, keeps you up at night the whole time, and has changed your life as you once knew it.

Nothing adequately prepares you for this life-changing event of tending to a baby who is completely helpless and depends on you 24 hours unrelentlessly. To not get the support or empathy from the ones who are closest to you and who are supposed to understand is devastating.

"I can see being overseas, educated in the medical field and exposed has done anything for Dr Kaloko. He is still very backward in his mentality. I feel sorry for his wife. Please do not ever discuss my issue with him ever again! He is the type of person who would say; "I didn't realize it was so bad", should I hurt myself or my child. He lacks empathy. I have been having panic attacks just thinking about waking up and living this same routine every day. Yet, I love Sany with my whole heart". I said to Ollie shortly after I laid Sankara in his bassinet.

"Don't worry about Dr Kaloko. I called one of your Aunts from Virginia. They are arranging for someone to come for a week." Ollie informed me.

"Just a week? I am going to need extra help for more than a week, Ollie." I replied.

"I know. We take what we can get until we figure something out". Ollie replied.

There was relief, however, after the third month. Sankara started sleeping through the night. He was babbling a lot, would recognize my face, and smile. He was fascinated by my voice and the silly things I would do with my face and the sounds I would make. He would stretch out his arms for me to pick him up. He became mesmerized by the TV, hypnotized by the vivid colors and sounds of the kids TV shows, especially *Barney & Friends*. The theme song on the show would make him happy and he would clap his hands in delight. Finally, I could steal away for a few minutes while his attention was captivated by the adventures of Barney. I could go brush my teeth, grab something from the refrigerator, or have a change of clothes. Some nights he would sleep so well that I would be scared that maybe he had stopped breathing. I would go to his crib and check to make sure everything was okay, and it was. Sankara was thriving and gave me much relief.

MOTHER-IN-LAW

Sankara walked at eleven months and would pull everything he could from the walls. We had to child-proof our house. We installed stair gates, cabinet locks, table corner guards, outlet plug covers and edge and corner guards. I used to take him to the boys section at Macys to try on a few outfits to wear to the Kingdom hall. Ollie and I would also take him to ToysRUs and buy plenty of toys. Sany had become such a curious toddler, he loved to learn, built impressive structures with the legos we bought. I found a lovely man who became his barber. He would spend time cutting his hair while engaging him with electronic games. After every haircut, he would give him a lollipop. Sany and I became inseparable. I was always with him. I knew the meanings behind all his gestures and sounds. And when some people couldn't make out his baby talk, I would easily translate. Ollie was a great provider but still not helping much with Sany. I knew he loved his son very much, but I also felt that he secretly believed taking care of Sany was my job, a woman's job.By the time Sankara turned three, I enrolled at the local community college. There was a daycare center right opposite the college. I dropped Sany off in the mornings and picked him up after my classes. He had become my best friend and I always wanted him with me. I took him shopping, dressed him up in cool clothes, and spent time teaching him his alphabet and numbers. He learned very fast which filled me with pride. I made sure he slept in his room at night even though he was in our master bedroom for most of the day. I didn't want him to take away from my time with his dad. I didn't want him sleeping in our bedroom and impeding the romance I had with Ollie. However, Ollie wasn't taking advantage of the same things as me. Most times he would fall asleep before I even put Sankara to bed. I would crave some intimate time with him, but he would fall asleep after he ate and wasn't prioritizing our alone time. One day, we took an out of town trip to Atlanta, calling it a family trip. He wanted his close friend Dule to meet his son and wife. We were gone for three days. His friend Dule had a new baby as well, his third boy. We had a great time meeting other

Sierra Leoneans in the outings Dule took us. We were nostalgic, theparties beingreminiscent of parties back home in Freetown, the aroma of the foods, the music, the clothes and the use of our local language krio. It was a far cry from life in Humboldt where we werethe only Sierra Leoneans besides the Kalokos.

After our three day visit, we set out to drive back to Humboldt. I was at the steering wheel for the six hours drive back. Ollie got out of the car to puff on a cigarette when I stopped at gas stations to buy gas or to change a soiled diaper. He had still not stopped smoking even after the birth of Sankara, andwould go smoke outside of the house or wait until he got out of the car.

We made it to Humboldt six and a half hours later. The first thing I did when we entered the house was check the blinking house telephone to hear our voice messages. One of the 14 messages caught our attention. It was from Ollie's Aunt Vicky in Virginia: "Hello? Hello? Hello Ollie, this is Aunt Vicky. I just got a call from your mother Doris. She told me she just landed at the airport in Memphis. She's going to need you to go pick her up. Call me when you get this message please."

I looked at Ollie with surprise. "Mom is here? She didn't tell us she was coming? We have to go get her from the airport."

"I'm not going anywhere else tonight, Zhu. Since she wants to be clandestine about her visit, she can take care of herself at the airport."

"Ok, I will go pick her up. Hold on to San-"

"You're not going anywhere else tonight, Zhu. You just drove for nearly seven hours. You're not going back on the streets at this time of night to get someone who is so inconsiderate. Let's all get ready for bed. I'll call Aunty Vicky in the morning."

All through the night, I kept thinking about what to do for Mom Doris in the morning, what time do I go pick her up? How do I set up the guest room to suit her? What welcome meal should I cook for her? What do I wear to the airport? Ollie could sense my anxiety and said to me, "Don't worry about too much Zhu-Zhu, we will handle everything in the morning. Now make sure you have a good night's rest."

We fell asleep in each other's arms. In the morning, I woke up to make Ollie his usual cup of Folgers coffee. He was very particular about me waking up and seeing him off with his coffee. Sometimes, I was too tired to wake up and see him off, especially if I had had a long night with Sankara. However, there was never a good excuse for him for why I couldn't see him off with his cup of coffee. He would have an attitude every time I wasn't able to do so. There was always a price for me to pay, either the silent treatment or him going to the guest room to sleep. Both actions I detested and viewed as passive aggressive. I did not believe in punishing one's spouse like you would a child. I believed spouses had to be able to express themselves in a safe place. I believe one must listen to their spouse to gain insight and understanding, that they must compromise and most importantly, resolve their problems quickly. I learned all of these things from the Kingdom Hall, based on bible principles. Ollie would always encourage me to go to the meetings at the Kingdom Hall but he never went with me there or to any other religious institution. However, he knew the teachings at the Kingdom Hall were beneficial to his marriage. He knew I was being taught to have deep respect for my husband, to be a capable wife at home, to be a nurturing and loving mother to our child. So, every time I missed a meeting, he would ask why I hadn't gone. I hated missing the meetings too, because I had help there. The brothers and sisters at the hall would help me with Sankara throughout the meeting. However, it was hard for me to get reinforcements about how to be a formidable wife when he wasn't getting taught how to be a good husband, how to communicate better, and how to be a good father. It became quite clear why the bible talked about not being unevenly yoked with unbelievers. Our marriage was like a person who was paralyzed in one leg. There was one good leg carrying the body, but there was also the paralyzed leg that you had to keep dragging along. Every time they preached about how the husband is commanded to love his wife as he loves his own body, to cherish his wife, to show her honor, I wished Ollie was there to receive the message. I was getting all the reinforcements while he didn't. It frustrated and saddened me. How come he gets to have a free pass and treat me anyhow, yet I have to follow the rules of the bible? I wanted consideration, reassurances and acknowledgements from him as well. I wanted him to be there to hear everything I was hearing. But I chose someone who valued my faith, but didn't care to share it. I was on my own.

"I want to go to Walmart to get some window curtains, bed sheets, toiletries and a trash bin for Mom's room," I said to Ollie in the morning. "I also want to cook sawasawa and foofoo after I'm done fixing her room. Then I will get Sankara ready to drive to the airport."

"No problem, I will leave some money for that. Make sure you drive carefully to the airport, there is no need to rush, take your time."

After Ollie left for work, I left for Walmart with Sankara. I bought new blackout window curtains for Mom's room because I didn't want the sun right in her face in the mornings. I figured she would pull the curtain if she needed some sunshine. I also got darker bed sheets so they wouldn't be easily dirty. I made the bed, added decorative pillows, vacuumed the carpet, and sprayed some air freshener all over, which helped it look cozy and nice. I then went to the kitchen and prepared the sawasawa, then I got Sankara ready for the airport. I strapped him in his car seat and drove away. My mother-in-law was waiting for us outside the airport hotel.

"Hello mom! Welcome to Tennessee! How are you, how was your flight?"

"Not bad. It's good to see you. How about my Oliver, what about Sankara? Where are the boys?" she asked.

"Ollie has to work this morning, and Sankara is in his car seat in the back of the car, you'll see him in a moment. Let me help you with your bags." I took the bags from her and headed towards my car and put them in the trunk. "You can have a seat by me, mom," I beckoned for her to take the front passenger seat.

"Not before I see my grandson. Hello Sankara. I am grandma Doris." She tried to take Sankara's hand but Sankara would have none of it, and he immediately started crying. "Don't be a naughty boy, come to grandma," she continued. Sankara's cries got even louder.

"It's okay, mom. In time, Sankara will get used to you. I bet it will take no time at all. C'mon to the front seat". I asked about her health and how things were back in Sierra Leone. However, I didn't ask her why she decided to come without telling us first. I felt that was a conversation for herself and Ollie to have.

As soon as we arrived home, I called Ollie at work to let him know we had made it back home safely. He thanked me for my efforts and said he would be home as soon as he saw his last patient for the day. I showed Mom around the house and then finally took her to the guest room which I set up for her. I told her if she needed anything else, she could knock on our bedroom door. I left her to rest while I retreated to our bedroom to watch my usual shows and played with Sankara. Soon we heard the garage door opening, and I peeped through my window and saw Ollie's car waiting for the garage door to open all the way. Sankara ran down the stairs to welcome his dad home. Once Ollie got out of the car, he scooped Sankara off the floor and carried him on his chest.

"Good evening buddy! How was your day, buddy? Were you a good boy for mommy today?"

Sankara was hyped and laughing. He loved when his dad held him high up. "Daddy!!!" he shouted.

"Sany!!!!" his dad replied. Ollie then walked over to me and gave me a side hug. "Thank you for today. How is Mom doing?"

"She should be fine, She'sin her bedroom. Go ahead and see her, I'll get your food ready."

He walked up the stairs to the guest room with Sankara still on his chest. He knocked on the door and announced himself. "Mom, it's me, good evening." His mom opened the door and let them in.

I went to the kitchen to warm up Ollie's food. Sawasawa was one of his favorite foods. I always served Ollie his meals, whether it was breakfast, lunch or dinner. I didn't just make the meals, I served them too. Ollie loved me serving him his food. He never pressured me to do it. It was something I started to do because that's what I saw my mother and the other women I grew up with do for their husbands. I loved serving him because I was particular about the presentation. I wanted the fruits in a small bowl by the big plate, veggies on the side of the big plate, and so on. I looked forward to serving him his food every day.

I did not know what Ollie and his mom talked about, but he came to eat his food about twenty minutes later. He always tried to feed Sankara bits and pieces of food off his plate. He watched the news, and then leaned on the couch and fell asleep. This was pretty much the routine. Ollie came home exhausted at around 7pm, we'd chat about how our day went while he atedinner, he'd hang out with Sankara for a bit, then fall asleep. I always had to wake him up to go to the master bedroom, otherwise I wouldn't see him in bed until 3 or 4am.

It had been close to three weeks since mom arrived from Sierra Leone. She wasn't talking to me much because every time she asked Ollie for something, he would tell her to ask me for it. Instead of her embracing this as a united couple who made decisions together, it upset her. I didn't think Ollie was doing it to upset her, but he was always gone and whatever his mom wanted, someone had to go get it for her. She couldn't drive anywhere and there weren't bus services in lil ol Humboldt. So, whenever Ollie would say, "Oh you need a new wardrobe? No problem, ask Zhuri. I'll give her some money and she will take you," she would reply, "Why do I have to ask Zhuri about everything? Is it not your money? Why does she have so much control over you? I knew this wasn't ordinary. Her parents must have put juju on you. You never used to act like this before, Oliver."

"I never used to act like this before because I was never married before. We never lived in the same house before except when I was a visitor at your house on holidays. I am seldom home, she knows everything about this house, because it is her home too. You cannot drive, who else do you expect me to ask? And please just stop about the juju thing, just stop!"

Mom would then angrily go back upstairs to her bedroom and lock the door behind her. She would not make it downstairs when we were around for a whole week. Ollie would ask me if I had seen her, and I would say no. Ollie would go knock on her door and say good evening or good morning and would leave when she answered him with her own greeting.

A week later, when I got home from college, I saw a utility truck in my driveway. When I got into the house, I saw two men working on the door in mom's room. They were changing the locks to her bedroom. I had not been told about this, so I went to our bedroom and called Ollie at work, askinghim what was going on. He said his mother had complained that there were some things missing in her bedroom. She had lost some panties, some writing pads, and a couple of cards she had planned to send to some friends. She told him we were the only two people left in the house when Ollie wasn't home besides Sany, so I must have taken them. Ollie said he thought she was paranoid and had some mental issues. He said he sent the utility guys to fix her door so he could shut her up. I immediately started crying. I started telling Ollie the things that I have endured with his mom without telling him because I thought things would change.

"She accused me of turning Sankara against her, Ollie. Sany is only three years old! She told me I must've told Sankara awful things about her and that's why Sankara didn't want to go close to her when she just arrived. Even as I told her it was stranger anxiety, she didn't want to hear it. She said, 'blood must recognize blood.' Then she told me I must have evil spirits because everything I chose for her bedroom was dark, dark curtains and dark sheets. She said my parents and I have used voodoo on you, she doesn't eat my food, and now she is accusing me of stealing from her bedroom? She never leaves that room except when we are not around, so when do I actually have the opportunity to go in there to steal from her? She is constantly in that room for days at a time. I didn't complain because I thought I'd kill her with kindness, but the more I tried, the worse it was getting. She has taken my kindness for weakness and is making me miserable in my own home." I explained with my voice squierking.

"Oh my God! I didn't know about all this. Why didn't you tell me all this, Zhu-Zhu? I must have a talk with her today. I want you to go give the phone to her right now! Oh my gosh! Give her the phone."

I gave the phone to one of the utility workers to hand over to her. She was on the phone with Ollie for two minutes and then she gave the man back the phone. I got the phone from the man and immediately it started ringing again. It was Ollie's office number on the caller I.D.

"Hello," I answered the phone.

"Hey Zhu! It's me again. I want you to do me a favor, I want you to leave the house with Sankara between 6 and 7 this evening. I will be having a harsh talk with my mom this evening and I don't want you or Sankara to be around."

"That's okay, Ollie. There is a bible study at the Kingdom Hall this evening so I'll take Sany with me." I told him.

"Great! I am sorry about everything. I will take care of this problem. Just trust me."

I found myself eating a lot around the time I was graduating from community college. I would later find out I was pregnant. It was the perfect time, just a month away from graduating. However, Ollie wasn't particularly ecstatic. He felt we needed to have planned properly for a new baby. He wasn't excited as he had been the first time around. This made me feel very much alone. Sankara wasn't thrilled either; "Nooooo, I do not want another baby! I just want you, me and Daddy". He said after I told him that we will be having a new baby. He touched my belly and pressed on it very hard as if to crush the baby. About two weeks after Ollie had his hard talk with his mother, I woke up one Sunday morning throwing up because of morning sickness. I went downstairs to get some juice in the refrigerator and saw two packed suitcases by my front door. I hurried upstairs and called Ollie who was already at work to do a 24 hour shift at the emergency room. He was working from 7 am to 7 am, so he left the house at 6am. I asked Ollie if he knew anything about the suitcases, but he said no. He asked me to take the telephone over to his mom's room. I knocked on her door and told her Ollie was on the phone for her. Once she picked up the phone, I left for the kitchen to get some juice. She later came downstairs and talked to me.

"Well, I want to thank you for my stay, but I had a dream last night and I saw my dead parents in my dream and they told me I shouldn't spend one more day in this house. Therefore, I'm leaving this house today. I don't know where I'm going yet, but I'm not staying in this house one more day. You see over there," she pointed to the African carvings by the fireplace, "that is the head station for the demons, that's their headquarters. I have been tormented by demons in this house, I am leaving. Thanks to your parents for sending those for you to bewitch my son in the disguise of decoration."

"Actually, those are all your son's property. And before him, they belonged to his father. After he died, Ollie took those as mementos to remember him with. I didn't know Ollie's dad believed in witchcraft. Apparently the carvings pick and choose who to torment. We've never had any problems with them until you said something. I cannot wait to tell Ollie about this."

She turned and walked away from me. A few minutes later, a taxi came and picked her up. She was gone, as abruptly as she came.

When Ollie came back after his shift the next day, he told me that he had found a hotel for his mother to stay at until he could book a flight for her back to Freetown.

"I am so sorry about all this Zhu-Zhu. I am sorry about everything she put you through. I really do not understand that woman anymore. Is it old age, paranoia or just a blatant control freak? I really cannot believe how she thinks". Ollie said, sounding very confused.

"She said my parents gave you the carvings and put voodoo in them. She said the whole pile of them by the fireplace is the station for evil spirits".

"Zhu, please stop, she tried to say that to me and I won't repeat what I told her. I do not believe my mother is sound-minded. There is a mental problem somewhere. When they can no longer control us, they come up with the most ridiculous excuses". Ollie said.

"I honestly thought I should kill her with kindness at first. I really did think being kind to her will win her over. That was the reason why I didn't tell you a lot of things. I thought I'd just bear with it until she realized that I wasn't her rival or a threat. I wanted her to see me as a daughter so badly but she was just so set in her ways, there was no helping her". I explained to Ollie.

"She wanted to be in control, that's all. Without control, she lost it. I hope you know that none of this was your fault, Zhu-Zhu." Ollie explained.

"Oh I know! I have always subscribed to the idea of everyone staying in their respective roles and not trying to usurp or hijack other people's roles. If you're a mother-in-law, stay in that role of a mother, grandmother and support system, do not try to be the wife or overseer of the new family your son just started. Contrary to her thinking, she still had a very important role of ensuring a healthy family dynamic with us, by being a consultant and a support system. She didn't need to be pushy, critical, possessive and accusatory. I must also stay in my role as a wife and mother of your children and not try to be your mother and of course, you should continue to be her son, my husband and my children's father. Once people start to overstep their boundaries and forget what their roles are, there is discord and the root of all sorts of other problems. I wanted her to feel secure in her role. I wanted her to be like my own mother, kind and supportive, but for some bizarre reason, she saw me as a problem." I responded to Ollie.

"Not everyone thinks like you, Zhu-Zhu. Some people think someone is always in their position or out to get them. The manner in which she came was very problematic, I was surprised you were still so eager to go pick her up from the airport and was shocked that you didn't accuse me of knowing something about it and not telling you. Anyway, she is gone now. We can go back to life as we know it again". Ollie said.

"I knew she could be difficult. I've heard stories, but I was going to kill her with kindness. As for you knowing something about it and not telling me. I never thought of that. I only just concentrated on making things work. She was already here, how can we all make it work? That was my thought process. But it was not to be."

Ollie was exhausted from his 24 hour ER shift. He ate his breakfast and went upstairs in our bedroom to sleep.

SHAREEF AND SAAMI

By the time I was close to 7 months pregnant, Ollie could see I was wobbling around with a big belly and a four year old. I had gestational diabetesbecause I had gained more weight the second time around. I would experience extreme tiredness, nausea, and blurred vision. I would get light headed and almost pass out. He asked me if I thought I was going to need help. I told him I wanted my mother to come so she could be a live-in help and be available to us 24 hours. Ollie thought it was a good idea and sent documents for my mom to go try for a visa. Before my mother went for the interview, I called to coach her. "Tell the consul your daughter had severe postpartum depression the last time she gave birth. She was depressed and cried most of the time. Stress the importance of support this time around. Make sure you say these things."

My plan worked, my mother got a three year visitor's visa. Ollie paid for her to come two weeks before I gave birth. I had gotten very heavy and my due date had come and gone. Unlike the previous experience with my mother-in-law, my mom was a great help. She didn't want me to get up to do anything. However, I had to still get up and make food for Sankara who wasn't warming up to her just yet. Every time my mom would try to make food for Sankara, he would yell; "Nooooo! I want my Mom to make it".

"Mom, don't worry, in due time he will get used to you. Sany is used to having just me and his dad around". I explained to my mom.

"Oh no, I am not worried about Sany. I just don't want you straining yourself. I want you to rest. If you need anything, just say so". My mom replied.

I didn't ask for much except my cravings for all the Sierra Leonean foods I had missed. My mom cooked whatever I craved. She made sure the house was sparkling clean. She did the laundry and folded them. She swept the patio and polished the furniture. Most importantly, she got along very well with Ollie. I would see them hanging out in the den chatting and laughing.

When I called my doctor two days after my due date had passed, he told me to wait two more days. He said if the baby didn't come in the next two days, he'd induce labor. Two days came and went and Ollie got me to the hospital to be induced. Eight hours after I was induced Shareef came into the world. He was a big baby being 10 lbs! Ollie chose the name Shareef because it meant nobility, distinguished, and protector. His size was fitting for the protector part of his name. He passed all his newborn wellness exams and we were free to go home the next day.

My mother was excited to see her newborn grandson. She immediately got him from my arms and carried him. Comparatively, Sankara was very standoffish to her when she had just arrived. He wouldn't let her touch him or make his food. My mother was looking forward to building a relationship with her new grandson, Shareef from the start. She volunteered to bathe him, dress him up, and rock him to sleep.

"What a difference it makes this second time around. Zhu-Zhu was a nervous wreck the first time around. She looks so calm this time around," Ollie said to my mother.

"I am calmer this time around because I have had tons of experience with Sankara and I know what to expect. I know Shareef is not going to sleep the whole night through, I know he's going to need several diaper changes, I know that sometimes no matter what I do, he's going to have crying spells. So, everything is not a surprise for me anymore. Most importantly, I know it's not going to be like that all the time. It's a stage, a phase, and everything is going to be alright."

"I am so glad about that new mentality, Zhu-Zhu. And of course, all that doesn't mean you will not get exhausted physically. When you do, mom is here to help."

"Mom? I'm glad she's here, but what about you, Ollie? He's your child too. Do you ever consider that you have to pitch in as well?" Ollie did not answer me. He just went upstairs and busied himself.

Shareef was a sweet little brother. He was always laughing, but had no interest in sleeping. It took long hours to get him to finally sleep and when he did, the slightest noise would wake him up. Things didn't change when he turned three months, or six months, or eight months, he would always wake up more than he slept.

I was just getting the hang of another baby when I found out that I was pregnant again when Shareef was 10 months old. I couldn't believe it. Because my mom was around to help, I slept with Ollie more. I never turned down an opportunity to have sex with him, I don't care how mad I was at him about anything. My religious upbringing made me aware of my wifely duty as a sexual partner to my husband. "Do not deprive each other of it except by mutual consent", the bible says in 1 Corinthians 7:5. And besides, I was very much in love with my husband even though he didn't help much with the baby. Sex was a fantastic escape for me. It made me feel good, desirable and would take away all my stress. Laying down next to my husband at the end of the day always made me horny. I always wore my preventive patch when I slept with Ollie and now I was pregnant again? I did not know how to tell Ollie. It was just the other night I overheard him making fun of an old friend on the phone, his wife was pregnant with their third boy. He mocked him mercilessly. Now, here I was with my third pregnancy before Shareef even turned one.

I knew I wasn't supposed to be nervous or scared to tell Ollie that I was pregnant, after all, am I not a married woman? And isn't there a disclaimer on all the birth control medications that it's not 100 percent foolproof? I had a bad feeling Ollie wasn't going to be very happy about this pregnancy, so I decided not to tell him just yet. Then one day, I went shopping and passed out at the mall like I did when I was pregnant with Sankara. The manager at Macys where I collapsed called Ollie to let him know. Ollie called one of the doctor's wives who lived right by the mall area to take me home until he got there. When we got home, Ollie asked me if I thought I was pregnant. I said yes and he just kept silent. Ollie would not speak to me besides the usual morning and evening greetings until I was five months pregnant. When he came home one evening, he saw an ultrasound picture of the baby on the bathroom mirror and asked me what the sex of the baby was. I told him it was another boy and he kept silent again. I had to deal with this cold and distant Ollie even as I continued to carry out my wifely duties of cooking, cleaning, doing laundry, and serving him his food. He would come home, greet everyone, play with Sankara and Shareef, watch his show on TV and then fall asleep. I was looking forward to being pampered and sharing the excitement of the impending baby, but I was alone in my feelings. I think Ollie must have thought I had been careless with my contraceptive. I felt incredibly lonely during my pregnancy. He was not open to everyday conversations, laughing or playing around with me. He thought the onus was on me to have prevented any future pregnancies. I guess this was his way of showing me if it ever happened again, I was on my own.

On a Sunday morning in July, I went into labor and gave birth to a beautiful baby boy who I namedSaami. It means one who is exalted. Saami was the smallest of my boys, being6 pounds and 3ounces. Sankara was 8 pounds and Shareef was the biggest at 10. Ollie was with me at the hospital. He seemed happy to welcome baby Saami. He cut the umbilical cord and carried him. This time around, it was only 6 hours of labor and this tiny, olive skinned, handsome, calm baby came into our lives. Saami had the best temperament. He seldom cried. He seemed always content to the point where Ollie joked that he could take care of Saami all by himself. I felt it was a corny joke, considering he never meaningfully helped at home with Sany and Shareef, but he was right about Saami being very easy. Saami would eat, play, smile, and just bounce around. We didn't feel like there was a new baby in the house. He grew up with Shareef and people would ask us if they were twins when he was two and Shareef three years old. Saami was speaking by the time he was sixteen months old. He was very sharp and tiny, so we nicknamed him 'lil skinny.' He was our little bring light who had come to join the Jones party and we loved him so much! Sankara who had been very apprehensive of having siblings had adjusted very well to his two little brothers. They played in the yard and he would make them watch Power Rangers with him. He was an avid fan of the Power Rangers series and he collected all the toys. He made them skip shows geared for their toddler stages and would have them watch his shows instead. He was the cool big brother who introduced them to cool shows and new things. They adored him. Sankara did very well in school and was constantly on the honor roll in elementary school. I remember how proud of him we were when he was also awarded the Spirit of St Joseph Award. This award was given annually to the student who best exemplifies generous, loving service to others, in the manner of St Joseph. I remember thinking, "I don't just have a smart kid, I also have a good kid and other people recognize it as well". I was truly happy that Sankara was the oldest as he set the best example for his little brothers. Our home was no longer lonely. It was filled with screams and shouts of excitement and sometimes of cries and tears after the boys scraped their knees or got into little fights. They were all used to their grandma by now and got away with everything. My mother became the enabler, while Ollie and I disciplined the boys. I also gave lots of hugs, kisses and reassurances. I decided I wasn't going to use corporal punishment with them, I had stern conversations instead. The boys would immediately start crying when their dad used a certain tone with them. That's when they knewthey were in trouble. When he yelled, "Sany!" sankara would immediately start crying because it meant he was in trouble. Most times, however, he was very loving and engaging with them. He asked them many questions about things I wouldn't think twice about asking them. If they were playing outside, he would ask, "what type of soil is this, Sany? How many types of soils are there? What type of flowers grow best in this type of soil? Is this flower an annual or a perennial?" I was always fascinated by how he made his playful interactions with them very educational. On days Sany didn't have school, Ollie would sometimes ask me to get Sankara ready in the mornings to go to work with him so he could observe him as he treated his patients. Sany looked forward to days like those because all the nurses would fawn over him and spoil him the whole time. I planned vacations to Disney world, art galleries and museums. We would take them to the zoo where Ollie would ask them all types of questions about the different animals. Even as we were getting our groove with parenting multiple children, I felt Ollie wasn't making time for us as a couple if I didn't make the effort. He was content with just providing for us materially. I wanted more than just material things. I wanted closeness and intimacy. I wanted him to take the initiative of planning a date or a getaway for just the two of us. He felt those things were for people who were dating and newlyweds, not a couple with a house full of kids. He thought my head was always in the clouds and not being realistic. "You have three kids, a husband and a full-time college student with a packed curriculum, when do you have time for romance?" He would ask sarcastically.

"We just have to make time for it. I still have time. My mom is here, we could have quick getaways or go out and not come back very early. I love getting dressed up for you and.."

"Ok, ok, Zhu-Zhu. You don't like going to nightclubs like I do, you don't like the bars I hang out in". He quickly interrupted me.

"I don't like the smoking, drinking and rowdiness in the bars and nightclubs, but we could go to a nice, upscale restaurant, we could go watch a show together or just spend a night in a hotel by ourselves. Just something for us". I tried to reason with him.

"I wonder how many married women with multiple kids your age back home still think like you do. We've been married for how many years now? You're still talking about getting romanced?" He asked in a dismissive manner.

"Ollie, I'm only 28 years old. You expect me to act like an old lady because I now have kids and I'm married? I still have the desire to feel sexy, to be romanced, those feelings didn't go away after I had children. I am a woman first before I am somebody's wife and mother".

"Let's talk about this another time, Zhu-Zhu. You're bound to bring this up another time soon." He said to me as he walked away. I shook my head in exasperation. Will I ever get to him?

SURPRISE FORTIETH BIRTHDAY PARTY

I was very cognisant of how babies could change a relationship and a woman's body. I had three children and was in my late twenties, 28 years old to be exact. However, motherhood had been good to me. It took me from the skinny, lanky girl to a curvy, voluptuous woman. I always had a nice shape, but the extra pounds accentuated my curves. My breasts got a little bigger and rounder, and my bottom got even more pear shaped, heavy at the bottom and a tiny waist. It was hard not to notice my figure when I went out, but I tried very hard to hide it under a coat or wear really baggy clothes just to be respectful of my status as a married woman. Other times, I just didn't care for the cat calls and honking of horns from random men. I also did everything to make sure I set time aside for Ollie and I. I made sure the children kept their bedtimes, so we could have time to ourselves before we went to sleep. I would also drop off the children at my parents' house, only two minutes away from our house. My father came to the US when Saami turned two years old after it was apparent my mother couldn't cope without him. She began experiencing heart palpitations whenever they argued on the phone. It became clear that the distance between them was doing a number on their relationship. They had lived together for over 25 years, so it was understandable how much they missed each other.My brother, Ahsan, had a small apartment not too far away and I helped him with the rent so my parents could stay there. It was a three bedroom apartment, but he lived there alone until my parents moved in because Ollie didn't want my extended family staying at our house. I would take the children to my parents' before Ollie got home, get really sexy, and cook a romantic meal witha bottle of wine on the side. I would make sure to cook early so the house won't smell of food. I would spray the house with scented air fresheners, then I would work on myself which included taking a shower, shaving my whole body, and using sugar scrubs to make my skin smooth to the touch. Then I would come out and dry my skin, then slather myself with scented lotions from Victoria's Secret before putting on some lingerie and wait for Ollie to come home.

However, when Ollie got home, he would be all but impressed. He would ask where the kids were, eat his food, and tell me how tired he was beforelater going to bed. I would go to bed very hurt, horny, and distraught . My self-esteem took a hit. However, like I did with his mom when she first came to America, I felt I should do even more. I would go to Walgreens and buy romantic cards, 'just because' cards, and sometimes I would show up at his clinic with a bouquet of flowers and freshly cooked food for his lunch. He would say thank you, but he was never saving the many cards I bought him. I would find them in his home office under the table, or on the floor somewhere. It hurt me really badly, but I became more frustrated because I didn't know what else to do. I was crying myself to sleep at night.

One day, when Ollie got home from work, I shared my frustrations with him. "We haven't had sex for almost two months now and it doesn't seem to bother you. I have tried everything, being sexy for you, taking the kids away so we can have some alone time, surprising you with gifts at work, yet it keeps getting worse! You seldom sleep in our own bedroom, you're always in the guest room or doing something in the basement." I was in tears as I continued, "this is affecting my self-esteem. I look at myself in the mirror and see nothing wrong, but the way you have ignored me, you make me feel like something is wrong with me."

"I have heard you, I will consider what you said. If you want the sex to resume, wake up early in the morning tomorrow and fix my coffee." He said devoid of any empathy or understanding for all I just said to him.

"But I do make your coffee! Not every time because I stay up all night working on my homework for college, and I have three kids I have to drop off in the morning. Sankara goes to a different school and Shareef and Saami go to another. You don't take any of them, I do it all and because I cannot make your coffee every day you have been withholding sex from me? You prefer to withdraw from me instead of helping me out so we can have even more time together?"

Before I finished talking, Ollie got up and went downstairs to smoke a cigarette. I went to bed in tears once again. He slept in our bedroom that night, but didn't touch me. I was at my wits end. I couldn't sleep much. What more was I to possibly do to make him realize that I was desperately going crazy from lack of attention, affection and sexual intimacy? I tossed and turned in bed to make him realize I was still not asleep should he want to be intimate, but it was not to be. I heard him snoring with his back turned against me.

When I stopped to buy gas on my way to university the next day, I heard a man cat-calling me as soon as I got out of the car. This was very typical for me. Even when I was on campus, I would have guys ten years younger than me try to talk to me. It was killing me on the inside because I wanted this attention to come from Ollie. I would hear men whisper to each other after I walked past them. One time, I was standing in a line, then I walked away and I heard the white guy behind me yell. "Damn!" I looked back at him and he apologized. "I'm sorry, I didn't mean to say that out loud." I continued to walk away. I was disgusted, not at him, but at my situation at home. Never once did I imagine I would have a sexless marriage, devoid of romance and intimacy, but I was more frustrated that my efforts didn't seem to be helping the situation at all.

In one of my classes, my Economics professor, Mr. Teague would innocently talk about his weekend while explaining something pertaining to the subject matter at hand. In his explanation, he would say "...and so, I took my wife's car, like I do every weekend, to wash and vacuum it, and I filled it up with gas. Then I helped her with dinner because she cooked last weekend. And I told her she could choose where we vacation this month, because I chose Dallas the last time." I couldn't believe what I was hearing. It filled me with so much jealousy and resentment. All of what he was doing for his wife was so considerate and it seemed like they shared the household responsibilities. Even though his wife didn't cook every day like I did, he still made sure he relieved her by cooking for her on other days. I would start daydreaming, wishing I had a caring, considerate, and nurturing husband like that. One who would not punish me indefinitely because I missed making him his coffee on certain days. I would go to my car after my class and just cry. I never told anybody what I was going through, not my parents because I didn't want them to not like Ollie, and not my friends because I always painted a picture of a happy marriage and never spoke ill of Ollie.

His 40th birthday was coming up in six months, so I called Ollie's friend Dule and told him that I wanted to plan a surprise birthday party for Ollie and would like his help. Dule was very sold on the idea and quite eager to help. I told him I would like to have some names and numbers of Ollie's other friends I was yet to meet so I could invite them too. I invited some of Ollie's family members who lived out of state and told them it was a big secret that Ollie didn't even know about, swearing them all into secrecy. From the little allowance he gave to me every month, I saved up to pay for the hall at a hotel, and also paid for Dule to come with a DJ. As far as the food was concerned, I was going to make all of it. As the time got closer, I asked some of his friends and a few family members if they would want to give a speech, and asked one of the ladies he worked with if someone from the clinic would give a speech. I also worked with Sankara, thinking it would be a nice touch if he said something brief or read a poem for his dad.

On the day of the party, I was busy cooking up a storm. I told Ollie I was cooking for an African Heritage event and that someone would be picking up the food. He knew there was a black-tie event afterwards. My mom got to the hall and so did my friend Salem who had come all the way from Florida with her husband. She got the hall ready with decorations and food set-up. Dule and the DJ set up the music and after everything was ready, Salem called to tell me the guests were waiting on us. I got all the three boys ready and Ollie came to the car in a black suit and white shirt, looking very dapper. I drove to the hall then called Salem to let her know we had arrived. Salem told me we could come in in five minutes. She told all the guests to get ready to say 'Surprise!' as Ollie walked in. I started straightening up the children's suits and told Ollie he could go ahead and save us a few seats. As he went in, I heard the crowd say 'Surprise!' He was stunned. He saw his cousins he hadn't seen in a very long time, old friends from school, and friends he recently just spoke to who told him nothing. He seemed overjoyed, laughing loudly and giving hug after hug. Dule then got on the mic and told the room that Ollie's lovely wife Zhuri, aka me, had planned this marvelous surprise party for him.

"When Zhuri called to tell me she wanted to plan a surprise party for Oliver, I did not hesitate. This man is a hard worker who just doesn't stop. He goes and goes and goes, just like the energizer bunny. He is lucky to have a wife like Zhuri to balance him out. Happy 40th birthday, Oliver! Man! You're getting old."

Oliver looked over at me and smiled. He took the mic from Dule and thankedeveryone who had traveled from out of state to be at his party. He admitted his shock. "Dule, man! I didn't realize you'd plot with Zhu-Zhu against me. I spoke to you yesterday man, and you didn't say a thing! And all of you who have come out of state, man I'm so flattered that you would do that for me. It really means a lot. And to my staff who are here and never said a word: you're all fired! And Zhu-Zhu, we'll talk about this later when everyone is gone." The whole room roared with laughter. "In the meantime, let's enjoy ourselves. Thank you Zhu and thank you to our boys who are looking like little big men tonight. Happy birthday to me! Let's celebrate!"

The DJ outdid himself with a medley of African and American songs. Everyone was on the dance floor. I got to dance with Ollie, and it felt so good to be so close to him and to have him show some affection publicly. I felt really good about the night. Sankara got to read his message to his dad and other friends and family members gave speeches. The party went on until the hotel manager came and told us at 3am that the time we paid for had ended.

Ollie invited some of the guests to the house after the party. They came with him and I could hear them till very late, cracking jokes and laughing. However, I had been in our room ever since we returned and Ollie hadn't even come upstairs to see me. The next thing I heard were cars leaving the driveway. Ollie had left with them, calling five minutes later to tellme they were going to finish the night off at the club.

Another disappointment once again, even with my best efforts, Ollie was paying attention to everyone else but me. Once again, I cried myself to sleep.

On Sunday evening after all the guests were gone, I told Ollie I wanted to talk to him after I had put the boys to sleep.

"Ollie, I was really expecting us to have an intimate time after the party. I was expecting you would enjoy the party, return home with your family and show your wife a good time."

"First of all," he promptly interrupted me, "I never asked you to throw me a surprise party. It was beautiful. I'm not going to lie, and it was definitely a nice thought, but I prefer you save the money I give to you instead of wasting it on parties."

"But it was MY money, Ollie. And I can use it how I choose. And I chose to make my husband feel special. It's not every day you turn forty." I started crying again and got up and left him and went to bed. I prayed to God asking him what else I was supposed to do, nothing seemed to be working. I was at my wits end. I felt like a complete failure. I felt useless. My soul felt empty and crushed. Surely there must be something I am not doing right? But what was it? He wasn't complaining about anything but his coffee. How much longer was I going to put up with this? Should I maybe just accept that our marriage is going through a phase or have we plateaued? The confusion in my mind was unsettling? I was embarrassed to complain about my husband not giving me sex. Would people think there is something wrong with me? How is this situation going to be solved because my libido wasn't going anywhere. The more he deprived me, the more heightened my libido and my need for his attention.

Before I could fall asleep, Ollie came to our bedroom and started taking off my clothes. I had mixed feelings. Was he doing this because he felt guilty? Does he really want to make love to me? Or was he doing this to shut me up? Tears rolled down my face as he completely undressed me. For the first time ever, I did not enjoy being intimate with my husband. There were a lot of doubts and so much hurt. I didn't feel like he cared about me anymore. In the ten years we had been married, I maintained the love I had for my husband since the beginning, I tried my very best to sustain the romance. I made sure I made time for him, for us. Nothing seemed to work and that frustrated me.

When I woke up in the morning, I showered right after Ollie showered and sat on our bed watching TV, makingsure I shaved my whole body very smoothly. When I got out of the bathroom, I poured some baby oil on myself and massaged my whole body. I was looking so supple, smooth, curvy and sexy. I went to the bed and as I twirled around. "Don't I look sexy for a woman who has had three kids?"

"That's what you're concerned about? There are women in Africa who cannot afford to feed their own children and you're focused on looking sexy after giving birth," Ollie replied.

"What! This is supposed to be an intimate moment between a married couple. Why should societal injustice be a part of it? You know what? You win. I am done trying to make my own husband see me, love me, desire me. I am done. Every time I leave this house and venture out, I get all this attention, but when I enter this house, it's crickets. Whatever your plan was, you finally succeeded in frustrating the hell outta me. Congratulations. I'm so done."

I left him in the bedroom and went to the guest room. I spent the whole day in the guest room after I dropped the boys off at their grandparents'. I was in there crying and contemplating my next move. I knew I couldn't continue like this indefinitely, but what was going to be my next move? Continuing like this will suck the life out of me. I was already without any joy, confidence or self-esteem. I would be like an empty vessel without a soul. I heard Ollie looking all over the house and couldn't find me until he went there.

"What are you doing here? Come back to the bedroom, you know you don't belong in this room," he said to me.

"I am not going back. You stay there all by yourself. I'll make myself comfortable here. And why do you care anyway? You don't seem to care about me any more. My feelings don't matter to you. I am done."

"C'mon Zhu-Zhu," he went over to the bed and picked me up even as I resisted. "This is not you, Zhu-Zhu. You are the caring, loving, nurturing, god-fearing wife. This is not you at all, a resisting, belligerent wife? Don't change to someone you're not. Everything is fine."

"Everything is fine for you, Ollie! You're the one having your cake and eating it too. You are not the one hurting, you're not the one crying yourself to sleep every night, you're not the one questioning your worth, your value. You're not the one whose self-esteem is in the gutter! You're now over 300 lbs, Ollie! You have gained over a hundred pounds since I married you. Yet, I have never made you feel less than, I have never made you feel unattractive. I never talk about your weight, I support you when you tell me you want to go on diets, I adjust my cooking to exactly what you want. I have done all I could," I yelled, tears running down my eyes.

He tried to explain himself. "You're not the one who gets to deal with people seeing us together and always asking 'Oh, she's your wife? I thought she was your daughter. Dr. Jones, that's your wife? Was she a model in Africa? She has had three kids? You look like her dad.' Do you know what that does to a man day in and day out?"

"Isn't a man supposed to take pride in the appearance of his wife?" I asked him. "Do you seriously want me to feel sorry for you because people ask you questions that you find embarrassing? Why are you punishing me for what other people say? I am not the one subjecting you to those questions, yet I pay the price everyday. I have to deal with a man who resents me, who pushes me away, who makes me feel unattractive and unworthy. All because of what other people are saying. I have been the one begging for sex, begging for attention, begging for intimacy with my own husband. I have gone to my wits end trying not to fall apart. You watch me suffer everyday emotionally. You tried to make me believe that I was the problem, even as I was doing everything in my power to connect with you. You have been emotionally manipulative and violent. I've been gaslit for so long and the buck stops here! There is nothing wrong with me Ollie. Nothing! I am beautiful, I am kind, I am lovable. Heck, I am damn sexy! I am hot! I will believe that about myself again. My gosh, you got me doubting who I really am."

"How did we get here? I promise things will be different…" He said.

"I don't care anymore. I want a divorce. We can co-parent. I promise I will give you every access to the kids. I will be your friend, there will be decorum on my end, no hurt feelings. I will conduct myself in such a way where it would be very easy to see your kids and be with them, but as far as"

"Since when did you stop loving me?" he interrupted me. In shock and disbelief.

"Since I got fed up with crying myself to sleep, since I gave in, not gave up, but gave in to the idea that things will never change. I am tired of my heart aching. I am tired of foregoing what I know I deserve simply because I love you and I want our children to grow up with their dad under the same roof. This has nothing to do with love. I will always love you Ollie, but love is not enough. There are other factors necessary for love to thrive, like care, concern, appreciation, respect, reciprocity. This is not about love, this is about choice. And for the first time, I'm choosing me. I am tired of hurting. I cannot control what you do, but I have control over whether I allow you to do it to me. I am taking myself out of the equation. Be however you wanna be, not just with me."

Instead of understanding, he became more frustrated. "I never thought I'd see the day you'll say this to me Zhu-Zhu! We have three boys and here you are asking for a divorce. I cannot believe you! I am going to go out for a drink."

He furiously left the room and I heard the car zooming away from our driveway. I breathed a sigh of relief. It felt good to actually verbalize what was already in my mind for so long. It was the scariest thing I had ever done or said. I couldn't believe I actually said it all. I returned to our bedroom and cried, because even though I was glad I let it all outI was so afraid. My world as I knew it was falling apart even though I had done all I could for us not to get to this point. Thoughts of the future without him and his financial support scared me. I cried to God for help.

INFIDELITY

Ollie apologized for everything and told me he didn't think I was getting to the point where I would give up on our marriage.

It is only the ones who are not suffering who continue to think the one who is suffering should value their marital status more than their own mental health and peace of mind. I took my marital vows very seriously. I did not believe divorce should ever be the first line of defense. Personally, I don't believe in inviting God and other people in my relationship unless I really mean it. However, there was peace of mind that comes with knowing that I had tried everything in my power to make my marriage work. I had called attention to him neglecting my needs countless times, both emotional and sexual. I had talked to him about helping with the kids more, prioritizing family time, I had called Brother McBeal from the Kingdom hall to counsel us as a couple. I had even asked his friend Khalil to talk to him. I had explored everything I knew how to do. I didn't want to lose my mind just to stay married.

I didn't understand the logic of men who did not want their wives to fulfill their sexual needs outside of the marriage, but would deliberately deprive them of sex inside the marriage. The narcissism is palpable. The voyeurism they exhibit taking pleasure in watching the pain and distress of their own wives. Mainly their religious wives whom they know have the desire to remain chaste and faithful to God and their vows, who have the strongest instinct to nurture and keep their families together. Even so, I considered giving our marriage another chance because my desire was not to get a divorce, but to make the behaviors that are causing discontent stop.

One afternoon, I was in our bed upstairs relaxing after cooking. My brother Ahsan was eating downstairs in the dining room. The house phone rang and it was Ollie's best friend Khalil on the other line. He sounded very upset.

"You might want to take yourself and the kids away before I come over there with a gun to shoot your husband," he began.

"What? What are you talking about Khalil? Why are you talking like this? What happened?" I asked rapidly.

"He has been doing this shit but the buck stops here! He wants to disrespect me? I will kill him! Get yourself and the kids out of the house before I get there," he continued heatedly.

"What happened? You know he is never here at this time, he is at work. But what has he done to you?"

"Let me tell you about your husband, all those times he told you he was attending medical seminars in other states, he was going with his girlfriend. You know the nurse Mindy in his practice? That's his girlfriend, and he travels with her. And before her, there was Shanda. That's why he did not like you showing up at his clinic. He has been doing this and I have covered for him, now he wants to do it with my fucking wife? My fucking wife? I'm going to kill this mothafucker!" I froze. Was I day dreaming? Was this really Khalil calling me in the middle of the day telling me so many devastating things all at once?

"Khalil? Oh my God, Khalil! I don't know what to say. I know he and Nyesha were late coming back yesterday but I didn't think anything of it because I trusted them both. I see you guys as family members now. I would never think…'

"So I thought, Zhuri, so I thought. Yesterday when Nyesha didn't come home till close to 9 pm. I questioned her about what happened. I threatened her and she told me that your fucking husband asked her to go to a motel with him. They didn't make it there because I kept blowing up her phone, but I don't do disrespect. He can do his dirt everywhere else but not with my Nyesha."

"You know what Khalil, I am going to call him right now. I am devastated. Let me call you back please. I need to call him right now."

I composed myself enough to go downstairs and tell my brother to leave because Ollie just called to say he was coming home with company. After my brother left, I went back upstairs shaking. My heart was beating very fast, the tears were rolling down my cheeks uncontrollably. I got on the phone and called his clinic. After the receptionist transferred the call to him, I broke down and told him everything Khalil had told me. He did not deny anything. He simply just said, "I am coming home right away."

I called Ahzan and asked him to pick up the boys from school and daycare and keep them at their grandparents. I did not want the kids or my brother witnessing us argue, scream and fight. I waited anxiously for Ollie to come home. Some things made sense and others didn't. I was devastated and confused. It made sense to me now that Ollie wasn't going without sex just because he wasn't having it with me. He was getting it from outside even as I begged and pleaded for us to be intimate. He was giving attention to other women as I craved his attention and affection. What didn't make sense was the type of women he was sleeping with. Here I was always working on my physical appearance making sure my figure stayed intact, no big belly, no excess weight, firm and supple skin, and always making sure I smelled nice. And these women, the women he was cheating with, they left more to be desired. It wasn't too long ago when Khalil had embarassed Nyesha by saying, "Look at Zhuri, she has three kids too, but she still looks the same. You, look at your stomach, you just keep eating."

I had intervened and chastised Khalil about not comparing two women against each other. I quickly told him our genetic compositions were different and that he should be more encouraging and maybe even workout with his wife. So, it really wasn't making sense to me that Ollie was cheating on me with these women. I needed to hear from him directly.

Ollie arrived home about forty minutes after I called him. He went straight to our bedroom and started apologizing. However he denied ever being with Nyesha. He said Nyesha didn't have a ride home and he wasn't leaving work immediately, so he told her to wait till he was done seeing patients. Nyesha and Khalil had relocated from Cleveland to Humboldt five years after we moved to Tennessee. Khalil found a job at a warehouse and Nyesha had asked Ollie to help her get a job as a nurse's aid. Ollie had promised to find out about the program and get back to her. They only had one car which Khalil was using to go to work, so after Ollie found a position for Nyesha close to where he worked, he promised to take her for the first week so she could finish her orientation.

Throughout that week Ollie arrived home later than the 7pm he would usually arrive. He got home around 8:30 or 9pm. I didn't think anything of it because I thought he was dropping Nyesha off at home and maybe sat down a bit to keep company with Khalil before coming home. Besides, they were like family, so I thought nothing about an affair between them. I had always chosen to trust my husband even though I had found a pack of condoms in his suitcase after he came back from a trip to Cleveland about eighteen months into our marriage. I had confronted him about it in tears and he told me they were unused. He said there were three in a pack and all three were intact. He said he just did it because his friends were pressuring him. He said it was a guy thing, they talked and acted a certain way when they were together. But it meant nothing, it's just something guys did. I accepted that explanation and thought nothing of it afterwards, especially because the condoms were indeed intact. I moved on without doubting my husband's love for me. Now here we were, with multiple allegations of infidelity. He continued to vehemently deny any involvement with Nyesha. I believed him. Maybe because I couldn't fathom a man in good conscience leaving his sexy, young wife for someone like Nyesha who was a little short and purgy.

But then there were Mindy and Shanda. He didn't deny those affairs. He apologized profusely.

"I don't know what to tell you. It happened. But with Mindy, it was innocent. I swear I didn't pursue her. Remember that time we had that big fight about your parents when I left home and went to a hotel for a few days? Well, she called me about a patient and said that I sounded low and sad. I told her I had just had a fight with you and was staying at a hotel. She asked me where I was, so I told her and she came over. That's how it started. I am sorry, I feel stupid. I have tried to end it many times, but she kept threatening to out me. She has threatened me that if I fire her she would report me to the medical board and labor department for unlawful firing. I didn't know what to do. At this point, I was just putting up with it. I am sorry."

I kept bawling the whole time he was talking. He paused and knew I was waiting to hear about Shanda. He tried to touch me and I screamed at him. "Do not touch me! You have made me go crazy! I have been here wanting you to touch me, make love to me, and have been trying to get your attention and all the while you were having sex with other women who look like... who look like...I am so done with you! And who the hell is Shanda?"

"Please Zhuri, I am sorry. Please do not leave me. Shanda was just an old girlfriend who came to see me just two times on my trips. I knew her before you. If I wanted her, I would've married her. She means nothing to me. It meant nothing Zhu-Zhu! I swear! You and the kids are my whole world. Please Zhuri, please."

I didn't talk to Ollie anymore. I just kept crying. I lost my appetite. Ollie left my side and went downstairs to smoke a cigarette. He came back up and continued to apologize. It was a relief to realize that I wasn't crazy. Nothing comes from nothing. I couldn't put a finger on what was wrong with us exactly, but I knew something was off. I had not questioned his fidelity because I wanted to trust him so badly. I wanted to believe he valued the life we had created together. I still believed in the fairytale of my prince charming leaving all the other women in America and England and going all the way to Sierra Leone to choose me. I refused to believe that feeling had left him. It hadn't left me, so why would it leave him? It had to be something else and I was spiralling because I couldn't quite figure it out. Now, I had such intense rage in my heart for him because he made me almost go crazy thinking something was wrong with me. All the while it was him, he was just watching me suffer, gaslighting me, making me feel it was about me not making him coffee sometimes. How wicked can someone be to watch your children's mother losing her mind for something you were doing to her, but all the while making her think she was the problem?

"If you forgive me, I promise you that you will look back ten years from now and be glad that you did. I will make it up to you Zhu-Zhu. I swear, I will. I will become a better man, a better husband and father for you and the boys. Please Zhuri, please."

I wanted to believe Ollie so badly. I wanted to be held tightly, to be reassured that this will never happen again, instead, Ollie was up and down the stairs and smoking one cigarette after another. He said he didn't know whether to hold me or to leave me alone.

"I know you need your space at this point. I will not bother you further. I will just go downstairs and will keep checking on you. I am sincerely sorry, Zhuri."

Again, I didn't say anything to Ollie. I was still stunned and it was amazing to me that after all these years, Ollie was still clueless about what I needed when I was stressed, depressed and utterly sad. I didn't prefer distance. I craved his touch, his reassurance. I wanted him to hold me tightly, look me in my eyes and tell me everything would be alright, tell me that it wasn't my fault. Yet, he honestly believed I was so mad at him that I couldn't stand him, so he was distancing himself not to get me even more upset.

After Ollie returned to work the next day, he called me several times to check on me. He kept telling me he would make it up to me. He reassured me he was finding a way to get rid of nurse Mindy without him violating any laws. I didn't even know what to say or think. How do you insist your husband get rid of a nurse he worked with who was set on exposing him for violating ethics and revenge against getting fired? And how do you deal with the knowledge of your husband going to work everyday with someone whom he has cheated with?

I stopped thinking about putting all the blame on him and started looking at myself. What did I do wrong? What else could I have done for that not to happen? Was I a capable enough wife? What did I lack that he was looking for in the streets? I couldn't come up with any answer. I had been the best wife I possibly could be. Wasn't I cooking for him everyday? Didn't I take care of the house and our three boys? Wasn't I surprising him with romantic gestures all the time, didn't I shop for all his clothes and shoes, didn't I welcome him with a hug and a smile every time he got home? Wasn't I always quick to resolve issues when they arose in our marriage? Where did I go wrong, what else could I have done to make him not look outside of our marriage?

I decided to book a room for us to go away for the weekend at the Peabody Hotel in Memphis. I needed it to be just the two of us and for him to answer my nagging questions. When I told my best friend Briana who lived in Los Angeles about my plans, she was livid. Briana was about 11 years older than I was.

"Zhuri! What is wrong with you? He should be kissing your butt and doing just that for you. He cheated on you for God's sake, why are you the one booking hotel rooms? He should be spoiling you, your every wish should be his command by now."

"He is trying Brie! I swear he has been trying. He calls very often and keeps apologizing, for the first time ever, he took the boys for their haircut, he even dressed them up himself, he keeps telling me he will be better. I just need to have some answers desperately. I am so confused, Brie, I just need some answers."

"Seems like you're making excuses for him and it seems like you have forgiven him so soon! He is still doing the bare minimum, if you ask me. This just happened a few days ago, Zhu! Let him earn his way back to you. Stop rolling the red carpet for him. Let him earn his family he has so frivolously put in harm's way."

"I just want answers, Brie. I am so confused. I want him to make sense of some of these nagging questions in my head."

Briana wasn't having any of it. "This is exactly why he married you, Zhu, this is why he married a girl a decade younger than him. He wouldn't do this to a woman his age and get away with it so easily. He knew exactly what he was doing. He didn't want a woman who was self-sufficient and would hold him accountable for his bullshit. So, he found someone who hardly knows the world and one who would depend on him entirely for everything and can be groomed."

I hated hearing that Ollie married me for anything else besides him being hopelessly in love with me, then and now. I truly wanted to believe the fairytale I had in my head of him falling in love with me so hard that he forsook everything he had in America, every woman he ever dated and could've married, but instead returned to Freetown to get me. I was the one for him. Wasn't a lot of thought given to whom one has children with? He didn't just frivolously choose anybody. He thought about this long and hard and I was the one he loved. That's why he married me.

I told Ollie about the weekend getaway I had planned. I told him we'd drop the boys off at my parents for the entire weekend and we'd be gone. I even made up a story to tell my parents why we wouldn't be coming back home the same day.

I toldmy mom Ollie's accountant messed up his taxes and he had to pay some hefty penalty. He needed some time away. My mom was all for it. She said,"That's why we are here, as a soft landing for you guys. Bring the kids over, you two go enjoy yourselves and you go take care of your husband,"

"Thanks Mom! You're the best! We'll see you tomorrow."

The next day, Ollie and I dropped the boys off at their grandparents.

"Mom and Daddy Swarray! I want to thank you for raising such a wonderful daughter. Something happened recently between Zhuri and I, and the way Zhuri has treated me during this hard time, this difficult time, has made me see her in a whole different light. I appreciate her so much!" Ollie said to my parents. I was stunned. I didn't expect him to say anything. He has never complimented me to my parents before. I hardly get any compliments from him.

My parents, thinking he was referring to his accountant screwing him over, replied, "You're welcome. That's what marriage is all about. You support each other in good and bad times. You make sure you relax and not worry about the boys. We will take great care of them. Enjoy yourselves."

I was happy to have some alone time with Ollie. I was looking forward to all of my questions getting answered. I naively thought that would bring me some relief and closure. I quickly realized that Ollie was the same man who was neglecting my needs and who had cheated on me. He was only doing the hotel getaway to appease me.He wasn't trying to make a move on me or anything. I was the one who initiated the lovemaking and conversation.He wasn't eager to show me that his neglect of my sexual and emotional needs were a thing of the past. He kept saying he would do anything to save his marriage, but he wasn't doing anything to me to prove it. I also realized Ollie doesn't know my love language. He didn't know what to do to appease me when I was hurt and distraught. He does what he thinks he is supposed to do, which is to apologize profusely. However, I didn't care so much for his apologies. I wanted clear explanations, a plan of action to change the behavior and lots of reassurances. I also needed his presence, not to give me space to overthink and come up with my own scenarios. I asked him if there was something I could've done to prevent him from cheating.

"You didn't do anything wrong, Zhu-Zhu. And I want you to understand that as stupid as I'm about to sound, I did not plan on cheating. It's more like women threw themselves at me and I didn't pass up the opportunity. I wanted to feel like I still got it."

"Have I ever made you feel like you haven't got it? Have I ever refused to have sex with you? Why do you need other women to prove to you that you still got it?" I asked with rasp curiosity.

"Zhu-Zhu, remove yourself from all this. Take yourself out of the equation. I already told you it had nothing to do with you. You have been the same person I married. I am accepting all the blame here. This is solely my fault and I will fix it, I promise you, I will. But you have to believe me when I tell you that I had nothing to do with Nyesha."

"I don't know what to believe, Ollie. I am just really confused. Nothing makes sense anymore. I will forgive you, but this can't happen again. I am willing to try one more time for the sake of the boys."

"Oh, thank you so much, Darling! I promise you won't regret it. You will look back 10 years for now and be glad you did." He said with his eyes wide open with shock and excitement.

I didn't get the closeness and intimacy I wanted but we made love a few times, walked up and down Beale street, and saw local artists singing the blues with cups nearby for cash gifts. We ate at a few restaurants and returned to Humboldt two days later with the renewed hope of turning over a new leaf. I told myself I wouldn't bring up what happened and just leave it in the past. I believed in forgiving and forgetting. Also, I thought if I was in his shoes, I would have wanted him to forgive me and not bring it up again. My JW upbringing always made me do things by the golden rule; "Do unto others as you would want them to do unto you."

And so, when I saw nurse Mindy at the local Walmart in Humboldt a few weeks later, I looked at her and just walked right past her. She saw me and looked quite nervous, thinkingI would approach her. I didn't; I just pitied my husband. I had wracked my brain before and even now, in close proximity, I did not understand what he saw in this woman. Was it because she was white? Was he trying to experiment? He told me he did all that in his college days, so I honestly couldn't understand why my husband had chosen to sleep with a woman who wasn't aesthetically pleasing at all. I have always been of the notion that one never approaches the outsider, whether it is a man or a woman. The outsider owes you nothing. They did not take any vows to uphold. They do not owe you any loyalty or explaination. Of course, they could've chosen not to be in relationships with married people, but they're the single ones. They can do as they please. The spouse on the other hand, can either choose to be faithful or put everythingon the line. If one cannot control the person on the inside, how does one expect to do it with someone on the outside who wants your life?

I walked out of Walmart with a renewed determination to make my marriage work.

FREETOWN

I hadn't been to Freetown in 9 years. I have had three children since I arrived in the U.S., earned an associate degree in business administration, and just enrolled in university to pursue my BA in Psychology. It hadn't made too much sense to go visit Freetown because my immediate family was all abroad. One in Europe, the rest in America. However, I told Ollie that I wanted to take Sankara with me to see my grandparents and other extended family members. I was eager to show Sany where I had grown up, the house I was raised in, the schools I went to and just interact with people I have missed for almost a decade. Ollie had already made two trips to Freetown back to back in two years. The first one he told me he was going solely because he wanted to rest and just relax on the many beaches. He took two weeks off from work and went. It was such a sad time for me. I missed him most of the time and couldn't reach him as often as I wanted because every time I would call his mother's house phone, they would say he already went out. I couldn't wait for the two weeks to be over so that I could see him again.

I remember going to Memphis airport to pick him up after his two weeks in Freetown. I was hoping that my husband would've missed me as much as I had missed him. I was expecting us to have an exciting welcome-back intimate session. It was a given for me. However, after we got home, Ollie changed and showered, gave me a bangle he bought from a street vendor in Freetown, and went to sleep. The next day, I was asking him about his trip when he casually said he bought some land at Juba Hill.

"You made such an investment without telling me first?"

"I'm sorry, Zhu-Zhu. I had to scope it up fast! Everyone was telling me it was such a good deal that if I wasted any time somebody else would get it, so I moved fast!"

"So, you couldn't get on the phone for 5 minutes and ask me, 'hey, Zhu-Zhu, how do you like the Juba hill area,' nothing like that?"

"Look Zhu-Zhu, I'm sorry okay?" He replied, looking indignant. "I did it for us. It was an investment for us. And I know what you're thinking, even though you were not around to sign the papers, they said I could still add your name to it when we are together in Freetown."

"You don't understand, do you Ollie? This has nothing to do with me wanting my name on the document. It has everything to do with you not respecting me enough as your spouse. It has to do with you not thinking my opinion matters or that you need the consent of your spouse to make big purchases." I said worn out by having to explain it to him.

"It will not happen again. I am sorry. I thought you would be happy that we now own a piece of land in Freetown. I am sorry."

I did not understand why anyone would marry a woman 10 years younger and instead of treating her as a marital equal, she'slike a child. Someone you do not confide in or think you owe any explanation.

My trip to Freetown with Sankara came around and we were going to stay with my mother-in-law because her rented house had modern conveniences. We would be visiting my extended family members during the day. I left Shareef and Saami with my parents as Ollie suggested. He had never been alone with the kids before, something that continued to frustrate me but I lived with it. I had never seen him change a diaper or just hang out with them unaided. Besides, he was going to be working so it was better that the boys be with someone who could take proper care of them. Ollie would stop by everyday from work to see how they were doing.

We first got to Ghana and had a three hour layover in Accra before finally arriving in Freetown. It was incredibly hot to the point where you just wanted to take off your clothes. We were approached by several young men who asked us to help with our luggages in return for tips. However, Ollie's cousin Simmy, who had gone to pick us up, told them all to scram. Sankara held on to my arm tightly, the scenery looking very strange to him. He had never experienced this type of aggressiveness in America before. Over there when you need assistance, you ask for it, people don't forcefully throw themselves at you. Simmy quickly let us know that there was no light at home.

"Light nor dae o," he said to me in krio. "But mek we see tay evening tem. If light still nor cam, ar go put on the generator for the pekin." For the sake of Sankara who was not used to blackouts, he would turn on the generator if light wasn't available going towards evening time. He said my mother-in-law was waiting for us and had prepared the guest room for us.

Everything looked very small to me now. Things that once seemed big looked very small. It was a treat to drive past familiar places as he drove us to Wilberforce. Passing by the post office, Law Court, the monumental Cotton tree in the heart of the city, Pademba road, Campbell Street, St. John, Youyi building, Congo cross bridge brought back so many memories of my high school days. These were the streets I walked through with my classmates, Qadir, Olu and Yaegar discussing how our day at school was or about our school assignments. It was where we talked about our dreams, where we laughed with reckless abandon. I saw a glimpse of my old secondary school Convent as we drove from St. John towards the Youyi building.

"Sankara! Look! That was the high school I went to!" I tried to nudge him before we drove past it. Sankara was fast asleep on my shoulders and didn't even move.

"Don't worry Zhuri. Sankara has two weeks to see every nook and kranny of where you grew up," Simmy said chuckling.

I saw the local street traders who come out in the evening to sell fry-fry, rosbeef, kankankan and stylishly peeled oranges displayed on the street side. "Simmy, can you stop so I can have some rosbeef. I haven't had those in forever. My mouth is watering."

"I hope you don't get a stomach ache. Because you've been gone for so long, your system might not be able to take it all in at once. Did you bring some pepto bismol?" Simmy asked with a wry smile.

"Don't be silly. I am still very much a daughter of the soil. This was one of the things I was looking forward to, street foods."

Simmy parked the car and I got so much rosbeef that the seller asked if I was stopping by the next day. "E don tay way ar dae fen dis kain custament. Sister, ar dae ya everyday, 6 o'clock sharp. Na for dae cam ep me buy. Ar go mek am fine for you."

I remember days when I couldn't afford to buy rosbeef. Now, I can have it in whatever quantity I want.

Simmy forewarned me not to take his Aunty and her antics personally when we make it home. "Enti you sabi da Mamie. Duya ar dae beg you, nor falla am, jus ignore am. We all know say e get-na-han, so duya nor pay am no mind."

"Thanks, Simmy. But I don't plan to be around her much. She can have Sankara all she wants, but I'll be going around to see some family and friends."

"Perfect! The less you're around her, the better. She can try to bond with her grandson if she wants to."

Simmy turned the generator on around 8 p.m that night. He saw Sankara and I sweating and shooing mosquitoes away. My mother-in-law served us the sawasawa she cooked. It was very delicious and tasted very fresh and organic. I savored every bite and looked forward to having more of it in the morning. Even though my mother-in-law had left our house abruptly with much bad blood, we both acted like it was all water under the bridge. I knew she didn't like me and I knew I couldn't stand her but we were both mature adults and had separately decided to co-exist until the two weeks were over.

Sankara and I slept under a mosquito net right next to a standing white fan oscillating back and forth. Sany asked me when we'll be going back to America as soon as we woke up the next morning.

"Sany! We just got here. I know you're not used to it here, but you have me every step of the way. We'll go back to America soon!"

"I want to go back to America. I miss Shareef and Saami and Paul and Jacob and Robert..."

"Okay Sany, I'm sure they all miss you too. You're going to love it here so you will have great stories to tell all of them when you get back."

I heard a knock on our door and my mother-in-law announced that Ollie's good friend Levi was here to see us. I wasn't expecting Levi but was happy he had come to see us. I reckoned he wanted to see Sankara the most. I told my mother-in-law we'd be out as soon as we washed ourselves and got ready.

Levi waited for us and when we got to the living room he said, "Well, well, well. Look who's here! Ollie Junior. You look so much like your dad, Sankara. Mrs .Jones! How are you doing, Zhuri? Welcome back home." He picked Sankara up and then hugged me with one hand. "It's so good to see you guys. Zhuri, are you ready? I have somewhere to take you. Ollie wants me to do it today, that's why I'm here so early."

"Levi! You and Ollie again! I have other plans, but if it won't take long, I'll go with you quickly."

Levi drove us about five miles from my mother-in-law's house. I wondered where he was taking us. The road he drove on was filled with potholes, and the speed of the car blew the red dirt from the road onto the car. The neighborhood looked very penurious. There were fullah shops and little petty traders on the road and street barber shops. Even though there weren't many impressive things about the area, there were nice sprinkles of big nice houses in the midst of all the chaos. "We're almost there. Do you see that huge house in front of us? That's where we're going."

"Okay, whose house is it? Who lives there?" I asked him.

"Don't worry, wait until we get there," he replied.

When we got to the house, I found out nobody lived there. It was a huge empty three storey house. It looked very beautiful on the outside, but inside there was still work to be done. The master bedroom was still under construction and so was the boy's quarter in the back. We climbed the stairs from the first floor to the third and then back again.

"Wow! This is really huge and nice. I just don't care for the neighbourhood it's in," I said to Levi.

"Welcome to your house, Zhuri! Welcome. This is your new house, your home away from home. Ollie bought this house and wanted me to bring you here to see how you like it."

My whole demeanor changed the instant he said that. "What? I cannot believe this. What? I just cannot believe this. Ollie bought this without…..That's okay, can you take me and Sankara back home please?"

"Is something wrong?" He asked me, looking confused. "You don't like it? It's a beautiful house, Zhuri. You should be glad your husband bought such a nice house for the family."

"Can you just please take us back home?" I demanded.

Levi drove us back. I didn't say one more word to him. When we got back home, Ollie was on the phone with my mother-in-law.

"Back so soon? Ollie is on the phone now," she told me.

"I will buy a phone card and call him soon. That's okay, I'll talk to him now." I got the phone's hand piece from my mother-in-law and took it to the guest room with me. "Ollie! Levi just took me to a house he said you bought. Tell me that it's not true. Tell me you were only contemplating buying it. Tell me.."

He interjected. "You don't like it? Zhu-Zhu! That house was being built by someone who had ran out of money and could no longer afford to finish it. As you saw, it is very big. I had to scoop it up before someone else did. It will save us from building from scratch."

"Ollie! Didn't we talk about this already? Didn't you promise not to make any more major purchases without my knowledge? And no, Ollie. I do not like the house. I hate where it is. I hate the surroundings. I hate the dirty gutters, I hate the potholes, most of all, I hate that other people know about the house before me. Ollie, has it ever occured to you that I need to have a say about where we live? This is the second time you've chosen where we get to live without even considering my needs, my input. I hate it."

"Oh my goodness! Every time I try to do something good, it just backfires. No matter what I do it just blows up in my face."

"Save me the victim speech, Ollie! Save it!" I said, very hot. "No one has any problems with you buying properties. This is about respect. You flounce your word to inform me about big purchases under the guise that they were hot on the market. It seems to me like you don't want to lose out on properties but watch out, because you will lose your wife. I am so tired of being so blatantly disrespected. Why am I even your wife? Why don't you confer with me? You really want me to jump and shout and be happy with you acting like a single man. I am done with this topic. Let me go about enjoying my two weeks vacation that you have already started ruining. I'm handing the phone back to your mother now." I couldn't believe I was having the same conversation with Ollie again. I couldn't believe his constant disregard for my feelings or my input. However, I didn't want Sankara to see that I was in a bad mood, so I decided I wasn't going to look hurt or sulky. I will have to deal with this another time. Right now, I want my son to have a good time with his mother in her country of birth.

I took Sankara with me down the road to get a taxi at the junction. "Old Railway line!" I shouted at a taxi coming our way. He stopped and picked us up. He quickly informed me that I may have to carry Sankara on my lap if he picked up more passengers heading to the Old Railway line. I was just fine with it. I wanted Sankara to enjoy the experience. Once we got to Old Railway line, I saw Lenny's house right there at the junction. It brought back such fond memories. I started recognizing some familiar faces and when I called out their names they were all pleasantly surprised. "You still remember my name after all these years?"

Everyone in the compound I grew up in was ecstatic to see us. They were so thrilled to see Sankara. They admired his American accent, but asked me if he understood krio and if he ate Sierra Leonean foods.

"He understands everything you say in krio. He just will not speak it back to you. But if you ask him to go do anything in krio, he'll do exactly as you ask. And yes, he eats all the foods. His favorites are okra soup and cassava leaves."

They all chuckled and felt comfortable talking to Sankara in krio. "Sankara, kushe o, how de body?" One of them asked him how he was doing.

"I'm good, thank you," Sankara responded.

They all laughed in unisom. "You're right! E dae understand krio."

We spent the rest of the days visiting my grandmother, who wasn't feeling well but was happy to see her first great-grandson. Sankara wasn't too thrilled that a frail, wrinkled, bedridden old woman was constantly reaching for him every time we went to visit her. Sankara couldn't imagine that this woman used to be young and vibrant at one time. She was a strong woman who raised 8 children on her own after her husband died. She was a professional cook who was booked to cater for prestigious occasions. She was a trailblazer who fought every obstacle in her way to put eight children through school. She was my hero, and it broke my heart to see a disease take away the best part of her.

After many rounds of Lumley beach and family Kingdom outings, we were two days away from returning to Tennessee. We couldn't wait! I started counting down just like Sankara. I had missed my life of independence where I did everything by myself so quickly and easily. I could wash my own clothes and dry them all within 90 minutes. I could blend my pepper, onions and other vegetables without asking someone to go do it for me. I could just walk into my shower and take a bath without someone fetching water for me first. There was constant electricity and I looked forward to being at my house without any interruptions from uninvited guests. The other day, a man who used to date one of the girls I grew up with heard I was in town and went to visit me. Even though he was told I had just left for the day, he waited for about six hours until I returned. I couldn't believe he had done that. I knew he wanted something more than to just see me. So after he told me he had waited for about six hours, I went to my bedroom, got $30 from my purse and gave it to him. The look on his face told me he felt it was worth it to have waited.

TEN YEAR ANNIVERSARY

We had quite a lot to show for our ten years together. We had three healthy, well-adjusted sons, a home of our own, Ollie had his own private medical practice, and was also the head of the nursing home and top physician at the local hospital. The boys went to private schools and I was only two semesters away from graduating with a BA in Psychology. It had been hard going to school with three pregnancies, postpartum depressions, and everything else in between. I was happy to have it over with. I was a top-tier student and was already getting offers for my Masters degree program. I showed Ollie one of those letters and he was all but thrilled. However, I didn't let that rob me of my joy. I became determined to finish so I could start working and be independent. The allowance Ollie was giving me every month couldn't even last for a week. I had to pinch and sometimes ended up at those predatory loan companies like Title Max for a quick buck! I didn't know what we had in the bank as everything was in his name. He opened a separate account for me where he would send my allowance every month. He also deposited money in it for me to pay the household bills, as he only paid the mortgage. The rest of the bills I had to write down every month end and he wrote a check for the exact amount.

One day, Ollie told me we had to talk. He never told me that ever! I am usually the one who initiates conversations, especially ones that have to do with our relationship.

"Zhu-Zhu, I have been thinking about us returning to Freetown to live there permanently." My eyes nearly popped out of my head as I listened to him. "We will always be coming back. I mean, the children were all born here, we will be coming for summer holidays here. But I want to return to relax, to rest. But most of all, I want to help the people back home with a top-tier medical professional and state-of-the art facility. I want to..." he continued.

"You can go Ollie. I am not going. I am not ready to go yet. Most of my friends my age are looking for opportunities to come here and you're asking me to go back? No, I am not going. But you can go, I will be here with the boys. You can come and go as you please," I said matter of factly.

He huffed. "I don't understand why you women find it so hard to return home. You will have a better life there than here, Zhu-Zhu. You will have your own house-girl, a watchman, your own driver, everything you need. You can't have that here."

"I never said I wanted those. I don't need a servant, I can do everything I want by myself, at my own pace. I love driving myself. It's the best part of my commute to my university, getting in my car, hot chocolate in my flask and listening to music or NPR news. It's the highlight of my day. I don't need any of those things, thank you. The boys and I have better opportunities here. I am not going. But you can go. We will be here," I told him resolutely.

He didn't try to convince me further knowing I was set on my words. He just got up and left. We did not speak on that topic again but he would drop hints every so often about someone who had relocated. I was never impressed with those stories. I had never cared about how other people were living their lives. I had mine to care about, three boys that were looking up to me and him. I had to make sure they had the best opportunities in life. Sankara was already winning many awards at his private school. He was on the honor roll and recipient of the St. Joseph's award, given to a student who has shown strength of character and always went above and beyond in helping others. I had always been the only one at these award ceremonies because Ollie was always at work. There were field trips to attend to awaken their curiosity in varying genres of study. I wasn't taking my boys to constant blackouts and uncertainty with water supply. However, I had no problem with Ollie going. I was already raising the boys by myself anyway. He was always quick to remind me that even though he wasn't hands on with the boys, his presence alone was beneficial.

"I may not be doing all these domesticated things with them, but trust me that my presence alone matters. Have you seen the statistics of children whose fathers were absent from the home?" he would ask me. I never indulged him in that conversation because for the life of me, I did not understand why someone would be so content with just giving their bare minimum and convincing themselves that just their presence is impactful. Why would you want to give your own children your bare minimum instead of all you've got? It was a conversation I never got tempted to partake in. It angered me. It seemed hypocritical to me that he wanted to go give other people the best of him, yet deprive his own children from seeing him everyday. Charity begins at home, they say.

About six months after our discussion about relocating the family to Freetown, I got an urgent call just after Sunday service at the Kingdom Hall. His doctor friend Jibola Udo called to tell me that Ollie had been flown to Jackson General hospital with shortness of breath and other symptoms. I was in the car with my mother and the boys, freaking out on the inside, but tried my best to stay calm on the outside because I did not want to alarm them. I told my mom that I would be dropping the boys off with her and go see Ollie who had fallen sick at work. I rushed to the ER at Jackson General and asked about him with tears rolling down my face. I was so nervous. They took me to him and one sight of him caused me to cry even more. He had sticky patches on his arms, chest and legs. The patches had wires connected to an electrocardiogram machine. A nurse was about to inject some drugs into his IV. He looked at my face soaked with tears and the first thing he said was, "This is exactly why I told you I want to return to Freetown. I am stressed out over here. This place will kill me. I am so stressed out."

"Shhhhhh! Don't say that! Concentrate on getting well first, Ollie. We will revisit that conversation, but right now I want you to hurry up and get well. Please Ollie, promise me you will fight to get better. You have to get better."

I stayed with him for four hours. His tests came back fine, but his doctor wanted him to change his diet and also told him he has to lose some weight and stop smoking. He gave me the prescription for some drugs and discharged him. On our drive home, I asked Ollie what he wanted me to cook for him when we got home.

"Do we still have some goat meat in the freezer? Some goat pepper soup would be nice," he said.

I helped him up the stairs to our bedroom and then ran downstairs to start on the goat pepper soup. I used the pressure pot to cook it very fast with all the spices he liked; season all, Mrs. Dash, maggie, habanero peppers, onions and tomatoes. Then I boiled some semi-ripe plantains to put in the pepper soup for him. He could smell the aroma all the way to our bedroom. I got some water on the side for him to drink after eating. After I served him the pepper soup, I made a dash for the pharmacy to pick up his medications.

"How are you feeling now?" I asked him after he finished eating.

"So much better. Thank you Zhu-Zhu, that was delicious. Thank you for all you did today. I didn't mean to scare you. I've just been so stressed out with work, my body couldn't handle it anymore."

I sighed in relief. "I'm so glad you're feeling better. You didn't mean to scare me but that was very scary, Ollie. Seeing you on that bed with those sticky patches and heart monitor, it scared the hell out of me. I cannot imagine anything happening to you, Ollie. I do not want to raise these boys by myself. And for the first time, I agree with you, just your presence matters. I cannot imagine losing you."

"You have to rethink going back to Freetown, Zhu-Zhu. I feel less stressed when I'm over there. I can just chill and have other people do things for me. Please say you'll consider it, Zhu-Zhu."

"Okay, I will consider it. I am not making any promises, just that I will consider it."

That night as I laid next to him, I started thinking about Ollie's mortality. What if he's telling the truth? How would I feel if he dropped dead from being stressed and overworked in America as he said. Will I ever forgive myself? If we were going to be coming back for three months of summer vacation, what was the big deal in returning? All these questions flooded my mind. I also considered things from the children's point of view, especially Sankara who was 10 years old and had made many friends. He did not enjoy his last visit to Freetown because he was so homesick. What if they never like it there? What about the many opportunities they would miss out on? What if they are not happy? As legitimate as the concerns about my children were, my decision came down to the fear of Ollie dying of stress and the guilt of not listening to him when he asked for relief. Wasn't he the one who brought me to America and introduced me to another lifestyle? Was I going to choose America over his health now? And what aboutSankara who I know would hate the thought of going to visit Freetown again, let alone live there permanently? However, my fear prevailed. I was more afraid of Ollie dying than anything else. I made up my mind to tell him we would go with him on certain conditions. Not in all of my contemplations did I think about myself once. I knew I didn't want to return, I wasn't mentally ready. I knew I wouldn't be happy over there because my whole life was now in America. My parents, my new kingdom hall family, my close friends were all over here with me. I wasn't ready to start over. Those were good enough reasons for me not to go, but I took myself out of any consideration. I put the interest of my husband before mine.

I picked Sankara up from school the next day. He was always so happy to be there. He loved his friends and his teachers. I knew I was going to break his heart when I told him about our plans. I thought of a way to cushion the pain.

"Sany, your dad and I want to go back to Sierra Leone...."

"Noooooooooooo!" he interrupted, tears starting to come from his eyes. "I don't want to go there. I want to stay in Tennessee with my friends. I love it here. I don't want to go. Please Mommy, please. Let us stay here. I love it here."

"Sany, listen. I know you love it here," I said to him, pulling him close to my chest and soothing his head. "I know you love it here, Sany, I love it here too. But we'll be coming in the summer. You can see all your friends in the summer and we'll visit more than one place. We'll go to Atlanta, Disney world, Los Angeles, and London. It will be fun. You're going to like it."

"But I wouldn't be here everyday. I want to be here everyday, mom. I want to wake up here everyday. Please don't make me go. You can leave me with grandma and Uncle Ahzan. They will take me to school, you and daddy can go. I don't want to go mommy."

"Sany, look at me, look at me." I pulled his little face wet with tears in my hands and looked him straight in the eyes. "Do you trust me? You trust mommy, right? I promise you if we go and you, Shareef and Saami are not happy and thriving, we will bring you right back to Tennessee. I promise you. Just give it a chance, Sany. If we go and you're not happy and properly adjusting, we will all come back here. You know daddy and I love you and your brothers so much and your happiness is the most important thing to us. I promise."

Sankara let out a long sigh. I could tell he felt powerless. He didn't seem relieved at all, only burdened by the news. He went to his room and didn't come out. I wasn't surprised by Sankara's reaction. I knew he wouldn't want to live in Sierra Leone permanently. However, he would have had the same reaction if we had told him we were moving to Atlanta or Texas or even Memphis. Sankara gets firmly attached and doesn't easily let go. He loved his school. He always wanted to be there. Even when he was not at school, he had playdates and sleepovers with his friends. He was happy with his life as it was, anything outside of that would take him out of his comfort zone.

I was sure that Ollie would put the needs of the children ahead of his own too. At least I assumed he would do anything to make his children happy.

"Ollie, I will go with you to Freetown under some conditions," I started after he ate dinner that evening.

"What? You have decided to come with me? Oh thank you, sweetheart. That's the best news today. I really did not want to go to Freetown like a single man without my family. You will-"

"Ollie, I am not finished," I interrupted. "I said with conditions. After I told Sankara about our plans to relocate to Freetown today, our poor baby was devastated. He started crying immediately. It broke my heart, Ollie, it really did. However, I have reassured him that once we are there, if they don't adjust well, are not happy or thriving, we will all come back. At the end of the day, it's not about us, it's about them."

"But Zhu-Zhu, you cannot let a 10 year old make the decision about where we stay. He is a child, he goes wherever his parents go. He doesn't get to dictate to us."

"I understand all of that Ollie, but ultimately it is about their welfare and happiness. I have seen kids who have problems acclimatizing, whose mental health suffer, children who regress or just develop behavioral problems. And then there are other kids who will smoothly adjust like nothing even happened. I just want you to be cognizant of the fact that we don't yet know how they will react. I want you to make their mental and emotional health a priority. I want to know that if things don't go as we planned and they cannot adjust well that we will come back with them. Also, I want to shop for everything they already have and love over here, so that when they get there they won't miss anything. We'll send all their toys, a basketball court for them to play in the yard, a trampoline, soccer balls, their *Barney* and *Teletubby* dvds, the snacks they enjoy, everything. I don't want them to get homesick."

"Okay, okay, if you think that's what it would take, fine. I will give you money to shop for the clinic as well. I love the art pieces you bought for the house, the color schemes and textures. I want you to shop for everything," Ollie said.

I actually couldn't believe I was talking to Ollie about going to live in Freetown. I tried to tell myself that we would be just fine even though I wasn't really sure. I hadn't lived in Freetown for a decade. I definitely wasn't sure about anything, but I was sure he would be able to take care of us.

My dad was less than enthusiastic when I told him about our plans to return to Freetown. "He is just trying to take you away from the people who love and care about you, that's all," my Dad said.

"How can you say that, Dad? I am his wife. We are his family. I know you will miss us, but that's no way to speak about him."

"Well, I've said what I said. He is trying to take you away from us, so he can do with you as he pleases and you're just too blind to see that."

I got so upset with my Dad that I walked out of their living room and stormed to my car. I remember my dad being very authoritative when we were growing up. He set the rules with very little regard for what my mom or any of us thought. How can he not understand it when another man says what he wants to happen with his own family? It was alright for him to unanimously dictate all that happened in his own household, but somehow has a problem with another man doing the same in his? The next day, I told my sociology professor, Mrs Nambuya about Ollie's plan for the family to relocate. She didn't wait for me to finish before interrupting. "But why, why now? The timing is off. You're how old? Somewhere in your twenties, only a semester or two away from finishing university with honors, why not let you finish first? What's the rush? What's there for you that is so important that you will forfeit your degree? You're one of the top students-"

"Mrs. Nambuya, he has told me I would come in the summer to finish my classes," I interrupted her. "We have it all worked out. He said we would come in the summer, he would work in the ER to make money, the kids would visit friends and relatives and I would complete my classes. It would be like the best of both worlds."

"Little girl, do you hear yourself? 'He said this, he said that,' about YOUR life. What about you, Zhuri, what do you say? What say do you have about YOUR own life? I know the likes of him. If you ask me, I'll say he is scared. He is afraid of what you are about to become, a free thinker, an educated woman who can be independent of him. Once you finish your BA, you can choose to go for your Masters in Psychology. You're becoming a powerful woman, Zhuri. He can see that, he doesn't want that, he wants to take you away from all that. Think, Zhuri, think."

"It's really not like that, Mrs. Nambuya". I said as a matter of factly, "My husband has been dealing with stress, high blood pressure and so much more. Life in Freetown will not be as stressful for him. Also, it will make him feel better that he is giving back to his people, the children will learn our culture as well and-"

"Look here, Zhuri. I am from Uganda. I am African too, old enough to be your mother. Listen to me. I want you to promise me two things. First, promise me you will complete your degree no matter what. Two, if you're wrong about him and you find yourself desperate and helpless, promise me you'll call me and I will get you out of there myself."

"Thank you Mrs. Nambuya, but that won't be necessary. But I do appreciate you caring so much. When I come back in the summer I'll make sure I go see you in your office."

"Don't forget to call me. Here's my number." She wrote on a piece of paper and handed it to me. "If you lose my number for any reason, make sure you call the University and ask for my extension. If I'm not in my office, please leave me a message. Got it? Have a good day, Zhuri." With that she walked away. I didn't understand why my Dad and Mrs. Nambuya's response to me going back to Freetown with Ollie had been met with so much contention and pessimism. Didn't the bible say married couples should stick together and become one flesh, forsaking all others? Why did they think my husband had anything but the best for his family at heart? Why would he want to hurt his own family?

Mrs. Nambuya and I bonded because of our African backgrounds. I was thrilled when she entered my sociology class and introduced herself as our professor. I listened with rapt attention as she briefly talked about her background before delving into the textbook. I introduced myself to her after class and we became fast friends. I wasn't expecting her to be thrilled about me leaving for Freetown, I knew she would miss me. But, I wasn't expecting her to question my husband's motives. Maybe she was just having a bad day.

The next couple of weeks found me very busy buying provisions in bulk at Sam's club. I bought large packs of juices, boxes of assorted snacks, gallons of olive oil, jumbo sizes of seasonings, packs of pancake mixes, big boxes of ramen noodles, boxes of black trash bags, big screen TVs, DVD players, speakers, packs of socks, briefs, toys, and children's books. I also went to Kirkland's and Pier One imports to look for decor for both our house and his clinic. I bought paintings, large clocks, flower pots, and swinging chairs.

A week after my many shopping trips for our relocation, I was suddenly awoken from my sleep with a racing heartbeat, chills, chest pains and a sudden sense of terror. I was genuinely afraid that I was dying or having a heart attack. My neck was sweating and I heaved as I tried to explain to Ollie what had just happened.

"It seems like you were having a panic attack, Zhu-Zhu. Are you okay?"

"No, I am not okay, Ollie. I am scared of this relocation. I feel like we are not completely ready. I don't think I will be happy and neither will the children. Besides, my dad and my professor Mrs. Nambuya, have been saying-"

"Stop right there, Zhu-Zhu! I was going to listen to you until you brought up other people in our family business. Their opinions do not matter, Zhu-Zhu. This is about us. We are making a decision best for our family, not your Dad or Mrs Whatever-her-name-is."

"I don't know, Ollie.."

"Zhuri! We will be just fine. Just trust me, Honey. We will be just fine. You will be living a luxurious life, complete with maids tending to your every need. You will be travelling more than you have ever travelled. You will have a good life. I know change is difficult but trust me, I will be by your side every step of the way."

He pulled me towards him and hugged me tightly as he reached for my lips to give me a peck. I laid down next to him and tried to fall back asleep. However my mind was racing thinking about the worst case scenario, what if the boys and I do not like it over there? I kept thinking about how we were all doing this to make just one person in our family happy, the one person who should in fact sacrifice his own happiness for us. Why was I having bad vibes about returning to my own country? Maybe it was because I wasn't doing it on my own terms or because I wasn't mentally or emotionally prepared to go. We were going mostly because we didn't want the head of our family to die from stress. It was all about him.

LEAVING HUMBOLDT

My Christian family from the Kingdom hall in Humboldt threw a going away get-together for us a week before we were to leave. The African Doctors Association also had a farewell party for us. It was a very somber time, especially for Sankara who hadn't hid the fact that he wasn't pleased about being uprooted from the life he had known for 10 years. Ollie gave a speech at the ADA's party, talking about his desire to go help the people of Sierra Leone, about how the country was suffering from a severe brain drain and how he hoped his decision will influence more African doctors to go home and serve. He said he'd be coming back often to work at the ER and exchange some ideas. He thanked everyone who had been encouraging and helpful throughout the whole process and said he was going to miss the people of Humboldt who had welcomed him and his family as their own. Everyone shouted, "We're going to miss you too, Dr. Jones!" He then called me and the children to join him on stage and introduced us to the crowd. "This is my family. They're going to make the relocation easier because I will have them there with me. My wife, Zhuri, my sons Sankara, Shareef and Saami." The crowd clapped as we walked to the stage. I didn't give a speech. I just waved to the crowd. Sankara looked like he didn't want to be there. I held Shareef on my hip and Ollie held Saami by his chest. After the acknowledgement, we all went back to our seats.

I had told Ollie that I wanted the children to spend at least a week in London touring before we finally returned to Freetown. He agreed. I made accommodation arrangements with his cousin, Hazel, to host us for the week we'd be there. Hazel and I had gotten close because she was a Jehovah's Witness and also because he said Ollie was his favourite cousin. We had become fast friends and would Skype every so often. I told Sankara that we were going to London and he would get the chance to ride the double decker buses, experience the London Eye, and visit London bridge and Buckingham Palace. It brought a short smile to his face as he mouthed, "Okay, Mommy."

One of Ollie's friends came to take us to the airport. We had packed the whole house up, shipped everything in two 18-wheeler trucks and were on our way to a new life in Freetown. My dad was beyond upset about our move and we had less than a pleasant goodbye from him. He didn't hesitate to tell me how weak-minded I was for listening to Ollie and following him back to Freetown. I simply ignored his comment as I hugged my mom and brother goodbye.

As soon as we arrived in London, I gave Ollie Hazel's number. He called her and I could hear Hazel was very excited in the background. She told him which train to take and which bus would eventually drop us close to her house. I was happy to finally meet Hazel. We had only just talked on the phone before this. After what seemed like an hour on the train, we descended and waited on a bus. Then two buses later, we were close to Hazel's house. Ollie was on the phone with her as she continued to give him directions. I saw a dark-skinned, 30-something year old woman with a phone in her ear talking and looking around.

"Ollie, is that Hazel?" I pointed to the woman.

"Yes! Hazel, we're here. Turn to your left."

She ran towards us and gave me a tight hug. "Welcome, welcome, welcome! I am so happy to have you guys. Ollie! Look at you! The last time I saw you, you were by yourself, a habitual bachelor. Now look! A family of five! You have done well for yourself."

"Incredible, isn't it? Boys, this is your Aunty Hazel. And of course, formally, this is Zhuri."

"Hello Zhuri! Look at you! You've had three boys? Well, I cannot tell," she said with the sweetest smile. "I have been hearing these boys in the background of every phone call, always running around or asking mommy for food and about changing the TV channels. Let me guess, you are Sankara," she said to Sany as she pinched his cheeks. "And now, these two, they look like twins. You are Saami and you are Shareef."

"No, I'm Shareef and the baby is Saami," Shareef said.

"Baby? Shareef, he's not exactly a baby you know. Saami is four years old now. Thank you for letting us stay at your place, Hazel. I felt bad after I asked because I remember you're not used to so many people at once at your house," I said.

"Don't be silly, Zhuri. You guys are family. It is always nice to see family. You're the reason why I am seeing my cousin Ollie again in so many years. I am so thrilled to catch up on everything. I have some food prepared. I don't know what the children like, but I bought some snacks just in case they do not like what I cooked."

I could see the children's eyes light up at the sound of the word snack. Hazel told us about the sleeping arrangement. She had me and Ollie in one room and got another room with make-shift beds for the boys. We were all jet-lagged and hungry. After our baths we got to Hazel's dining room for dinner. The food she prepared wasn't exactly Sierra Leonean, nor was it English. She cooked some chickpeas and lamb with some spicy condiments to go with them. I had never had chickpeas before and did not usually eat lamb, but Ollie who was the most adventurous eater was quickly finishing everything on his plate. I struggled to eat my food, as I preferred rice. I ate all the lamb and left the chickpeas in plain sight. The children said they wanted KFC, so Hazel gave them some of the snacks in the meantime.

Hazel and I kept company for a couple of hours before I left her to put the boys in bed. By the time I made it to our room, Ollie was already fast asleep. Once I woke up in the morning, Ollie had already left the house. He said he was going to see his longtime friend, Marc. Here I was again with the responsibility of taking care of the boys solely by myself. It had not occurred to him that I was also as jetlagged as he was and that I had friends in London I could be visiting too. He just thought that the children were my responsibility when it came to nurturing and raising them. Hazel noticed his absence as well and asked, "Is he always like this?"

"Like what?" I tried to clarify. I was tempted to ask, *where do I start?*

"You know, leaving you with everything. Yesterday, he didn't help with the dishes after dinner and today, he has been nowhere around to help with the boys. Do you do it all? The housework, I mean."

"Yes, Hazel. I do. I got tired of asking and it's easier this way. I used to think that because he works outside of the house and is the sole breadwinner, I'll take care of everything in the house, but he doesn't even seem to think he should help with the boys. It's so frustrating, not to mentiondisappointing. He still has this mentality that it is a woman's work."

"But you are letting him get away with it, Zhuri. He gets away with it. You have to put your foot down." Hazel told me matter of factly.

"Too late now Hazel. We're on our way to Freetown where he says we will have our own personal house servants. He has never been one to help with the kids, but somehow I've managed. Sometimes he would tell me he wants to take the boys to the movies, what he means by that is I wash them, change their clothes, comb their hair, and all he does is put them in the car and take them to the movies. When they return, he takes them out again. I have to change their clothes and get them ready for bed."

"That is crazy, Zhuri! This is not the 16th century. He knows better than that."

"Sometimes he invites me to come with them to the movies and I refuse. I will tell him, 'that's okay, you guys have a boys day out. I'll be here resting.' Then he would complain that I don't want to spend time as a family. But, spending time as a family would entail me taking the boys to get popcorn and snacks, or taking them to the restroom while he relaxes. So, I turn him down every time."

"So, where is he now?"

"He said he is with his friend Marc. Don't worry yourself, Hazel. I'm used to this. The boys and I will be just fine." I retorted.

Hazelshook her head in disgust. I could sense she wanted to say much more, but shecensored herself and tempered her anger. I wonder if she thought I was an enabler. I knew I hadn't enabled Ollie's behavior but I would understand if she felt that way. She took the boys and myself sightseeing. We went to Madame Toussaud's Wax museum, Big Ben, Buckingham Palace, St. Paul's Cathedral, and Hyde Park. The boys enjoyed going to the upper level on the double decker buses. Sankara seemed to have forgotten that he didn't want to go to Freetown, he was having so much fun in London.

Ollie did not come to Hazel's house until one day before our return to Freetown. I had cried myself to sleep every night in Hazel's house as

I laid in her guestroom night after night without Ollie. He told me his friend Marc was taking him around to see different friends and going to clubs at night.

"I know you don't like going to clubs, and it's always too late to go back to Hazel's place. She lives almost an hour away from Marc's house, but I know you guys are comfortable." He told me on the phone the third night away. I decided not to argue. I already knew the drill. It immediately occured to me that things were not going to get better, it was about to get worse. It was Ollie's world now and we'd either dance to his beat or be miserable. He didn't care.

Ollie and I were not intimate the whole week we were in London. When he finally came the day before we travelled to Freetown, we were all busy packing our suitcases. We had to go to bed early to wake up on time to beat the traffic to the airport. It was the happiest I've seen Ollie in a while. His smile was different; it was wider, lasted longer and there was a twinkle in his eyes. He was happy that his plan had worked. I couldn't help but feel happy for him, even though I was still very nervous, I was pleased that I had made a decision that was going to make him happier and healthier. Wasn't the reason he said he wanted to return was because he felt happier and less stressed there?

When we got to the airport, the airline didn't want to seat the kids because they didn't have Sierra Leonean visas on their American passports. I was travelling with my Sierra Leonean passport and green card, and Ollie Ollie had both his British and Sierra Leonean passports. I had a bag with a number lock where I had kept all our passports. Ollie asked me for the code and I told him it was the four digits of his birth year. Ollie asked the desk agent for a supervisor or manager to speak to. When the manager came he told the agent to go ahead and check the boys in because he had called Lungi airport and they had told him that we could purchase visas on arrival. We breathed a collective sigh of relief as I took everyones passport and put them back in the number lock bag after immigration stamped them and cleared us to leave. Ollie sat with Sankara on the plane, and I sat with Shareef and Saami on both sides of me. In six hours we would be in Freetown.

BLINDSIDED

Shareef and Saami tried to stay up coloring their puzzle books the flight attendant gave to them, but after their first meal on the plane they had the itis and quickly fell asleep. I was swished in the middle and could hardly move or even get up to go to the bathroom. I tried to fall asleep, and may have dozed off a couple of times, but the seat was so uncomfortable and I had a sprained neck. I decided to just read to pass the time. As I was getting engrossed in the book, the pilot got on the speaker telling the flight attendants to prepare for landing in 30 minutes. He urged all to put away their tray tables and put on their seat belts. He told us it was going to be a little over 100 degrees in Freetown and reminded us to complete our landing forms. "Not long now," I thought to myself. I was nervous about what lay ahead. I was going to make the most of it, especially for the sake of the boys.

Freetown was hot as usual. The boys had just woken up and were still rubbing their eyes. They looked around and saw people hustling around, drivers honking their horns loudly and yelling at another, and little children all over the place, some selling fruits, others just idling by. Ollie's cousin Simmy had come to pick us up. They were standing in a distance laughing while Ollie smoked a cigarette. Ollie looked very relieved to be back. He came over to us and asked how everyone was doing.

"I'm really exhausted to be completely honest. I cannot wait for the ferry to arrive so we can be on our way to Freetown," I replied.

"Things don't work as fast here, Zhu-Zhu. It's one of the many adjustments you will have to make. Sometimes, they will say the ferry will be around in an hour, but you may not see it in an hour, most likely two hours or so," Ollie said.

Ollie's mini-lecture did nothing to help my lassitude. I was feeling quite lethargic and wanted to go lay down. I refused to say anything else.

Simmy spoke up. "The boys can sit in the car and sleep, we can just straighten our legs while we wait for the ferry."

"Zhu-Zhu, I have something to tell you, but I'm afraid to say it. What I mean is, I don't know how to tell you," Ollie began as all three of us, including Simmy, were standing outside the car.

"What is it? You've never not been able to tell me anything. What is it?" I probed Ollie.

"I don't know how to tell you. Simmy, you tell her."

"Uhmmm, it's just that mom, Aunty Doris, Doc's Mom, left the house Doc is renting for her a little over a month ago and has taken up residency at your house. She said the house she has lived in all this while has evil spirits in it and she will not return there. Doc has been trying to call her ever since to convince her to move back, but she has refused to pick up any of his calls. So, Doc asked me to look for another place to rent for her. It has not been easy trying to find a place to her liking, so she is at your place at the moment. But, we are still looking for somewhere to move her to," Simmy explained.

I sighed heavily in disappointment, palm on my face. "Well, Ollie had over a month to tell me this but did not. I could've just stayed behind to complete my classes in uni while you guys looked for a place for her. But I'm here now, there's nothing I can do about it now."

"I'm sorry, Zhu-Zhu. I was scared to tell you. I figured if I told you then you would not have come with me. You would say something like what you just said. I just wanted my family to be with me, my whole family. Levi is helping me look for a place for her to move to, so it will be sooner rather than later, I promise."

"Like I just said, there is nothing I can do about it now. I'm already here." I opened the car door and took a seat. I was annoyed that Ollie hadn't fixed the issue before he brought us to Freetown. He knew how paranoid his mother could be. He knew about her false accusations and her penchant for meddlesome gossip and baseless insinuations. I do not understand how he thought this living arrangement would work, even for a short while.

By the time we crossed over to Freetown, it was evening time and the city was dark. However, I could make out some landmarks as we drove to the house on the west side. I knew we were close when we started tumbling from one pot hole to the next. When we arrived, there was a security guard outside the gate who opened the door for us. He enthusiastically greeted us. "Good evening Sir, good evening Ma. Una welcome, sir. Me name na Sorie. Welcome Ma."

"Good evening," I replied to Sorie the gateman. He offered to help us with our suitcases. The boys were still sleepy, and we were both jetlagged. I followed Sorie closely as he took our luggages up the stairs. Once we got up, I asked him to open the door to the master bedroom and leave the suitcases there. The master bedroom wasn't completely finished. There was a bag of cement by the corner, and in the middle of the room was a queen size bed, unmade. I called out to Ollie to tell me where we would be sleeping and about the boys' rooms.

"The only room that's completely ready is that one," Sorie pointed to the room right of the master bedroom. "That is the room Aunty Doris already occupies." He volunteered the information.

Ollie came upstairs and told me he was trying to figure things out himself.

"Trying to figure things out yourself? Ollie! We have three boys here tired, hungry, and dirty, and we don't have any sleeping arrangement? And the master bedroom is unfinished? Was this your grand plan? Why did you bring us now? You are so selfish! Nothing is ready. We could have stayed in America and you could've been here making sure everything was completed and sorted out before we came to join you. Now we do not even know where we are sleeping. Great!"

"Hey! Go easy on me, please! Like I said, I'm trying to figure things out. I will have Simmy bring you some beddings to put on this bed here and you can have the boys ready for bed."

I continued to yell at him, completely irate. "I cannot believe this! I really cannot believe this! Oh my God! Why did I even listen to you and come? I should've never come, let alone bring the boys into this chaos."

"Hey! Watch your mouth Zhu-Zhu. This is just a small inconvenience that will be sorted out before you know it. People over here tend to do the work when you're available to monitor them, not when they're left to their own devices. I will get everyone working tomorrow and by the week's end everything should be perfect!" He said resolutely.

"You're just very selfish, too selfish. You had all the time to make this right, but you chose to blindside me. It's not going to work. I hate it here already!"

"I cannot believe you!" He said gastly. "You're so ungrateful, Zhu-Zhu! You literally have a 3 storey house the size of a mansion and you're pulling a fucking fit about minor inconveniences. How many women would love to be in your position? How many women would want their husbands to buy them a mansion, give them maids and money and everything they want?"

"Don't talk to me like that. Just because you're in Freetown now, you think you can talk to me and use foul language. The boys are around, so don't talk to me like that. Also, you can go find those women who would love to have this mansion and several servants because I do not want this life."

Ollie stormed off to go smoke a cigarette. I was very well familiar with that move by now. I stood in the house beside myself, wondering how I could have been so wrong. I have never felt more stupid and naive in my whole life. I stood there in stupor. I didn't understand how I couldve been so dumb and gullible. Why did I believe everything he told me? How do I even begin to get myself and the children out of all this orchestrated scheme?

My mother-in-law must've overheard us arguing outside, but didn't open the bedroom to come meet her grandchildren. I thought this was very odd behavior. My parents would run a mile to meet their grandchildren, especially the last two they hadn't met. However, I knew she was very peculiar and keenly calculating. All of this had been orchestrated by her devious mind. She knew her presence would cause enough trouble to drive a wedge between her son and I, and maybe even guilt him into choosing her over his own wife and children.

I got the bedsheets from Simmy and made the bed in the master bedroom. That night, the very first night of our arrival in Freetown, all five of us shared the queen size bed in the master bedroom. I could hardly sleep because it was so hot and there was no electricity to power the electric fan in the room. Also, I was in regret mode. I was thinking about all the ways I could've just stuck to my initial instinct and just refused to return to Freetown with Ollie no matter what.

The next morning, I took the boys to the bathroom to wash them. There was a huge drum with water in it and an empty bucket nearby. I got some water from the drum to fill the bucket and washed Shareef and Saami. I told Sankara what to do and he just heaved a long sigh and closed the bathroom door behind him. I could tell he was sad and disappointed, and I felt very guilty that I had allowed this to happen. I got dressed and told them I would be making them breakfast downstairs in the kitchen. When I got to the kitchen, Simmy told me that most of the provisions I had shipped were not in the pantry or cabinets in the kitchen, but locked away in the room my mother-in-law was occupying. He said she had told him they would be safe there from the rest of the construction and cleaning staff who came around every day. I told him that I needed the olive oil I shipped to fry the fresh eggs he had just bought from the neighbor next door. I also needed the pancake mix to make the boys some pancakes. I wantedthe boys to have some semblance of familiarity about what they ate. Everything didn't have to change for them in one instant, that would be traumatic. Simmy advised me to wait until my mother-in-law woke up to ask her for the items I needed.

"Oh no Simmy, that is not happening. It is already past 10 a.m. She knows her grandkids are here, two of them she has never met. She hasn't come out to meet us and ask how our trip was, and now we have to wait till she decides to leave her room before my kids can have breakfast? Oh no, I'm going to knock on her door and ask for my stuff," I defiantly told Simmy.

"Okay but Zhu, know that I understand that woman more than you do. She is doing this for a reason. You have to know how to deal with her to get what you want."

I didn't listen to Simmy, I walked up the stairs to the room she was in and knocked. She asked who it was, I announced myself, and told her I needed to get the provisions to cook breakfast for the boys.

"Welcome Zhuri, sorry I haven't made it out yet. What do you need and how much of it do you need exactly?" she inquired.

"I need everything I bought on the outside in the kitchen and accessible to me and the kids. I just need everything," I told her waiting outside her door.

"I can pour some of the oil for you and give you some soft drinks from the refrigerator and-"

"I do not want anything poured out. I wanted those provisions I spent weeks buying, everything the boys and I are going to be needing. I do not want any of it rationed out to me like they're not mine."

"Can you please get Simmy here, please?"

I yelled for Simmy to come. He told me to go back to the boys downstairs while he sorted things out with his aunty. When I saw Simmy in the kitchen again, it was with a cup of olive oil and four soft drinks.

"What is going on?" I immediately asked Simmy.

"Zhu-Zhu, I will call Doc and explain things to him. I told you this is how my aunt is. She only listens when Doc speaks, so I'll let him know. Go ahead and cook breakfast for the boys. You will have your provisions, just let them have something to eat first."

I made the boys some pancakes and eggs and gave them soft drinks. I was really mad that my mother-in-law really had the effrontery to invade my home, take the best room, and now thought she would have control over the things I sweated to get for my household. She had another thing coming because I was determined not to let her get away with all this. Her plans were not going to work if I had anything to do with it.

I immediately thought about our passports. I knew I wasn't going to last in Freetown. I knew I wouldn't tolerate my mother-in-law's evil ways. But most importantly, I knew I owed it to my boys to get them out of the mess we had brought them into. I went upstairs to the master bedroom to look for the bag with the number lock where I had kept our passports. I did the number combination and clicked it open. To my horror, there were no passports inside. I turned it over and emptied all the contents on the bed. There were no passports in it. I wanted to panic but decided to wait and ask Ollie if he had them by any chance. I had not spoken to Ollie after our initial verbal altercation, and he hadn't been in the house the whole day afterwards. When he came back in the evening I told him that I haven't seen the passports and wanted him to question the staff that came in whether one of them may have taken them.

"I took them! I have them. After that nonsense you pulled about wanting to go back, I took them away. They're with me now, so do not worry about them. The boys will never go back to America until they're adults and old enough to make that decision to go," he said to me with authority.

"What? You lied to me! You lied to me! You told me that if the children and I were not happy, we could return to America. You told me that we would be visiting every summer and that I will go back to finish my last two semesters in the summer."

"That's when I thought you would be reasonable. As it is, you're out of your mind. I have moved out of the house for the moment. I will be staying at the house my mom moved out of since the sleeping arrangement is still not ideal. I have the passports there with me, so please do not waste your time turning this house upside down because they're not here." Ollie said with so much hate and disgust in his voice.

In that instant, I thought I was in an alternate reality. I didn't want to believe what I was hearing. I felt the rug had been pulled under me. I was in a nightmare and wanted to just wake up. There was so much hate in Ollie's voice when he spoke. I knew it was hopeless to try to convince him to act reasonably. Somehow we had arrived in Freetown and he had turned into a complete monster. I had only seen him this way once in Tennessee, the very first time he had hit me. I was mad at him for leaving me and Sankara at home when he went out and did not return until about 6 a.m in the morning. Sany must've been around eighteen months old. I had struggled with him the whole day, then after he came in the evening he ate dinner, slept for a few hours, and told me he wanted to go to the club. I never minded him going to the club. I had only gone with him twice and knew I didn't like it, but I was never one to stop someone from enjoying something because I do not enjoy it myself. I only asked that he returned home at a respectable time. I had been up until 3 a.m before Sany fell asleep, hoping he would come at any time during that time. I couldn't sleep the whole time as I laid in bed tossing and turning. At about 6 a.m in the morning, I heard the garage door opening.

I left my room and went downstairs to confront him.

"Why are you only coming in now? It's 6 a.m in the morning and you're supposed to be a married man with a new baby, where the hell have you been," I yelled at him.

"Don't yell at me! You know I was in the club. I lost track of time-"

"You lost track of time? You are a husband and father with a new baby for God's sake. How the hell do you lose track of time? You don't think I need help? You think you're the only one in this house who gets to enjoy free time?"

"Get out of my face, get out of my face!" The next thing I felt was a back hand slap on my face. I held on to my face and looked at him in disbelief. "You slapped me, you slapped me?" I ran and grabbed a bulky book from the library in the living room and hurled it at him. He dodged it. I saw his shoes he had just taken off, grabbed it, and hurled it towards his direction. It hit him on his back and he came running towards me. I ran up the stairs and could hear him running after me. He yanked my hair and said, "I will really mess your face up if I wanted to. Where is this behavior coming from? This is not you, Zhuri."

"It's coming from you thinking you can treat me any kind of way and I should just take it. It comes from you thinking I should just stay calm and get on with the business of being a good housewife no matter what you do. It comes from me knowing I deserve to have a life too. I simply just got angry this time and you hit me? You hit me? An educated man from Cambridge, a whole medical doctor running after me and hitting me because I dared to ask questions and be upset for once. I am calling the cops."

"I am sorry Zhu-Zhu. I don't know what came over me. You know I've never done this before. I just felt attacked by you. You're right, you have never fought back before, you have never been like this. I just wanted to nip it in the bud. I will never put my hands on you ever again. I am sorry, please do not call the cops. If you do, they will seize my medical license and we will not get our green cards. Think about that. One call from you and we will lose it all."

I decided not to call the cops that day, but wondered why the burden of him retaining or losing his license lay with me. Why should I adjust my response to his violence so we are not denied our greencards? Shouldn't he modify his behavior and be accountable for his behavior? Now, I realize I should have nipped that behavior in the bud by calling the cops and letting him suffer the consequences. Most importantly, I should've never agreed to come with him. Now, I have to deal with his abuse on a magnified scale. How did I wind up here? My mind was racing.

DON'T KILL MY MOM

When we woke up the next morning, my mother-in-law had released some more of our provisions to Simmy. Even though I was tempted to go to her bedroom and just get the rest of them, I decided that had become secondary. I knew my life was going to be hell in Freetown and my priority became focused on getting our passports back by any means necessary. As I was dressing the boys to get them ready for breakfast, I heard a knock on my door.

"Who is it?" I inquired.

"It's me, Olivia," the person answered on the outside.

"We'll be out in a sec, hold on." I finished dressing the boys, then went and opened the door. I saw a distant cousin of Ollie waiting for me. She immediately approached me and said, "My Aunty Doris called to let me know that you have been disrespecting her ever since you got here. I'm here to warn you, if she ever calls me again about you disrespecting her, I will come up here and beat you into a pulp." She said in disgust, rolling her eyes and sucking her teeth afterwards.

My boys could sense the aggression in her gait and voice and kept asking me what was going on.

"A sensible person would've come and asked questions to gain understanding. So, she has called you to have you beat me up, huh? I will call Simmy immediately and let him know. Boys, c'mon, let's go downstairs and have breakfast," I said as I guided the boys towards the kitchen downstairs. I asked one of the servants to get Simmy from the boys quarter in the back. He came immediately, "Good morning, Zhuri. Is everything ok?" He asked.

"Your cousin Olivia just knocked on my door to let me know that she will come and beat me into a pulp the next time my mother-in-law calls her to complain about me. I am just letting you know so.."

"She called her too?" Simmy interrupted me. "She told me to do the same but I quickly told her you are my brother's wife and I will do no such thing. That would be disrespectful to Doc who is like a big brother to us and because you never did anything to me. Why would I just beat you?"

"The fact that she thinks you guys can beat me into submission and subservience is astounding to me. This is coming from an educated woman who has resorted to thuggery because she doesn't see herself getting away with all the shenanigans she has under her sleeves. Well, I will let you guys know that-"

"Zhuri! Zhuri!" Simmy interrupted me again. "Listen to me, Zhuri. You're the one who called me, right? Now listen to me. Nobody is going to beat you up as long as I am in this house. Also, I will be seeing Doc in a few hours. I will let him know that Olivia has been here to threaten you. She will have to answer to Doc. As for Aunty Doris, please continue to ignore her. Please, please, I'm begging you for the times I wouldn't be around and she pulls something, just ignore her please. Promise me you will ignore her, please."

"You know what, Simmy. It's pretty sad that my husband who is supposed to be here to protect us has absconded. It's also pretty sad that he created this whole mess of a situation and has left you and I behind to fix it. As for your aunty, I have nothing more to say to her. I don't even want to be here. I just want me and my children's passports so I can leave him and his mother to be together and live happily ever after. Isn't that what his mom wants?" I paused for a moment and looked him in his eyes. "Please I beg you, when you see Ollie, please beg him to give back our passports. That is all I need from him, nothing else," I implored Simmy.

"I will give him your message Zhuri. Don't worry about it. I hate that this is happening. It's not good for the boys to see all this. They should be carefree and try to make new friends."

"I will be taking them out when I leave and we will come late in the evening just to sleep. I do not feel safe here," I told Simmy.

That afternoon I took the boys to my old friend Aziza's cousin Sadia's house which was not too far away. I explained to Sadia everything that was going on. She was very saddened by it all, but told me not to worry.

"I will not sit quietly and let him and his mother treat you like some girl they just picked up from the streets. Your father was a very nice man and helped me through some difficult times. I will not stand by and let someone take advantage of you in his absence. I will let my husband know when he gets home from work and we will sort this whole thing out," Sadia reassured me.

It was a relief to be in Sadia's house, especially for the boys because Sadia has three boys the same ages as my boys. Her boys spoke English at home, so they communicated effortlessly. I felt solace at her house and in her company. She generously shared her provisions with my boys and would send them out to play. When we were left together, she would share similar stories about some of the friends we have in common who have gone through the same fate as me.

"I don't understand why this is happening to you guys, you know, the good ones. You got married a virgin and Marcella and Eve were such good girls as well. They went to scripture union every week and were just delightful. I really do not understand why these men, your husbands, do not seem to treasure you guys. It really baffles me."

"Sadia, this is what happens when our culture and parents groom us girls to matriculate into good women and good housewives but do not do the same for the boys. You know the proverb, 'my cock will roam free, you who have a hen make sure you tie her for her own safety'. Our boy counterparts were never subjected to any of the stringent rules we were subjected to. Our parents reasoned boys couldn't get pregnant, so there was no risk of them getting spoiled or damaged. They went out as they pleased and came home as they pleased with no questions asked. We grow up to be good women but our choices of husbands remain the unruly, untamed boys who are only men in stature but are yet to mentally and emotionally matriculate to manhood."

"That's an interesting take on it. But don't you worry, Zhuri. You can come with the boys here every day. They will be happy to be around kids their age."

"As long as it doesn't bother your husband. I don't want him coming from work everyday and we are at his house. He needs to rest after a long day. So, I will bring them everyday, but I will only stay till 5:30 p.m. I want to give him time to relax and bond with his family."

"That sounds good. Be strong, Zhuri. Everything will be just fine in due time," Sadia said as she squeezed me tightly.

We returned home from Sadia's house at about 6 p.m that evening. I let the boys change and washed them. As I was dressing them in our room, I heard Ollie's voice downstairs. When he made it to our room he asked the boys how they were doing. They ran to him as I folded their clothes which my cousin Steven had washed. Steven was a year younger than me. I had told him about the threats I was receiving and he decided to come stay at the house to be with me and the boys to make sure nobody bothered us. He told me he would be sleeping on a mat in our master bedroom through the night and leave for work in the afternoons.

"So, Simmy told me what Olivia did today, I have talked to Olivia personally and warned her not to get involved in our marital business. I don't care who calls her."

I totally ignore Ollie. I continued folding the clothes when he yelled, "Zhuri! Do you hear me? I am talking to you.."

"What exactly do you want me to say to you, Ollie? Where do I begin exactly? The part where you brought us to Freetown knowing months in advance that your mother has invaded my home? Or the part where you stole our passports and proclaimed the kids will never go back to America? Or the part where you left me open to the devious devices of your mother and other relatives to do to me as they please while you conveniently lounge and pass the day at her place?"

"Oh, so we're talking about deceit?" He asked with nonchalance. "We are talking about deceit? Well, tell me who Keza is? The one who has been sending you all those romantic emails and what about Alanna. She likes you too, doesn't she? Are you guys lesbians? What about all those Facebook likes? You didn't think I knew, did you? You think I'm stupid? Well, I put spyware on the laptop I gave to you for your birthday two years ago and everything you did or said on there I knew. So, don't you stand there on your high horse." He ran towards me and slapped me on my face. I touched my face, feeling a stinging sensation on my left eye where his slap landed. I started running away from him. He came after me yelling, "You think I don't know? You think I'm stupid? I knew about all your affairs and you think I was going to have you divorce me in America, so you can have my money! You lie! I picked you up from the gutter and I have brought you right back to it," he continued. By this time, I could hear our oldest Sankara running after his dad as he ran after me. I could hear the terror in his voice.

"Dad! Dad! Please don't kill my mom. Daddy please don't kill her. Mom! Please leave this house so my daddy won't kill you."

Simmy came running from the boys quarter and intercepted Ollie. "You will kill her, you will kill her. Don't you see how much bigger than her you are? If you keep putting hands on her in anger you will surely kill her and live to regret it. Zhuri! Leave! Go to your friend Sadia's house. Stay clear until he calms down."

I heard the boys crying in distraught. I also heard Ollie talking to Simmy telling him that I had been unfaithful to him. He was explaining to him about the messages he had found on my email and the many men and women who interacted with me on Facebook. I was dumbfounded. The physical pain from his blows had nothing on my mental state. I kept thinking about how utterly unsuspecting and credulous I had been. My unworldliness was nauseating to me. I was repulsed by myself. How could I have been so over-trusting of him? How did I get in this nightmare and most importantly, when was it going to end? Again, my mind went to the passports. I thought of them as my way out of this nightmare and by any means necessary I have to find a way to get them back.

I took a taxi to Sadia's house. When she answered the door, she screamed, "Who did this to you? Did that mother-in-law of yours really send someone to beat you up? Tell me, who did this to you?"

"Ollie started beating me up and I fled" I answered, sounding deflated. "He slapped my face and-"

"No, he didn't! What a brute! An international doctor beating up his wife? So, he knew he couldn't get away with it in America. That's why he brought you here? We will go to the police in the morning. We will-"

171

"No, Sadia. Not until I get my boys first. I don't want him to take the boys away from me too. Wait till I get my boys. He accused me of cheating and he said he has been spying on me for two years." I burst out crying.

I now understood why my emails always looked like someone had read them. Usually an unread email is bold when it comes through until one reads it. However, I always thought it was a technical error. I never would've thought my husband would hack my computer and put spyware to read my correspondence. This man preferred to degenerate into a voyeur instead of solving the problems that were in his marriage that I so boldly and frequently articulated. I had naively told him about Keza, a fellow student I met in uni. Keza and I had become fast friends because I had shown interest in his home Country Rwanda's civil war. He came to the US at 13 years old after the war. We traded harrowing stories about the cruelty and inhumane atrocities both our countries have endured. I told him about rebels in Sierra Leone asking their hostages whether they wanted long sleeves or short sleeves before butchering them. If they chose a long sleeve, it meant their limb would be amputated at the wrist, but if they chose a short sleeve, their limb would be amputated by the elbow. I told him about the rebels invading family homes and asking sons to have sex with their mothers or sisters and if they refused they would be shot to death. Sometimes rebels would lock families inside their houses and then burn the houses down. There were also stories of rebels encountering pregnant women and then argue amongst themselves about the sex of the baby, then they would cut the pregnant woman open to find out the sex of the child to settle the argument. Keza wasn't shocked or dismayed. This was all too familiar to him as well. He told me abominable stories about the civil war in Rwanda. They were just as ghastly and horrendous as the stories I told him about the atrocities inflicted by the rebels in Sierra Leone on innocent civilians. He told me how some Hutus turned against neighbors they had known for decades and allowed them to be slaughtered or betrayed their whereabouts which led to them being sought out seeking refuge in churches, school buildings and stores and then brutally murdered. Our harrowing experiences bonded us. We could talk about everything after that. I had confided in Keza about my marital problems, about not feeling beautiful because my husband refuses to touch me. He would react with eyes and mouth wide open.

"What? A fine babe like you? Do you know what the guys say about you behind your back? Are you sure your husband is not gay? Have you seen yourself, Zhuri? The American guys here ask me if all the women in Africa look like you."

"I don't know, Keza. I think it's a control thing. He does it when he wants to but not when I want to. It's also the fact that he doesn't even care if he meets my needs or not. That's where I am baffled. If I wasn't meeting his sexual needs, I would be worried. But he carries on like nothing is amiss."

"Zhuri, that man is either gay or he is screwing some chick. Mark my words. Men love sex and he has a young, hot wife. It doesn't make sense, I smell a rat."

"I don't think he is cheating. Maybe he is just punishing me. Either way, I cannot continue this way for too long. I have this hollow feeling in my heart. This unrelenting sadness and also a yearning for emotional and sexual fulfilment. I'd rather we divorce and I find someone who matches my libido. My self-esteem has taken such a hit, Keza."

"We will continue this conversation after my class. I wish I didn't have class right now, but I have a quiz in like five minutes. When is your next class?" Keza asked.

"Not until thursday. I'm off tomorrow but I'll see you in Childhood Psych class then. Don't forget to study for the test."

I had spoken very fondly of Keza to Ollie, but I had no idea that would make him suspicious. On my day off one day, Keza looked for me in class but didn't find me, so he sent me an email. 'My beautiful African Goddess. I hope you know that your absence robs me of all that is sweet and endearing. It was not a good day today because you denied me the sight of your violent physique. Until I see you again, please take care of that fine body of yours and know that you are beautiful.' I melted reading Keza's email, not because I wanted him, but because he was saying everything I wanted Ollie to say to me. He was evoking the feelings I wanted to feel from Ollie. He struck my ego, he made me feel beautiful. "Awwwww, Keza. You just melted my heart. That is so sweet of you. I am glad someone noticed me. I will see you tomorrow. Thanks for checking on me." I clicked send and hurried back to Keza's message. I read it over and over and over again to the point where I was looking forward to Keza's emails. I knew they would lift up my spirits every time and make me feel 10 feet tall.

Alanna had sent me a text after I confided in her about my problems with Ollie. "Just know that I would've wifed you and had my way with you EVERY chance I got. Lol." I replied to Alanna, "Lol. Too bad, too bad, you're not a man. Thanks for making me feel better, Als." Ollie had no context for my texts and emails, he was just spying on me while he put a password on his phone and left it in his car most times. I had always trusted him until he proved otherwise. As a doctor, privacy is huge in his profession. Patients always had to sign documents about their medical treatments. I never in a million years would think someone like him would go out of his way to violate my privacy like this. I've had to deal with years and unending months of unrequited sexual intimacy with him. I made myself understand that rejection is tough. It was not easy to accept at any time that someone I was pining for, wasn't pining for me. The only thing that brought me peace was the fact that I had communicated my feelings with him numerous times and he hadn't followed through with his promises to try harder. I am only responsible for my actions and I had made peace with myself that I wasn't going to continue to put myself in a space where I would be rejected for no reason. Keza's emails made me feel happy, beautiful, sexy, worthy, and I looked forward to them because they reminded me of what I already knew about myself. Those emails quickly became the highlight of my days.

So instead of Ollie confronting me about the emails in America, his revenge was to bring me to Freetown and attack me for emails and messages he had no context of and then divorce me so I got nothing! He didn't want me to have any of his properties, he didn't want me to receive spousal support after 11 years of marriage, and he didn't want to pay child support, All of which he would have been made to pay in America. So, this was his masterplan? I felt like Ollie had a plan B whilst

I was all in. His plan B was if things don't go his way in the US, they will go his way in Sierra Leone. I believed we had reconciled after his infidelity, I believed we were trying to make our marriage work, I believed him when he told me that if I forgave him, I will look back in ten years and thank God that I did, I believed he had been sick and my sole purpose in returning was to make sure he was healthy. I never thought twice about anything else. Now I was going to start all over, with him having all the advantages. He was exactly where he wanted to be, he had all the money, all our things have been shipped to Sierra Leone, all the properties are in his name and all I have is my being. I didn't care about anything he had. I only cared about our three boys and my resolve to have our freedom. I will have to think about what lies ahead later. At the moment, I was in survival mode. I wanted our passports and that is where all my focus and effort will go.

AMERICAN EMBASSY

The next day, I went to the American embassy with my bruised face and swollen eye to ask for help. On one hand, I hoped it would help my case, but on the other hand, I also became oblivious about how I looked. I wasn't even feeling any physical pain from my swollen face and the bump on my eye. It was almost like for that time period I had congenital analgesia. My concentration became solely about recovering our passports. I was unaware of anything else. Even as I received stares, I assumed it was because of my rapid weight loss and ill-fitting clothes. I wasn't thinking about a bump on my face. Normally I was super self-conscious about my appearance, I always wanted to look stunning when I left the house. However, now was not the time. I hoped my look and demeanor convey desperation for immediate help. Whatever else someone thought of me outside of that, was unimportant to me. I didn't care if I was gossiped about. It's amazing how things we thought are important become really minute and almost irrelevant in the grand scheme of things. I would have been hurt by rude stares and gossip before, but now, I could care less. There were more important things on my plate, like finding a way to escape from Freetown with all my kids intact. I had waited in the reception area for about 15 minutes before they called me into a corner office. I told the consul I desperately needed help to go back to America with my children.

"Mrs. Jones, how did you get to Freetown?" he asked me.

"I came with my husband and three boys. My husband told me we were coming here to help the people and that the boys and I would go to the states on summer holidays. Once we got here, I found out that I had been duped and blindsided by him. He has stolen our passports and told me we would not go back to America, and when I protested his treatment I got beaten," I explained with tears coming down my eyes and nose.

"I am so sorry to hear that Mrs. Jones," the Consul replied with a dejected and despairing look. He paused for a moment and after a long sigh, he continued, "but unfortunately, since you came here on your own volition, there is nothing we can do. He did not kidnap you or your children, so there's really nothing I can do about it except advise you to report the matter to the nearest police station. Do you have your husband's phone number? We would like to reach him and ask him to return the passports because they are not his property. They are the property of the United States government."

I couldn't believe what I just heard. Did he just say there is nothing he could do except send me away to thelocal police?

"I have his number, sir, but I do not want him to know that I came here. I will be in big trouble if he finds out I came here."

"Don't worry about it, Mrs. Jones. We pride ourselves on our proficient handling of clients' privacy. This will be between you and the embassy. Do you have a number I can reach you to check on you and the children sometimes? And also, can you provide us with a number of a friend or family member that you trust in case he takes your phone away and we cannot reach you?"

I gave him Sadia's phone number and looked him dead in the eyes and said, "Please help us, you have to help us. You are our only hope. Do everything you can, please."

"Like I said Mrs. Jones, we cannot help you since you came here on your own volition, but please go to the police station and file a complaint. Take care of yourself and the children. Best of luck to you," he responded with a bit of sadness in his eyes.

Just like that, I was dismissed from the embassy. I took a taxi to the house feeling so defeated. When I got in, Sankara ran to me. "Mom, mom, are you ok? What happened to your eye? Are you okay mom?"

"Sankara, don't worry, I am fine. I bumped into something yesterday. The swelling will go down soon. Where are your brothers?"

"Shareef and Saami are with Uncle Simmy upstairs. He is trying to fix the dvd player so that they can watch Barney and Teletubby."

"And you think you're too big now to watch *Barney*, huh?" I tickled his tummy.

"I wanted to play basketball with Uncle Steven, that's why I came downstairs," Sankara replied.

I left Sany downstairs and headed upstairs to see the boys. They ran towards me and just hugged me tightly without letting go.

"We will be fine, I promise you, okay? Do you trust Mommy?" I asked them and they nodded their little heads.

"Now, go sit down and watch your show. Thank you Simmy for all your help."

"They're like my own children, Zhuri. I will do whatever I can to help them settle down," Simmy replied.

He then switched to speaking krio, maybe because he didn't want the boys to understand what he was about to say. "Zhuri, ar nor lek how ar dae see you so. You don loss borku weight. You look so sad. You en Doc really get for do somtin bot dis. Wetin una dae pan so nor good o." After Simmy's small talk about me losing a lot of weight and his suggestion that I try to make up with Ollie, I simply nodded my head and didn't say anything. I appreciated his kindness to me and the boys, but I realized that his goal and my goal were in complete contrast. I had no energy to try to convince him to think otherwise. I knew he couldn't convince Ollie to do anything since he was under Ollie's roof. He would do what Ollie says at all times, but I was grateful that in spite of the pressure on him to turn against me, he was still being kind to me. However, I did not look to Simmy as an ally to accomplish my goal of fleeing with my boys. But, I knew I had to keep playing the game of being nice to him until I no longer have to be around to play games.

I left the boys in the living room watching their show and went to the master bedroom to unwind. However, as soon as I locked the door I cried into the pillow. I felt there was a heavy weight that I needed to release. I cried because of my regret of being so naive and stupid that I fell for Ollie's trick to bring us to Freetown. How could I have been so dumb? I pondered to myself, was I dumb for believing in him or for projecting that everything I felt for him, he also felt for our family? I cried the most because I had disappointed the boys. They deserved at least one parent who they could trust to do right by them, at least one whose word was a bond and they could always rely on it. Even as I promised them that everything would be okay, I did not know how it was going to be okay but I knew that I was up for the fight of my life and wasn't going to give up. However, the response from the consul at the American embassy was a severe blow. They were my biggest hope, my way out, and to hear the consul say they couldn't help me set me back woefully. Now I would have to think of another game plan.

Later, I went outside our compound and called Sadia to tellher about what happened at the embassy. She was disheartened and told me she would pray for me.

"Thank you, Sadia. Please continue to pray for me. I gave the embassy your phone number. There is a slim chance that they might call you. Please tell them everything that you know."

"Oh I sure will, Zhuri. I was wondering all night last night that what is happening with Ollie is not natural. It seems like someone must have taken him to the underworld, voodoo, or witchcraft. How can a man behave so repugnantly to his own family so quickly? I suspect his mom or maybe another woman who might want him to herself," Sadia told me.

"I really don't care about that, Sadia. At this point, my only focus is to go back to America. I feel like if I entertain anything else, it will take away from the focus and energy I have to give to that mission. I have three boys to set free from domestic abuse, three boys who need to be raised without giving them the responsibility of saving their mother, three boys who should roam their home carefree without the fear of physical abuse to them or their mother. That is my focus, everything else is not important at this time."

After I spoke to Sadia, I called one of the brothers at the Kingdom Hall. Brother Watson was an American missionary that was also a close family friend to my parents. He listened to me intently and later responded with so much empathy. He promised to come see me and the boys the next day. It was a relief to hear him say that because I knew he was going to have much needed encouragement and some practical advice for me.

The next person I called was my former friend from St. Edwards, Olu. We had kept in touch when he was going through hard times after he lost his father. He struggled to pay his fees in college. I had helped him by sending a hundred dollars a few times. That was about six years ago. Now, Olu was a celebrated erudite and skillful lawyer in Freetown working at a private firm as second in command to the owner.

"Hello?" I heard Olu as he answered his phone, not recognizing the number. Maybe he thought I was a new client.

"Hello? Olu? This is Zhuri!" I announced with excitement in my voice.

"Zhu-Zhiski, Zhu-bella, my Zhu-zhiski!" he responded with his many nicknames for me.

"Yes! I'm back! I'm here with the boys-"

He did not wait for me to continue. "Where are you guys, what area? I will come see you after work."

"You will? Oh, thanks Olu."

"Why are you thanking me? I haven't seen you in almost 12 years. I will come to you anywhere I can."

I gave Olu our address and told him to call me if he got lost. I went back into the house relieved. I knew a few heads were better than one and with trusted people who cared about me, I was sure we could all come up with some good ideas. As I climbed up the stairs to the bedroom, I saw Simmy waiting in the upstairs living room. He told me Ollie wanted him to inform me that he had invited some of the elders of our families to come to a family meeting at our house at 6 p.m the next day and wanted me present. I acknowledged that I would be at the house in time for the meeting with the elders.

I went to the bedroom and started counting down the time until I saw Olu. I was embarrassed to have him see me this way. I had lost 17 lbs in just 10 days, and some of my clothes didn't fit me the same way anymore. I had imagined when Olu and I would finally meet after so long, I would be glamorous and fashionable. However, I was in survival mode and embarrassment about my deteriorating new look beingan impediment became secondary. I spruced myself up and told the gateman to let my friend Olu in when he arrived.

About two hours later, I heard a car drive through our gate. I didn't recognize the driver, but then a man descended from the back seat of the car. It was him, it was my friend Olu! I ran downstairs as I heard him ask one of the servants downstairs about me.

"Olu!, Olu, Oluuuuuuu!" I ran towards him and we hugged tightly.

"Zhu-Zhiski! Look at you! You're not like other people who go to America and get fat! You have kept your figure even with three boys. Where are the boys? Wait! What's wrong with your face? What happened to your face?'

"I'll tell you about that later. Come with me, the boys are upstairs." I pulled Olu by his left hand and walked ahead of him upstairs.

"This is a nice house, Zhu-Zhiski. It is huge. You guys have done well for yourselves."

"Thanks Olu."

The boys were standing at the top of the stairs waiting to see what was causing all the excitement downstairs. "Saami, Sankara, Shareef, this is your Uncle Olu. We used to go to the same school a long time ago, before you were all born. Olu, these are my boys. Now boys, say hi to Uncle Olu"

"Hi Uncle Olu," all three said in unison.

"Oh wow! My name sounds so sweet in their American accent. Hahaha! Hello Jones boys. Let me guess, you are Sankara?"

"How did you know?" Sankara asked in his Tennessee accent.

"That's because you were the first we all heard about. These two didn't come until years later. So, we all know Sankara," Olu explained.

"That's right, Olu. This is Shareef and this is Saami."

"Come over here and give me five," Olu asked them.

After meeting with the boys, Olu and I went to sit on the veranda. He seemed very impressed that I had birthed three boys already and seemingly done with that part of my life.

"Zhu-Zhu, you have done well. Most of your friends are only still looking for steady partners and you're done with all that already"

"Everything is not what it seems, Olu. All that glitters is not gold."

"What do you mean by that? Is everything okay? What happened to your face?" he inquired.

My eyes instantly welled up with tears. "Everything is not okay, Olu."

"Zhuri! What is wrong? Can you talk here? If not, we can go outside and talk."

I immediately got up, indicating that I would rather talk outside. We got out of the compound to a safe distance outside the house then I poured my heart out to him. I told him about Ollie's deceit in bringing us to Freetown, about the stolen passports, the slap that swelled my face, the threats from his mother and cousin, about the spyware he installed on my laptop and about Keza's emails.

"Wow Zhu-Zhu! This was the least of what I was expecting. I was hoping to get here and just give you a hard time messing with you about the good old days. I am so sorry he did all this to you, but he will not get away with it. He brought you here knowing your whole family was now in the US. Your parents and siblings are not here to help you, but I am here. I hate someone who takes advantage of the vulnerable. I am about to teach this fool a lesson. I will show him that he may have the money and status but this is my stomping ground. I will show him that I get what I want here. Just leave everything to me from here on out. I will help you and the boys, I put my life on that."

"Thank you, Olu. Please do not forget to keep checking on us. If you don't hear from me by phone, please make sure to see us, just in case he takes my phone away. Please, Olu, please." I pleaded with him with desperation in my voice.

"Zhuri, you have my word. Do I ever call you Zhuri? I never do; I always call you by your nicknames, but I just called you Zhuri because I mean business. Someone needs to teach this fool a lesson. He messed with the wrong girl. I hate men who take advantage of vulnerable women with a passion."

After Olu left that evening, I felt very relieved. It didn't go unnoticed that other men were the ones I looked to for protection instead of the one who was supposed to protect me. There was my cousin Steven who slept on the floor in our master bedroom to make sure I was safe, there was Simmy who would come running to protect me, and now there is my friend Olu.

That night, as the boys and I laid in bed. My 4-year-old Saami said something that stung me and filled me with guilt and sadness. "Mommy, I wish I was a bird so I can fly back to Tennessee."

"Oh Saami, me too, baby, me too. Don't worry, mommy is finding every way possible to go back, okay sweetheart?"

That moment was another reminder that I had to do everything in my power to protect myself and my sons. I pulled him closer to my chest and rubbed his head until we fell asleep.

GLIMMER OF HOPE

My cousin Steven always woke up before we did. He dutifully made sure he filled the drum in the bathroom with water and got our bucket ready for us before he left for work. He called around 10 a.m every morning to make sure we got up alright and didn't have anybody bothering us. I made breakfast for the boys and then put their Disney shows on the dvd player. I tidied up our master bedroom and then called Sadia to let her know we would not be going over to her house at midday like we usually did. I laid in bed crying to Jehovah to give me wisdom to navigate our way out of this fog of a nightmare we were in. Just as I was done praying, my phone rang. I looked at the caller ID and saw it was the American embassy calling. My heart started pounding.

"Hello?" I answered.

"Hello, Mrs. Jones?" The lady on the other end of the line asked.

"Yes, this is Mrs. Jones, Mrs. Zhuri Jones."

"How do I know it's really you?" she inquired.

"Well, I was at the embassy yesterday and…"

"Okay, okay Mrs. Jones, that's why I am calling you. Can you come to the embassy today or tomorrow at 2p.m?"

"I will come today at 2 p.m."

"O.K, I will let my boss know to expect you at 2pmGoodbye."

I immediately opened my room door to make sure nobody had been listening to my conversation with the embassy. The coast was clear. It was just the boys engrossed in their Disney show. I closed the bedroom door and got down on my knees, put my hands together, my face towards the ceiling as I repeated under my breath, "Thank you, Jehovah, thank you Jehovah, thank you, Jehovah! I know you're going to make a way for us. Thank you in advance, Jehovah."

When I got up, I sat on the bed and started pondering about why exactly the embassy had called me. Surely it was not just to find out how I was doing, or they would have just asked me over the phone. It was not to turn me down because if that's the case, they need not call me since they already said there wasn't much they could do. Why did they change their mind all of a sudden?

I heard a knock on the door and Sankara told me that a man named Brother Watson was waiting for me in the living room.

"Hello, Brother Watson. Thank you for coming to see us."

"It is my absolute pleasure, Zhuri. How are you? I am so sorry about this," he pointed to my swollen face. "Is it okay to talk here? I just want to share some encouraging words from the scriptures."

"It is fine, brother. The boys are here, we all need encouragement at this time."

Brother Watson shared the scripture at Ephesians 5: 25-33 where the bible implored husbands, among other things, to love their wives as they loved themselves. Right in there he read with emphasis, "For this reason a MAN WILL LEAVE HIS FATHER AND HIS MOTHER and he will STICK TO HIS WIFE, and the two will be ONE FLESH." He also read Ephesians 6:4: "And fathers, do not be irritating your children, but go on bringing them up in the discipline and admonition of Jehovah."

"Zhuri, Jehovah is the originator and creator of marriage and the family. He provides guidelines about how to operate within the family. Every family member has a role to play to make the marriage successful. If we abandon his instructions we are doomed to fail. Jehovah wants marriages to succeed. I can tell you that love is patient and kind and long suffering, but it doesn't tell us to put up with abuse, especially physical abuse. I want you to know that whatever decision you decide to make about your marriage, Jehovah will be there to support and guide you."

"Thank you Brother Watson. I've known about these scriptures since a young age. I knew they would be practical when I eventually got married. I was looking forward to being cherished by my husband like the scripture said. I tried my very best to make it work, Brother Watson, I really did. I gave it my all, there is really nothing else for me to do. I won't put myself in harm's way anymore."

Brother Watson prayed for me before he left. He said I could call the police and then call him if Ollie comes around to beat me up again. He also told me if I needed to stay somewhere else, he could ask someone at the Kingdom Hall to take me in for a while. I profusely thanked Brother Watson and then walked him to the gate.

"Alright Sister Jones, I will be checking on you again tomorrow morning. But if you need me at any time, please don't wait till the next day, just call me."

"I will, thanks Brother Watson. Give my love to Sister Watson."

When I got upstairs to my bedroom again. I felt relieved. I called Sadia to tell her I'd be dropping the boys off to her to go to my appointment at the American Embassy.

"Sadia! Guess who called me? The American embassy! They want to see me at 2 p.m today! I will be dropping the boys off at your house in a few."

Sadia didn't share my excitement. She sighed very deeply and asked, "Zhuri, are you sure it's the embassy? They already turned you away. How do you know it is not Ollie who paid someone to pretend that they were calling from the embassy so they could lure you away?"

"Oh Sadia, I need you to be happy for me. I am very sure it is the embassy. I saw their number on my Caller ID. I will show it to you when I drop the boys. I will be there soon!"

"Zhuri, are you sure? I am so terrified for your safety."

"I am positive! Besides, I will be taking a random taxi to the embassy. Nobody is sending me a ride to go anywhere else and I'm not meeting anybody anywhere besides the embassy."

"Okay, I will see you guys soon!"

I told the boys I was taking them to Aunty Sadia's house. They were happy and asked if they could bring their DVDs with them. I got the DVDs out and took them with me to get a taxi to Sadia's house. I then dropped them off 20 minutes later and went outside to get a taxi to the embassy. I arrived at the embassy 10 minutes before my appointment and went to the reception window to let them know I was in the building. A few minutes later, I got called into the consul's office.

"Mrs. Jones, ever since our last conversation yesterday I could barely sleep". The Consul started, his voice and demeanor exuding so much concern. "Your story haunted me the whole night, your swollen face, the black eye and those poor kids. I just couldn't rest. I am one of three boys who was raised by a single mother who had to seek refuge at a domestic abuse shelter because of my mother's abusive boyfriend. I know how these things can be. None of this is unfamiliar to me. So, the first thing I did this morning was to send word to Washington about your case. I called your husband yesterday and asked him for the passports, but he has declined to bring them to the embassy. Washington has given me the go ahead to reissue new passports. I am going to need a few things from you. First, I will need you to bring your oldest boy here tomorrow, the 10 year old, as we will be interviewing him. If you coach him before you get here, the interviewer will know, so please don't. Secondly, I will need a police report about the stolen passports, the threats from his relatives, and when he put his hands on you. Third, take this. It's instructions about the correct passport pictures to bring. There are a few suggested photo studios whose passport pictures meet our standards. Make sure you have the passport pictures with you when you come tomorrow. Oh, and we suggest you have a lawyer as well. Do you already have a lawyer?"

"Yes sir I do, a very reputable one too. Thank you so much, sir. Thank you! I will let my Lawyer know and I will bring my son tomorrow."

I took another taxi straight to Sadia's house. I could see the relief on her face upon my return.

"What now? You're so brave Zhuri. I was paralyzed with fear but you are brave and courageous."

"My dear Sadia, this is no time to be paralyzed, it is no time to let fear overcome me. I have a mission, remember? And I have good news. The embassy has agreed to give us new passports."

"You're lying! Are you for real? Oh my God, Zhuri, please do not let the boys know. I am afraid they will innocently divulge it to their dad."

"I will not let Shareef and Saami know, but I have to tell Sankara. The embassy has asked to see him tomorrow. He has to know something. I am not scared that Sankara will spill the goods to his dad. Trust me, Sadia, Sankara want to go back to America more than anyone. Our secret with the embassy is safe with him. I know my son."

"Are you sure? You know how kids talk too much about everything," Sadia said, still skeptical.

"I am very sure, Sadia. I know my Sankara. Our secret will be safe with him. I have no worries."

I got the boys out of Sadia's house and waited right in front of her gate at Wilkinson road for a taxi. We had to be home at 6 p.m because of the family meeting Ollie said we were having.

When we got home, the boys stayed in the compound to play basketball and I went straight to my room, deleting the incoming call from the American Embassy on my phone. I also went over my text messages to make sure none of the messages were incriminating. Later, Simmy came upstairs to let me know that Ollie and three other people were in the den on the second floor waiting for me. He told me he was taking the boys with him, so I did not have to worry about them.

When I got to the den, I saw my eldest cousin Saana, my Uncle Ibrahim, and an older friend of Ollie's named Ayo. I greeted them respectfully and found myself a seat close to my cousin Saana. Ollie then started, "My elders, I have called you here today to tell you about my wife Zhuri whom I plan to divorce soon. Zhuri here has not been a faithful wife to me. She has been unfaithful, an accusation of which I have plenty of evidence." At this point, he got some print outs from a folder and started distributing them to all three of the elders he had called. "I am also led to believe that she may have also had a lesbian affair during the marriage. I came across a text message where another woman was talking about 'wifing' her." All three of the elders gasped in disgust and disbelief. "Oh, that is not all. Zhuri has been very belligerent of late. She is disagreeable and argumentative about everything I say or do. She has become very combative and disrespectful, not to talk about being ungrateful. Zhuri has the nerve to go to the American Embassy to tell them I stole her and my children's passports." He then got up and rushed towards me. Sanaa intercepted him. I stood up ready to make a dash for the door. Uncle Ibrahim told me to sit back down. "Zhuri, who I treated like a Princess, who I brought from nothing. Zhuri is now reporting me to the embassy..." He got up again to rush at me, but my Saana stopped him again.

"Okay, okay," Uncle Ibrahim interrupted Ollie. "We have heard from you, Ollie. Thank you for inviting us here. It shows you respect your elders and you respect tradition. We have heard your side of the story. We are very pained by what we heard because that is not what we know our daughter to be. She wasn't raised like that. However, we are not doubting your story. Over a decade in America may have corrupted her mind. I will now ask our daughter Zhuri to tell her side of the story.

"She has nothing to say!" Ollie quickly interrupted. "All she is going to do is sit here and lie. She has a boyfriend in America who she wants to go back to. They have it all planned out. They want to go start their own family. But she will not take my children with her, over my dead body."

"Are such plans in the papers you just gave to us?" My Uncle Ibrahim asked him.

"It's not on paper, but why would she want to go back to America? You think she hasn't talked about future plans with her boyfriend?"

"With all due respect, Oliver, Zhuri has her parents and siblings all in America. That is a good enough reason to want to go back. They have been her support system since she was born. Let us not jump to conclusions that she wants to join a boyfriend before hearing from her first," Sanaa said to Ollie.

"It doesn't matter now, does it? We are here now and she is not taking my boys anywhere. I repeat, she is not taking my boys anywhere. Over my dead body!"

"Uncle, Saana, Ayo, the reason why Ollie is not allowing me to tell my side-" I began, but Ollie interrupted me again

"It's because you will lie, you will just lie about everything. You are not taking my boys anywhere with you, get that through your thick head."

"This man that is accusing me of infidelity has cheated on me multiple times. Not with just one woman, not with two or three, not just with strange women. He cheated with his nurses, family friends-"

"Shut up! Shut up! You're trying to deflect from your infidelity."

"After I found out this man cheated on me, I treated him with compassion, kindness, understanding, I made-" At this point Ollie rushed towards me.

Saana stood up and said, "It's obvious that Oliver is not interested in Zhuri telling her side of the story. Those are very disgusting things you accused my cousin of, Oliver, repugnant and off-putting. To not let her tell her side of the story is despicable to say the least. I also see Zhuri with a puffy face and black eyes and several times you have made attempts to pounce on her. That is a very disrespectful thing to do, especially in front of her family. Zhuri, you don't have to stay here tonight if you don't feel safe".

"I think Zhuri should come with us until her husband has calmed down," Uncle Ibrahim agreed.

Ollie dismissed their concerns. "If it makes you all feel better, I don't stay in the house. I have been living over at the house where my mother moved from. I am just here today for the meeting. So, there is nothing to worry about,"

"Steven has been sleeping on the foot of our bed. He has been there for us. I just want the children to have some type of security and stability. I don't want them all over the place. They have been going through a lot these past few weeks. I want them to have some kind of familiarity. I will stay with them and Steven will be with us," I tried to assure the elders.

"Do you not feel uncomfortable that a grown adult man is sleeping in the same bedroom as your wife? Is that what you want your kids to see and experience?" Saana asked Ollie with disgust.

"Well, I'm sure no incest will occur," Ollie retorted.

Saana was done with the conversation. "Uncle Ibrahim, let us go! I am disgusted! Zhuri, please take care of the boys, okay? I will call you first thing tomorrow morning to make sure you're okay."

"Thank you Saana. Thank you Uncle Ibrahim. Thank you Ayo. Good night everyone".

I excused myself and went upstairs to the master bedroom, locked the door behind me, and started crying quietly. I couldn't believe Ollie's false accusations and concocted tales. Even the emails with Keza, they were filled with praises about me. They may have been inappropriate coming from another man, but I had gotten to a point where I thought I needed to be stimulated mentally and emotionally, otherwise I believed I would go crazy. Time and time again, I talked to Ollie about him not spending time with me, him not touching me for months. Many times he left me in the master bedroom by myself and slept in the guest room instead. No matter how much I kept my figure in shape, smelled good, looked good, took the children to their grandparents so we could have alone time, cooked whenever and however he wanted, nothing was good enough. I was pouring and pouring into an empty bowl and I got nothing back. Keza's emails gave me something to look forward to, they helped restore what I already knew about myself, even if I didn't believe them anymore. Keza's emails were my sanity. After I discovered Ollie cheated on me multiple times, I was still gracious to him. I gave him the respect of not shaming him in front of my brother, my boys or my parents. I lied to my parents about going to Memphis to keep his dignity intact. I even allowed him to go back to work with a nurse he had slept with because she was threatening to ruin him by suing him. Every day in spite of my hurt and heartbreak, I put his interests before mine. To now see Ollie doing the complete opposite to me is heart wrenching. The problem with me is, I project a lot of myself unto other people. I always felt if I would respond or act a certain way, that was exactly how other people would act towards me. I had given my husband love, dignity, strength, loyalty and forgiveness when he needed them the most, even when he didn't deserve it, and what does he give to me in return? He had given me betrayal, dishonor, shame and deceit. But this was no time to lull in self pity. I gave in to tears and regret a little bit because I am only human, but I must focus on getting away. I called Simmy and told him to bring the boys upstairs after I heard Ollie's car zoom away.

"Mom!" They ran into my arms as they entered the bedroom. "Are you okay, mom?"

"Of course, I'm fantastic! Are you guys okay?" I started tickling them. They saw that I was smiling, so they started giggling.

Steven knocked on the bedroom door before he opened it to come inside. The boys went to hug him. We didn't stay up for long that night. Steven locked the door with the key and we all went to sleep.

The next morning I got the boys dressed and took them to one of the photo studios recommended by the American Embassy. Then, we returned to Sadia's house where I dropped off Saami and Shareef, then took a taxi with Sankara to Imatt where the embassy is located. On our way there, I told Sankara, "Sany, I am taking you to an office where they will be asking you questions. I don't know what the questions will be, but make sure you answer them truthfully, okay. The people who will be asking you questions want to help us get back to America, so make sure you are polite and answer all their questions, okay baby?"

"Okay mom. When will they help us get back to Tennessee?" he asked.

"I don't know yet. But as soon as they can. Just make sure you do your part, okay baby?"

"Yes, mom. I cannot wait to go back to Humboldt," he said.

"Me too, Sany, me too."

The taxi driver was looking back as we spoke from the back seat fascinated by Sankara's American accent. I could tell we were almost at the embassy as soon as we started ascending the hill. I looked into my purse for the taxi fare and gave it to him. "Tenki. Just drop we na de gate." After thanking the driver when we arrived at the gate, the security officer recognized me from the day before and let us in.

I was told once we got in Sankara would be interviewed away from me. He would be in a separate room interacting with a psychologist while I would be in another room watching them interact. I would be able to see them, but Sankara would not be able to see me so that I would not be able to affect his answers in any way.

"So, what's your name, handsome?" The psychologist started with a big smile. I smiled as I watched them. I wasn't nervous at all. I knew Sankara was going to tell them everything they wanted to know.

"Sankara."

"Sankara. What a unique name. I've never heard of it before. How old are you, Sankara?"

"I am 10 years old."

"Oh wow! And you're so tall already! Do you have any brothers or sisters?"

"I have two brothers, Saami and Shareef. I don't have a sister even though my mom would like a little girl."

"Is that so? What about you, would you like a little Sister, Sankara?"

"Hmmm, I don't know. Maybe. I heard that little sisters are annoying though. But maybe ours won't be. I don't know. Maybe."

"That's good enough. Sankara can you tell us about your life in Tennessee, especially at home. What was it like?"

"I was very happy. I played with my brothers in the den, we watched Disney Channel and PBS Kids. Oh! And Nick Jr too! We went to McDonalds and Chuck E Cheeses, I had sleepovers with my friends from school, my mom cooked all the time, we went to the Kingdom Hall, we played music in mommy's car and sang along, we went to gramma's house. I miss Tennessee." In that instant, he went from excitement to sadness.

"I'm sure you miss Tennessee. Can you tell me what you did with your dad as well?"

"My dad? Hmmm, lemme think. Oh! I know! Sometimes, my dad took me to his clinic. I stayed with him the whole day. The nurses would bring me food. I liked it."

"What else do you remember about life at home, Sankara. Was everything fine at home?"

"Yes, everything was fine. That's why I miss it so much." He bowed his head.

"Thank you so much, Sankara! What a smart boy you are! I will take you back to your mother in a few minutes ok?"

"Okay."

I was beaming the whole time as I saw the interview on the circuit TV. I wondered what they were going to conclude after talking to Sankara. I didn't have to wonder for too long since theconsul came to the room I was in with Sankara.

"He did very well, Mrs. Jones. The psychologist said he was very organic and didn't seem coached at all. By the notes, it seemed that you guys provided a loving home for Sankara and his siblings for him to miss it so much. Whatever was going on between you and your husband, you both did your best to shield it from the children. That is very commendable. I believe children should be children and not be exposed to adult problems. We will have the passports ready in about 7 to 10 business days. We will call you as soon as they arrive."

"Oh thank you so much sir, thank you, so much! Thank you, thank you!" My gratitude was profuse.

"Don't forget that we need the police report on file. Make sure you have it with you when you come back."

"Most definitely! I will do that first thing tomorrow."

Afterwards, we descended the hill from the embassy like gazelles galloping towards their prey.

"Sankara, I'm so proud of you! The consul said you did well on your interview," I commended Sankara, not letting him know I was watching the whole thing from another room the whole time. I didn't want him to think we set him up.

"Thanks mom! When are we going back to America?"

"As soon as we get our passports. Now Sany, listen to me, I want you to keep this between us, okay? If Daddy knows about this, he will not let us go back to America. He will seize the new passports too. Do you want to go back to America?"

"Yes, mom. I want to go back right now."

"Okay, then don't tell your dad or anyone else, especially your dad. Do not tell him."

"I won't tell him, mommy. I won't, I promise."

"I trust you! This will all be over soon, Sany. Just trust me, okay?"

"Okay, Mommy."

POLICE REPORT

I called my friend Olu the next day and told him everything the consul said. He volunteered to help me without me even formally asking. He said he had talked to the owner of his firm, another astute lawyer, and he had agreed to take on my case pro bono.

"What? He has? Olu, I don't know how to bless you. You know I do not have any money. He took all the money, over $205,000. He opened a separate account for me and would only give me $200 a month allowance," I stated as I started crying.

"No, Zhuri. Do not cry. Remember what I told you. I hate anyone who tries to take advantage of another person. You are MY person. I will fight for you like I have never fought for anyone else in my career. Can you come to the office by 11 am tomorrow? Mr. Turay wants to meet with you."

"Olu, stop asking me if I can come. I will do any and everything I need to do to get my children out of here. I will need you to help me file a police report as well. The embassy requires one."

"We'll have it all sorted out tomorrow, Zhuri. I'll see you at 11?"

"Yes, at 11."

I breathed a long sigh of relief. It seemed like everything was coming together. I didn't know how to tell Olu I wouldn't be able to pay for his services while in Sierra Leone, so hearing him say his firm would take up my case pro bono eased my worries.

I heard a text message come in and nervously checked my phone. It was my dad! He and my mother were deathly scared for our safety, so I immediately called them. He shared with me that Ollie had sent an email to my brother Ahzan telling him that he and his family were all safe from their clutches now. He reiterated to him that the boys will never go back to America until they were old enough to make that decision. I couldn't believe that being in Freetown had made Ollie so brazen with his antics. He seemed so power-drunk. I had not even found the right time or right words to tell my family what I have come to and what I was going through and he had gone ahead of me to tell them we were now stuck with him without their interference anymore. My dad told me that Uncle Ibrahim had called and told him that Ollie had tried to hit me several times even in their presence. I tried to allay my dad's fears by telling him Steven was always with us for protection and disclosed to him what I got from the embassy. My brother Ahzan got on the phone to tell me that he was getting one of his friends to get some thuggish 'eastern boys' to go beat up Ollie just as he had done to me.

"No, Azhan, no! Don't do that! Don't! If you love me and the kids, please do not do that. That is their father! We must all concentrate on one thing, getting us out of here! That should be the only focus. Don't worry about me, Steven is here, Saana is here, Olu is here. They are looking out for us. Please don't ask anyone to do anything to Ollie."

"Well, I was going to give him a dose of his own medicine," he continued.

"No! No! Do everything you can to get us out of here. Let me speak to dad."

When dad came on the line, I told him not to let Ahzan send anyone to beat up Ollie.

"Dad, I want you to do me a favor. Call my university tomorrow, and ask to speak to Professor Nambuya. Tell her you are my father, explain to her what has happened to me and the boys. She promised to help me if anything happened. If you don't get her, please keep trying until you reach her, okay? She gave me her phone number but I do not have it now, just call the university then ask for her extension. Please."

After that phone conversation. I took a taxi to Sadia's house with the boys. I just needed to rest. The boys were always happy to come along and even though I was afraid of Sadia's dogs, the boys never cared. They just wanted to play with their friends. I left them in the yard with Sadia's three boys and went to sleep inside.

We returned to our house in the evening to spend the night. The boys were already looking forward to going back to be with their friends the next day. I told them I'd be gone for a long while before I picked them back up. However, before I could complete our plans with them, Simmy knocked on the door to let me know that Ollie wanted to spend time with the boys the next day and wanted Simmy to take the boys to him in the morning around 10 am. It was a welcome surprise for me. I didn't get nervous about Sankara telling his father what happened at the embassy even if his father blatantly asked him. I trusted in my gut that Sankara so desperately wanted to go back to Tennessee that he would do nothing to jeopardize that.

"That's fine, Simmy. I will get them ready in the morning."

After handing the boys over to Simmy the next day, I took a taxi to Olu's law office. It was a very busy building with a couple of other businesses. There was a long queue leading to Olu's office door. A few people who were tired of the long wait saton makeshift benches waiting for 'de Pa,' as men of status and authority are referred to in Freetown. I called Olu on his cellphone to let him know I was waiting outside. In less than a minute, a man came outside and got me. "Udat name Zhuri Jones, de Pa go see you now." I raised my hand and followed the man through the door leading to Olu's office. I could hear some of the people who had been waiting longer murmuring that I had just arrived but was getting seen almost immediately. I ignored the murmurings and made my way to Olu's office.

"Zhu-zhiski!!! Welcome to my humble office. How are my Americanas, my Yankee boys?"

"They're with their dad today, thank God. We'll have time to do all we need to do today. Olu, I am so tired. I want all this to be over soon! I have lost so much weight, Olu. Look at me, look at my pants. I have to fold them and tie them. I am so embarrassed. Even Sadia was mentioning how much weight I've lost in only a few weeks. She was chiding me to start eating the other day, but I have no appetite, Olu. Not until this is over."

"Zhuri, I need you to trust us, okay? I know you trust me as a person, as your friend, but I need you to trust me as a lawyer too, okay? Trust that we will vindicate you. This is a David and Goliath situation. Oliver has all the money and the big, expensive lawyers he can buy, but you have the best lawyers. You have God on your side, Zhu-Zhu, God is for the underdogs as much as we are. By the time we are finished with Oliver, he will be running for the hills. Sometimes I've had to tamper my tactics because I remember he is the boys' father. If that was not the case, I would've adopted some ruthless tactics to teach him a lesson. Come with me, let me introduce you to Mr. Turay."

I followed Olu down a narrow hallway about 20 feet from his office. He knocked on the door and announced us.

"Come right in!" I heard Mr. Turay say from behind the door.

"Counsel, this is my dear friend Zhuri Jones I was talking to you about. Zhuri, this is my boss and counsel, Mr. Turay."

"Good Morning Mr. Turay. So nice to meet you. Thank you very, very much for taking my case pro bono. I do not know how to bless you two. I am so very grateful. Thank you so much, from the bottom of my heart thank you."

"Don't worry about it. After Counsel Williams here told me about your story, I wanted to help you. A similar thing happened to my favorite Aunt Rafiatu a long, long time ago. I was just an 11 year old boy then. A rich businessman came and married my beautiful Aunt Rafia and took her abroad. They would later have four children. He became abusive to my aunt and when she decided to leave, he convinced her to come home with their children for summer holidays. After they arrived, he seized their passports, destroyed their travel documents and left her penniless. My aunt fought tirelessly, but her husband had all the money and more connections. I saw my aunt struggle to cope and before we knew it, she had a nervous breakdown. She was not the person we used to know and love. She started struggling to sleep and developed severe insomnia, and her bubbly personality disappeared. She would have debilitating anxiety and significant mood swings. One minute you'd think she was coping, the next she'd have uncontrollable crying spells, blamed herself for being "so stupid." She had massive guilt about not trusting herself and her own instincts. She became a recluse. Her husband had custody of the children because he had his lawyers prove her unfit to care for them. Their children were 11, 8, and the twins were 6 years old. She had taken care of them all the while as a stay-at-home mom. That's all she knew how to be; a dedicated, nurturing mother and wife and when she was treacherously stripped of it all, she lost herself. My aunt later suffered from severe depression and had a brain aneurysm five years later and died. She was only 36 years old. I never got over how abysmally she was treated by someone she loved and trusted. I think my aunt died from shame, guilt, disappointment and a broken heart. It was a pivotal moment in my life. That's when I decided I wanted to become a lawyer when I grew up. I was too young to help my aunt Rafia at that time, but I vowed to help somebody like her one day. I hate people who take advantage of other people, especially their own family members. This case is very personal for me. I will not stop until we do everything in our power to prevail." He took a breath before continuing. "So now, tell me what do you want out of the divorce? How long were you married?

"I am so sorry about your Aunt Rafiatu. I understand why she blamed herself. I feel the same way sometimes as well. We project our good hearts onto our husbands without measuring risks. We believe they have the whole family's interest at heart just like we do. We believe their intention is never to hurt us even as they hurt us, emotionally, physically and verbally sometimes. However, I do not want anything. I only want my children. That's what I want, the children. We were married for almost 12 years. We're five months shy of our twelve year anniversary."

"Oh no, Mrs. Jones, you're getting more than your children. You were married to this jackass for over a decade and you want nothing? Hell no! Tell me about the assets in the marriage."

"Well, he has-" I started, but Mr. Turay interrupted me promptly. "You mean we had? It is all community property, Mrs. Jones. He does not have anything by himself in this marriage. So, tell me again about your assets."

I took a deep breath and started all over. "Well, the last bank statement I saw, he had, I mean, we had about $206,000 in the bank. But it was his personal account, he only gave me monthly allowances. He has a private medical clinic in Humboldt. Then he came alone to Freetown and purchased land at Juba Hill, bought the house we live in now and of course the hospital he will be practising at. I was made aware of these purchases only after the fact, so I never signed any documents, my name is not on them."

"It doesn't matter if your name is on them or not, they were bought during the time of your marriage, so they are equally owned by both of you. It's community property. Also, since he was the one taking care of you financially during the marriage, we are going to ask for spousal support akin to the standard of living you have been accustomed to and he will be forced to continue to pay for your university education like he promised your father and yourself until you have enough training to become self-sufficient. Then we are going to ask for child support. He has never spent a night by himself with the boys, you have been doing it since they were born. He has to support the lifestyle they have been accustomed to. Is there anything else you want to tell us that we have not covered?"

"Not really. Thank you, sir. I really just want to have my children's passports so we can go back to Tennessee. I really don't care about his money or his properties. The boys are my riches, they are my everything. I choose them. I just want to be able to go back with them, please just help me do that," I answered tearfully.

"Of course. I know what you want Mrs. Jones, but you get a lawyer to know what the law allows, what is possible to do within the law. That's where we come in. We will send a letter to the embassy notifying them that we represent you, so they will start communicating with us directly. We will do everything to make you have a happy ending after all this is over."

"Thank you, sir. Thank you Mr. Turay. God bless you, sir, and you too, Olu, thank you."

As I walked with Olu back to his office, I was stunned about what just happened. I knew Olu would be there for me in any and every capacity, but I wasn't expecting a total stranger to be so passionate about helping me. Olu read my mind and said, "You're thinking about Mr. Turay, huh? You know Zhu-Zhu, the bible in Exodus 23:20 says: 'See, I am sending an angel before you, to keep you on your way and to be your guide into the place which I have made ready for you.'' God takes care of His own, Zhu. He saw your heart, he knew your intentions, he had people set up in place to help you because you were ignorant of Ollie's devious machinations. In Genesis 50:20 it says; "as for you, you meant evil against me, but God meantit for good." No weapons formed against you shall prosper, Zhu! By the time we are done with that man, he'll be the one fleeing just as the bible says in Proverbs 28:1. Now, let us go to the eastern police station to start this process."

"Olu!" I said, giving him a side eye, with my hands on my hip, "Since when did you become a pastor? Look at you, dazzling me with all these biblical quotes. And what do you mean by starting the process? Won't I get the report today?"

"Zhu-zhiski, unfortunately, things don't happen as fast here as they do in America. The process here is rather slow and you must shake everybody's hands before things get done. You know what I mean by shaking hands, right?

"I know. I am sorry I am not in a position to do that, Pastor Olu."

"Haha! You got jokes. I am not a pastor, Zhu, but my faith in God is very strong. It is what has carried me all these years after I lost my father. The way some things have worked out for me, the way some people were positioned to help me out, the way I was at the right place at the right times, it was none of my doing, Zhu-Zhu. Only God."

We arrived at eastern police station around 1p.m. Some of the staff there were familiar with Olu because of how closely law enforcement officers worked with lawyers. They addressed him as 'de Pa'. I blushed at the reverence with which they treated him because I was reminiscing about the Olu I went to school with. The boy who was overprotective of me and would walk me home often. He always had a matchstick at the corner of his mouth and a folder in his hand. We would walk from Maypark, Kingdom to Old RailWay line, talking and laughing about any and everything. Most times he came in the house with me, other times he would just continue the journey to his house through King Harman road to New Englandville Road. He was always fun and vibrant, extremely intelligent, yet so unassuming. A few years later, we were here and people were referring to him as 'de Pa.' He let one of them know we were there to file a police report. I was asked to go to a small office and wait for a police officer to come. Olu put some money in my hands and told me to use it as I saw fit. By the time I wanted to say thank you, he said, "Zhu-zhiski, you can handle it from here on out. I have to meet with a client at 2p.m. Let me know how it goes. Call me as soon as you're done. And please, remember the scripture at Romans 8:18;

"For I reckon that the sufferings of this present time are not worthy to be compared with the glory which shall be revealed in us". Hold on a little while longer, my dear Zhu-Zhu, God's blessings are about to blow your mind. Your breakthrough is coming". He squeezed my shoulders and then dashed off.

I knew the money he gave me was for me to 'shake hands' with some of the people that worked at the station. I went into the office alone and just waited. The office was not what I expected. The floor was bare. There was no linoleum, carpet or tile on the floor, there was an unevenly hung picture of the President on the wall. There was no computer or typewriter in sight; however, there were two chairs and a large table by the wall which had piles upon piles of documents in folders. There was no phone on top of the desk or a stapler or a box of pens. None of the basic things an office space needs. Fifteen minutes later an officer came in. I greeted him and he asked me if I can speak krio very well.

"Of course! Ar dae talk am good, good wan." I assured him I could speak krio really well.

"Correct! That accent threw me off a bit. Before you tell me what happened I want to let you know that you have to buy an exercise book to write your statement. I already have one here you can pay for," he said.

I couldn't believe what I just heard but I went with it. There was no time for me to ask why the police station didn't provide the basic things needed for everyday function. I told him I would take care of it. What stunned me next was the officer asking me to spell some words correctly for him as he wrote. I would be in depth with my story about what happened and he would say something like, "How do you spell punch, is it ponch or ponched?" I would stop my story to spell the word correctly and then continue only to be interrupted again to spell something else. After 45 minutes we were done.

"So madam, the next step is for you to pay Le150,000 to get it typed by the secretary. Also, there is going to be a fee for us to put the police seal on it to make it legal and valid. You should be able to have it by next week or so." he informed me.

"Next week?" I asked in disbelief. "No, that's too late, officer. I need this document immediately. The American Embassy has asked for it. They need it right away, sir."

"Well, madam, you get for show usef o. De secretary get borku tin dem for type, so for lef dem fos en type u yone, you need for show usef." The officer told me in subtle terms that I'll have to pay more money to get my document ready fast. I counted the money Olu had given me, it was Le350,000. I gave it to the officer and said, "This is for you and the secretary, how soon can I get my report?"

"Come back tomorrow this same time, it should be ready," he said with a broad smile.

I felt relieved, as it seemed like everything was working out afterwards. I would have the police report ready for the embassy tomorrow and that would fulfill all the requirements they needed to give us our passports. It was Tuesday, so by Friday next week we should be able to get our passports and leave for America. I became nervously excited because until I had the passports in my hand it was all wishful thinking. Even after we got our passports, how were we going to flee? I had no money to pay for flights for the four of us. I reminded myself not to become overwhelmed with the details. First things first, we have to have the passports.

When I returned home, the boys had not returned from their father's new place. I went to the master bedroom to rest. After about twenty minutes, there was a knock on my door and my mother-in-law handed me a bulky envelope, then snickered and went into her room. My hands were shaking like a chronically ill Parkinson's disease patient. When I opened it, I realized they were divorce documents. Ollie had officially filed for divorce on the grounds of infidelity. I couldn't believe it. It was as if someone kicked me in my stomach. The man who had cheated on me with multiple women, the man who I've found condoms in his suitcase, is divorcing me on the grounds of infidelity. I started crying uncontrollably but as quietly as I could. I didn't want to give my mother-in-law the satisfaction of hearing me being distraught, devastated, and shattered like I knew she wanted. I was crying because of the unfairness. I cried because I was pining for a husband who was emotionally and sexually unavailable, for the deceit of bringing me all the way to Sierra Leone to get a divorce when I had asked him for one in America. I was crying because I fell for his devious ploy with three children in tow. I was crying because I put myself and my own interest last and was looking out for him. Even though I knew I didn't want to make the move and Sankara didn't want to make the move, I put his own interest ahead of all of us. As I thought I was choosing the right course, making sure he had less stress and better health, all the while he was thinking about how to leave me desolate and penniless. If he wasn't going to have me anymore, he wanted me stripped of everything; money, dignity, and even the place I have called home for over a decade. I couldn't believe someone I have shown mercy and dignity was not only treating me this way, but had the nerve to plot against me for months.

I got on my knees with my hands stretched upwards towards heaven and prayed to God. "Jehovah, you know my heart. You know I always meant well for my husband, for my marriage. You know I tried my best to be the best wife I could be to Ollie. You're the one who searches the heart, you know my intentions for my husband were always good. Not one time have I entertained any evil thoughts against him. I would rather go away from him than hurt him. Jehovah, I need you to fight for me, please. I need you now like I never did before. Fight for me, O God. I am in this desolate place, but only you can turn things around for me. Please fight for me, so your name will be glorified. I will let everyone know that you, the only true God, made a way out for me when there seemed to be no way out."

By the time I was finished praying my whole face was soiled with tears. I went to the bathroom and washed my face. I called Olu and Sadia and let them know what just happened. They were not surprised but were worried about my mental state. Sadia offered to come and pick me up, but I told her I was in no shape to leave the house; I just wanted to cry it out. Olu told me to bring the divorce papers to his office the next time so he could respond to it. I was grateful that I had Olu to respond on my behalf, but it was the first time in my life I realized the stark unfairness of life. Didn't my parents promise me that if I married as a virgin I would meet a man who would value and cherish me and treat me like a valuable possession? Why was all my kindness and understanding being met with such viciousness and ingratitude? No matter what you do, life hands you what it hands you, and you better be able to roll with the punches. It's a dog eat dog world and survival is only for the fittest. Nothing is promised or guaranteed in life and damn our parents for giving us a formula for a good life, when they themselves have no idea what lies ahead. There is no formula. If anything, you prepare your children for life's unexpected challenges. You tell them to turn to God, if you believe in one, their faith and their strength, you teach them to be resilient, to think positive, to strive for the best and when things don't turn out the way they had hoped for, you teach them to make the most of how things turned out. You teach them to be emotionally self-reliant. You teach them to be happy on their own and not look for happiness in other people or things or accomplishments. Happiness is not outside of us but within us. Happiness isn't something that Prince Charming brings to young women as a reward for being prim and proper. Happiness isn't somewhere waiting for us after we fall in love, get married, earn a degree, or win a gold medal. Happiness isn't in the future. It is not something that comes to us after we accomplish milestones. It is inside of us, readily available, and we must learn to tap into it to activate it. You teach your children to enjoy the moment they're in, to live in it, soak in it, savour it all before it all becomes a blur. Teach them it is ok to think first of themselves, not others. It is not selfish, it is selfcare. Teach them to learn how to say no and mean it. You teach them to cherish what they have while they have it. I realized at that moment, I have to unlearn everything that I have been conditioned to believe and start all over again. I needed to be strong and resilient and continue to fight.

NO WORD

By Thursday the next week, I was devoid of all hope. I had lost about twenty more pounds, I barely had any breasts, and I could feel my body getting lighter, my face sunken. I knew from living in America that when you're told something will take seven to ten business days it's just a safe estimation, usually it gets done in three or four days. I had not heard anything from the embassy. Fear gripped me as I made my way to Olu's office to find out if he heard anything from the embassy. Fear and I had become strange bedfellows by now. It played with my psyche, my sanity. It tossed and turned me every which way and I had become a slave to its wimps. Olu told me he hadn't heard anything from the embassy. I was broken.

"Olu, I cannot take it anymore. Look at me, Olu. I have lost so much more weight. I'm going to die here, Olu. I do not care anymore, I am taking my children and running away to Guinea. We cannot live like this anymore."

"Zhu-Zhu, you cannot go into another country without documents. You can slide maybe because you're Sierra Leonean, but what about the boys? They are American citizens and they will need to have their passports."

"I will slide with them into Guinea and we will wait for our passports there, but I cannot be here anymore, Olu. Look at me, I'm slowly wasting away. I'm dying, Olu. He wants to kill me, Olu." I paused for a moment to observe his reaction. "Look at me! You can't even look at me, can you? Even you cannot bear to see me like this." I said in despair.

"Zhuri, I have to be in court in 15 minutes. I need to wrap up a case, but it shouldn't take me very long. I will send the driver to take you to Sadia's house to rest for the day. Tomorrow will be the tenth day and the end of the deadline for you to get the passports. I want you to go to the embassy in the morning and demand to speak to the consul to find out why they haven't called you to pick them up after all this time. We will go from there after we get a response from them. Remember, 'all things work together for good for them that love God'. He tried to reassure me by quoting a scripture from the bible..

Olu walked me to his car and opened the back door for me. I went in and he put some money in my hands like he did the week before. I thanked him as he closed the door and told his driver to be careful. When I arrived at Sadia's house, she got upset, "Zhuri, look at you, why are you doing this to yourself, Zhu-Zhu? I have told you to take heart. You're letting this situation get the best of you. You're beginning to look like a skeleton, is that what you want? Do you want him to see you like this and think that without him you cannot survive? I need you to be stronger than this and eat. I am going to feed you. Come here and sit down, I have some food."

I immediately bursted out crying. Sadia held me close."It is going to be okay, Zhu-Zhu. Nothing lasts forever. He used your kindness and naivete against you and he seemed to have won for now, but God has the final say, Zhu-Zhu. Do not feel defeated before you are actually defeated. You're doing all the right things except not eating. Do you know how many women would've just left their children and ran? Do you know that not many people can fight the big guns? But look at you, you have become resolute about not leaving your boys behind, no matter what Ollie throws at you. You are determined and unwavering in giving your boys the life they once knew. You're strong, Zhuri, mentally strong and resolute. I need you to physically match that, okay?"

Sadia took a spoon of rice and plasas and started feeding me. Every time I opened my mouth for another feeding, she would say, "There you go! That's what I'm talking about." I felt like a little child all over again. I couldn't even manage to eat properly. However, my study about mental health in university quickly kicked in. I recalled there was nothing wrong with receiving help when one needs it or asking for it. I had always been one who was always eager to help other people, but I always felt like I was a bother or an inconvenience when I was in a vulnerable position. I told myself that this time, it was ok to not be a martyr and just receive the help, nurture and care I was getting from Sadia.I finished the food after much coaxing from Sadia. I told her I wanted to sleep. I went to her bedroom and slept for hours. She woke me up to let me know it was 6pm and I had to go make sure the boys were fine. I thanked her and took a taxi home.

ESCAPE

The boys got home an hour after I arrived back home with their Uncle Simmy. They told me they had spent time at Lumley beach and Family Kingdom. Sany said their dad bought them pizza but they were not able to finish it because it "tasted weird, not like Dominos." However they loved the roasted chicken, fries and soft drinks. They said they were tired because the sun had beat them. I understand how brutal the heat in Freetown can be for someone who wasn't used to it. I told Sany to go take a cool bath first and I'll bathe Saami and Shareef afterwards. Once they were all clean and felt refreshed, they fell asleep sooner than I had anticipated. So, I stayed up to chat with Steven a little bit. He was worried about my drastic weight loss. I assured him I would try to eat and not worry so much.

"There's just too much on my plate, Steven," I told him, sighing. "I didn't plan on any of this. It's really not easy for me. In the twinkle of an eye my whole life changed, in a place I haven't lived in my adult life. I've learned how to wangle in America, not here. Adjusting is taking a toll on me. Also, I don't know if I wanna adjust. I refuse to adjust. Adjusting would make him win. It would mean he planned this warped life for me and I don't get to have my say, but to just fold and adjust to his ploy. I refuse to!"

"Zhu-Zhu, I don't care what you do, I just want you to stay alive. I want your children to have a mother. So whatever you plan to do, I am behind you one hundred percent, just make sure you do not die in the process. Be healthy."

"I am trying. I have to go to the embassy in the morning to find out about our passports. I am excited and nervous at the same time."

"Do you want me to come with you? I can come with you," he offered.

"I don't mind at all. I will drop the boys off at Sadia's place at 10a.m. and we'll take a taxi there afterwards."

We dropped the boys with Sadia and headed for the embassy the next morning. Sadia said she had been so nervous for me that she had diarrhea all night but had prayed for me the whole time. "Be careful, Zhu-Zhu! Call me as soon as you find out anything".

My heart was beating so fast as Steven and I descended the taxi at the embassy. I got to the window inside the embassy and asked to speak with the consul. The consul beckoned me to a corner window not generally used.

"Good morning sir. I am here to check on the passports since today marks the tenth business day."

"I am so sorry we didn't call you Mrs. Jones, we do have the passports, they arrived four days ago. However, through his lawyers, Mr. Jones sent the embassy an injunction from the court forbidding us from issuing passports to his minor children," the consul explained. I immediately started crying.

"Please Sir, he is using the courts to bully me. He has all the money and can buy lawyers to do whatever he wants-"

"Mrs Jones, do you have a Lawyer of your own?" he interrupted me.

"Yes, I do. Mr. Olu Williams of Turay and Associates."

"Can you get him on the phone right now? No, give me his phone number so I can call him." I went through my caller ID and read Olu's phone number to him. "Okay, I am calling him now. I will put the call on speaker so you can hear our conversation."

"Yes sir," I replied with tears streaming down my face. After two rings Olu answered the call.

"Hello?" I heard him speak.

"Hello? Is this Mr… I mean lawyer Olu Williams?"

"Yes, this is he."

"Mr. Williams, I am calling from the American Embassy. I am here with your client Mrs. Zhuri Jones, do you represent her?"

"Yes, we formally sent a letter to the embassy stating that we are her legal counsel."

"Excellent! Now, here is the situation Mr. Williams. Almost a week ago, her husband, Mr. Jones, through his lawyer, sent a notice of an injunction forbidding us from issuing the passports to his minor children. That is why we didn't call Mrs. Jones, because we were stumped by it and did not know how to move forward. Can you tell us anything that is within the laws of Sierra Leone that will make it possible for us to give these passports to Mrs. Jones without being in violation of the court in any way?"

"Most definitely! After Mr. Jones served Mrs. Jones with divorce papers, we responded to his divorce petition, thereby notifying him that we now represent Mrs. Jones. We were supposed to be copied about any filings which pertained to our client and given notice of a hearing. Obviously, they flouted the rules and did what they wanted to do regardless. But what I can tell you is that you have every right to give those passports to Mrs. Jones and not be in violation of the law because what you have in your possession is a notice of an injunction, which only means one is being filed. It has not been ruled upon by a judge yet, so there is no judgement. What you have there is just a sheer notice. For a judge to rule on it, both parties have to bring their arguments before him. That has not happened since the other party hasn't even been given a notice of an injunction being filed. A judge cannot charge you for violating anything because he hasn't presided over the case, nor issued a judgement," My Olu explained so eloquently.

"Thank you, Mr. Williams. We will give Mrs. Jones the passports right away!"

The consul then turned to me with a sigh of relief on his face and said, "Mrs. Jones, I am going to give you the passports, please make sure you look at each one carefully and make sure names and dates of birth are correct. Then sign here to confirm that they were issued to you." I looked them over and signed the sheet and gave it back to him. "Good luck, Mrs. Jones. I really wish all the best for you and your boys. I really do."

"Thank you, sir. God bless you, sir. Thank you so much. Thank you," I said to him. I took the passports that were in a blue envelope and put them inside my pants. The consul didn't look at me strangely. He understood that I would do everything in my power to make sure the wrong hands did not come across them ever again.

As I walked by the hallway making my way out, a few of the Sierra Leonean employees at the embassy asked me if I finally received the passports. "Den gee u de passport dem Ma?"

"No, they told me to come back next week," I told them. I had received word that Ollie had bribed some of the staff at the embassy, that is how he knew they were going to issue passports to me. The embassy was telling me that our dealings were confidential but they did not understand that every time they dealt with me, a couple of locals who worked there basically read my file and told Ollie everything that transpired. I wasn't going to let them know I had the passports. I intentionally gave them the wrong information so they could text him or call him now to let him know I would have to come back next week.

I met Steven outside who gave me the biggest hug. I didn't have to tell him I got the passports, he could tell by the smile on my face and how relaxed my demeanor was. I called Olu immediately and thanked him.

"Olu! Oh Olu, thank you! Thank you so much, Olu! You are my angel. Thank you, Olu. I do not care about the divorce case anymore. I am going away with my children. I am leaving right away, Olu. I am taking the boys to Guinea. We will wait there until we can get a flight to America. Don't say anything to anyone, Olu. We're out of here!"

"I will act exactly how they have acted. I will initiate no communication. I am leaving for Bo in the morning anyway, so if they call my office or come by, I will be conveniently gone. Take care of yourself and the boys, Zhu-zhiski. I told you God was on your side, didn't I?"

"Oh yes! Thank you, Olu! I will let you know when we make it to Guinea."

"Sounds good. I love you, Zhu-zhiski! Take care of yourself, dearest."

I called Sadia and Saana to break the news to them. They were over the moon for me. Saana volunteered to get the taxi that would take us to Guinea. Steven said he would come with us to Guinea and stayed until we left for the US. I told Sadia to get the boys ready. Steven and I went home to get a few items, just some things to fit in a backpack and my handbag. I got some of the boys' underwear and clothes in the back pack and put my address book, a bottle of children's Motrin, some of my jewelry and makeup in my handbag and told Steven I was ready.

"What about this big, nice suitcase? What about these shoes? Look at all your shoes and clothes, Zhu-Zhu. At least take-"

"Steven! Focus! We are running away, we are sneaking. I don't want anything that will make them notice we are leaving. I want this room to remain as it is. Do not worry about my shoes or clothes, I can get more when I get to America. None of this is important to me anymore. Now, stop looking at them like you're Lot's wife and let's just focus and get out of here."

I could tell from Steven's expression that he couldn't believe I was leaving all my valuables behind. I didn't care about anything I was leaving;. I was focused on getting my boys out of Sierra Leone safely.

After we got to Sadia's house, Saana called to say he was on his way with the taxi that will take us to Guinea. Sadia begged me to go to the Guinean embassy next door to her house and get Guinean visas for the boys.

"That would make it less stressful for you, Zhu-Zhu, please. The people at the border can be difficult. What if they give you problems? I am insisting that you go get them visas."

I agreed with her and we went to the embassy and Sadia paid $150 for the boys' visas. When we returned home the taxi was waiting for us. I finally told the boys we were leaving Freetown and would be in America not very long. Sankara ran and hugged me so tightly. His brothers came after and we all hugged each other. Sadia and Saana couldn't help tearing up.

"Okay, okay boys, go say goodbye to your friends."

I hugged Sadia tightly and thanked her for everything. She told me to be careful and to take care of the boys. However, we couldn't let each other go. Our voices quivered when we continued to speak, both of us were crying and maybe for different reasons. I think Sadia was crying because she felt powerless that she could no longer help us and wasn't sure what lied ahead for me and the boys. I was crying because she had been nothing short of an angel to us and had been there exactly at the right time when we needed help. Saana hugged me tightly and then opened the car door for us. He put some money in my hands and told me he had already paid the driver for the trip from Freetown all the way to Guinea.

"Steven, take care of them okay? Make sure nothing happens to them," Saana said to Steven.

Steven nodded. "I will bro, I will be with them until they return to America."

And just like that, we were on our way from Freetown and away from Ollie. I knew he was going to be devastated when he finally realized we had left, but I didn't care anymore. The James Baldwin quote I had studied my last semester came to mind immediately. "People who treat other people as less than human must not be surprised when the bread they have cast on the waters comes floating back to them, poisoned." It was so strange to me because for the first time, I wasn't putting his interests first. I was in survival mode. I had no idea how we were going to make it to America, but this was a good first step. The children were happy in the car. I saw their eyes light up and shine for the first time since we arrived in Freetown. There was so much hope and endless possibilities in those eyes and their smiles warmed my heart. I sat in the back seat with all three of the boys, while Steven sat in the passenger seat in front. As we were getting close to Waterloo, Sankara's phone rang. His dad had given him a phone during their last visit, so he could reach him directly. He looked at the Caller ID. It was their Uncle Simmy. I told him to answer it.

"Hi Uncle Simmy!"

"Hi Sankara, how are you guys? Your dad is here with me, hold on."

"Hi Sankara. Are you guys having fun?

"Yes, dad. We are with Mom."

"Yes, I know that. Look, tomorrow your Uncle Simmy will pick up all three of you and I will be taking you all to Number 2 beach. You guys are going to love it! It is so beautiful, better than Lumley beach."

"Alright dad."

"Alright, buddy! I will see you guys tomorrow."

"Ok, dad. Bye."

"Bye, Sany."

As soon as Sankara hung up the phone, we all started laughing.

"He'll see you guys, alright! In America one day. Zhu-Zhu, you were right about Sankara, this boy is really smart. I was always nervous he would say the wrong thing or give something away unintentionally," Steven noted.

"I know my child. I know he wants to return to America more than anything, so I know he will not ruin it for himself or for us. I remember the terror I saw in his eyes when I broke the news to him that we were relocating. His little heart was broken. And for his parents to come here and the focus not be solely on acclimatizing them, that's traumatic. Upon leaving Tennessee, none of us besides Ollie prepared for physical abuse from him and his other relatives. We did not plan to come to an unfinished house, to have his mother in our house, to have our provisions seized by her and only rationed out to us. I did not plan to be incommunicado with my own husband. I didn't know he would separate from me after practically begging me to make this move with him and leaving everything behind including my education. I did not plan to be without money and at the mercy of people. I did not plan for a grown man like you to sleep in the same room with me and my children for me to feel protected from him and God knows who else. I did not plan on hiring lawyers for a divorce. Heck, I did not plan to run away but here we are."

"God saw all this before it happened, Zhu-Zhu. He knew your heart. You shall prevail. This is only the beginning."

The boys were sleeping an hour into the almost six hours drive to Conakry, Guinea. When the driver stopped to get some gas in Port Loko, I woke the boys up so they could stretch their feet and look at the scenery which was much different from Freetown. There were more thatched houses in Port Loko and the locals were speaking temne. The petty traders were selling a range of goods, from palm wine to cassava bread, to fry-fry, to boiled ground nuts, to popcorn to ros-beef. Sankara pointed to the lady under the shade of a mango tree fanning the hot flame coals on her make-shift stove top grill. She had some already grilled ros-beef she set aside as she mounted some more on the grill.

"Mommy, can we have some?" Sankara asked.

I instinctively replied, "Of course, you can have some," but then I realized we were running away and I had only limited funds. I had the money Saana gave to me and also what Olu had given to me from time to time. I had no idea how much exactly. But it would be about $150 to $200, hardly enough to take care of us. I was going to call my dad and brothers to see if they could send us some money and also to find out about his call to Prof Nambuya. I had so many missed calls from my dad which I had yet to return.

"You know, Sankara..." I began, but then Steven, noticing what I was about to do, interrupted me and said, "Sany, you boys can have all the ros-beef you want, let's go!" They all ran to Steven and I saw them skipping to the ros-beef seller with reckless abandon. I looked at them looking so relieved and happy and just being children. My heart was full. This was exactly what I wanted for the boys, for them to enjoy their childhood, for them not to carry the burden of brokering peace between adults, for them not to grow up too fast but to be oblivious to the pangs of adulthood, of the real world, of the passage of time. I wanted them to use their imagination like Barney taught them to, to go to fantastic places where dinosaurs are purple and one can sing and play with them and Clifford the Big Red Dog can talk to children. I wanted them to be pure, their minds not corrupted. I wanted them to be unaware of the imperfect world we live in while they were still very young children.

I called my dad while the children were eating their ros-beef to let him know we had escaped. I could hear the very loud cheer from my mom as well who was listening in on the conversation. Dad had good news as well, he had spoken to Professor Nambuya and she had vowed to keep her promise to me. She asked dad how many of us would need help and my dad had told her it would be the four of us. It was a tall order because she had only promised to help me, I never interpreted what she told me to include more than me, but she told dad she would raise some funds with the other professors and students and would let him know how much they came up with. I told dad to call her on Monday and let her know we had escaped and were stranded and wanted to get out as soon as possible before we got discovered.

The driver beckoned for us to get back in the car to continue the journey to Guinea. There were only a few hours left before we made it to Guinea. Ollie wasn't going to find out we had not returned home until the next day. The thought of it immediately put me in panic mode. I couldn't relax like I wanted to. I felt a cold sweat run down my brow. I had never been to Guinea before. Steven knew someone who agreed to let us spend the night with them before we set out in search of Monsieur Barry's house the next day.

The next few hours of driving went by quickly because it was night time and there weren't many cars on the road.

"Welcome to Conakry," the driver announced as we approached the border. I got out our passports to show the border security who just scrolled through them and waved for us to drive on through. Conakry was pretty dark from the blackout that night. The driver stopped at the address Steven gave him and I woke the boys up.

"Sany, Shareef, Saami, wake up guys. We're in Guinea! We're no longer in Freetown. We're in Guinea now," I told them.

"When are we going to be in America?" Saami asked as he rubbed his little eyes.

"Soon, baby, soon. We're going to spend some time in Guinea but we will be in America soon, okay, baby?"

"Okaaaaay," Saami replied as he held my leg.

"Shareef, come here. What's wrong, why are you so dull?" Shareef didn't reply but came and held my other foot. "Your hands feel so warm, Shareef. Are you ok?" I asked him

"I just feel so weak," he said.

"My gosh, I think you have a fever, Shareef. I have some children's motrin in my bag. Let's go inside and I will give you some."

Steven stayed behind to talk to the driver and a few minutes later, I heard his car zoom away. Steven's friend was by the door waiting for us. He welcomed us and showed us our room. It was a small three bedroom house, sparsely furnished. There was a kerosene lamp in the living room because of the blackout they were experiencing that night. No sooner had Kortoh said he was going to get another lamp for our bedroom, the electricity came on.

"Oh, you guys have brought the electricity with you. You have good luck," Kortoh said.

"Well, I hope our luck continues and doesn't run out. We really need it."

"There is a fan in your room. Steven told me you guys are from America, I know the heat will bother you a lot, so feel free to use the fan now that the light is back on".

"Thank you so much, Kortoh. My son here is having a fever. The fan will help a great deal."

We entered the guest bedroom and Kortoh had it cleaned with a gara bedsheet on the bed. There were water stains on the walls, but the room didn't smell moldy. There was a small table by the window and a sleeping mat beside the bed. I laid Sankara and Saami who were still sleepy on the bed. I told Steven to wet one of the towels I brought with us and bring it back. I gave Shareef some of the motrin and started fanning him. I put the wet towel on his chest after I took his shirt off. Steven told me he will be sleeping on the couch in the living room every night until we leave for America.

I turned the fan on and had it oscillating, then I turned off the lights and tried to fall asleep with Shareef next to me. It was a difficult night because Shareef's fever would ease for a few hours and come back even worse. I kept giving him the motrin, but was afraid of what would happen if we ran out. By 11 a.m my phone started ringing. I got a call from Olu who was conveniently in Bo on business. He said Simmy had called him asking about us and he told him he had nothing to say to him that would not violate client/lawyer privileges. Olu said he had not even told his own mother who was the closest person to him about our whereabouts. Later, Sadia called and said Ollie and Simmy had just left her house looking for us. She said she gave them the note I wrote before I left her house. Sadia had asked me to write a note saying goodbye to her as if I went to say goodbye but had missed her. I had written: "Dearest Sadia, I cannot thank you enough for everything you did for me and the boys. I am so grateful. The American embassy has given us our passports and we are leaving for America right away! It was urgent and we had to leave immediately. I just stopped by to say thank you and to say goodbye to your boys. I will call you once we reach America. Zhuri."

Sadia said Ollie had stormed out after seeing the note. "This is just a ploy. They have not left for America. They're still here! She must be hiding at some boyfriend's house with my children. I will find her! Wait till I find her! They cannot be on their way to America, there was an injunction, she has no money for airfare. She has nothing!"

"I have nothing else to tell you, Dr. Jones. This was the note my gateman gave me when I returned from service yesterday," Sadia said she told him.

"Your friend is playing with the wrong person, the wrong person. Wait till I find her, just wait till I find her!"

Sadia said he stormed away and asked Simmy to take him to someone else's place. He tried calling my phone, Sankara's phone, and Steven's phone, but none of us answered. Later Saana texted me. "The devil just left my house. I told him he better find you guys after he came looking for you. Please make sure you leave Conakry as soon as you can." My contact with all three of them made me very afraid. It was very real that Ollie was actively searching for us. I knew I had to go find my father's old friend, Monsieur Barrie's house to see if he could hide us until we found a plan to safely leave Conakry. Ollie was desperate and would do whatever it took to discover us. I became paranoid that someone might crack under pressure and tell him where we were, not Saana, not Sadia, but maybe the taxi driver who took us, or someone who knew Steven's whereabouts. I knew we had to move fast! Surely Monsieur Barrie who was a retired Major in the Guinean army would be able to help us. My dad and Monsieur Barrie knew each other after he, my mom and brothers fled to Guinea during the civil war in Freetown. He was impressed that dad could easily speak french, so they became fast friends, surely he must be able to hide us until we confirmed travel arrangements to the US.

MONSIEUR BARRIE

"Zhuri!!! Comment ca va? Ca va bien?" Monsieur Barrie asked how I was doing in his native French as he got up and hugged me, followed by his wife Madame Barrie and their five children.

"S'asseoir!" He told me to sit down, pointing to an empty couch in the living room. My boys immediately followed me. I struggled to speak the very little French I knew to thank him and tell him I was fine and these were my boys with me. "Merci, merci beaucoup. Je suis très bien, merci. Je parle un petit peu de français. Ce sont mes fils, tous les trois".

"Ils sont beaux, tres beaux," Madame Barrie chimed in saying my boys were handsome.

"Merci, merci beaucoup. Je... je.." I tried to start telling him why we were there, but they saw I was struggling, so they called their daughter Umu who was in university studying English to become an English teacher. "Ne t'inquiete pas, Zhuri. Umu parle anglais et français. Elle sera notre interprète."

"Hi Umu. Please let your parents know that even though I said I was fine, we are not really fine." Umu translated what I said and I noticed a worried look on their faces. I explained our ordeal to Umu bit by bit as she translated everything I said. At certain points, they would sigh collectively, other times they would gasp in disbelief, yet in other parts of the translation, they would say, "Ah, non!'

Madame Barrie was so moved, she got up from her chair and came to hug me. "Tout ira bien." She assured me that everything would be alright and that I had come to the right place. She said nobody would bother us in their house.

"Mom is getting a room ready for you and your boys. She doesn't want you to leave the house, if that is fine with you, Zhuri".

"That is perfectly fine. I just want the boys and I to be safe until we can leave Guinea," I answered. "We will try to do our best to stay out of your way so they do not bother you, but they are such good boys." After Umu translated what I said, Monsieur Barrie said, "Oh, don't be silly my dear Zhuri. We have raised five children ourselves. We understand children. Do not worry about anything. You are safe here, completely safe. Usually, my security is only here at night, but I will tell them to take turns being here during the days and nights. Do not worry, nobody will bother you in this house. Now, come over to the dining table and eat. Madame Barrie is bringing food for you and the kids. Umu, show her to the guest room."

Umu led the way to a narrow hallway which led to the guest room. It was painted light blue, and had a huge king size bed in the middle with gara sheets and matching pillow cases. There were two night stands on either side of the bed, and a big built-in closet made from oak. Instead of a fan, the air conditioner was blowing cool air.

"I love this room, mommy! Can we just stay here and not go back to the other house?" Sankara asked.

"That's okay, Sany. We will stay here until we can leave. It is safer here. The house is enclosed by a high fence and there is security always by the gate. Now, I just need all three of you to be good, okay? Don't jump around, don't throw things, don't spill juice on the floor, just be the good boys I know you all to be. Shareef, your fever is still high, so I will bathe you first and have you take another dose of motrin."

"But I don't like medicine, mommy," Shareef protested.

"I do not like medicine either, Shareef, but you have to drink it so you can get well. Come on, take a quick shower, then go eat some of the delicious food Madame Barrie is setting up and then take your medicine. Ok my baby?"

I washed Shareef and put him in a big white t-shirt that Madame Barrie laid on the bed. She has brought some of her husband's t-shirts so the boys could have a change of clothes.

By the time we got back out to the dining room, Madame Barrie had a huge spread of food for us on the table; yestisse fish stew, kansiye with rice, salad, soft drinks and fried chicken. We were so hungry. However, the boys were not familiar with the other foods, so I was relieved when they started eating the chicken and drinking the soft drinks.

Madame Barrie came out with an arm full of traditional African gowns and dresses. She told Umu they were for me and would buy some clothes for the boys in the morning.

"Please tell your mom I cannot thank her enough. I wasn't expecting all this, only a place to hide. But the food, the bedroom, the added security, the clothes. Please tell your parents that I am very grateful."

"Ah! Non! Ne t'en fais pas! Tu es une famille." Monsieur Barrie told me not to worry about it. He said I was family.

I felt really relieved for a while. Now all we had to do was wait for Shareef's fever to go away and hear from Prof Nambuya. I just had to hear from Prof Nambuya to see what progress was on her end. Shareef's fever wasn't going away and I didn't want him hospitalized in Guinea.

PROFESSOR NAMBUYA

I asked the family to excuse us after eating and immediately called dad to ask how far he has gotten with Professor Nambuya with regards to her promise to help me. He said he had just talked to the professor andthat she asked for my contact in Guinea, and had promised to call me after her last class in about an hour.

"It sounds very promising, Zhu-Zhu! She seems ready to do whatever it takes. Make sure to take care of the boys, especially Shareef. Don't worry too much about how you're getting back here, just know that it is about to happen," my dad tried to reassure me. After talking to my dad, I went back to the dining room to clean up after ourselves. However, it was all clean by the time I returned. I was looking forward to hearing from Professor Nambuya as I was ready to stress the urgency of our situation. My thoughts were all over the place. I was scatter-brained and about 30 minutes later, just like a dream, my phone rang. It was a U.S telephone number. Surely it had to be Professor Nambuya.

"Hello?" I answered on the second ring.

"Hello! Zhuri? I'm trying to reach Zhuri Jones please."

"Prof! This is Zhuri. It's me, thank you for calling."

"Zhuri! My gosh! Are you okay? What about the kids? Are you safe?"

"Prof! Yes, we are safe, at least for the moment. We arrived in Guinea yesterday. My second son, Shareef, is sick. He has this constant fever that won't go away. I am scared, Prof. I have called friends in Freetown and word is, my husband is in hot pursuit of us. We have to leave here as soon as possible. Please help us! You were right about him, Prof. You were right. He had other motives, he wasn't-"

"Zhuri!" Professor Nambuya cut in, "I am sorry to hear all this, but I don't want to be right at your expense. I really wish things were different. So, there's four of you needing to get out fast, right?"

"Right! Myself and my three boys. I am so nervous, Professor Nambuya. I am terrified. I don't want him to catch us and I don't want Shareef to get worse here in Guinea. I have no money and I don't speak the language. I will never forgive myself if anything happens to Shareef."

"Zhuri, I need you to breathe. This is not just your battle, okay? I don't want you feeling overwhelmed. You have enlisted other people who have your best interest at heart. People who really want to help you and are doing everything possible to help you. So, do not burden yourself with anxiety. Now, I thought I would be helping only you, but as it turns out one person has turned into four people. I have $2500 I want to send. However, I called the airlines and the cheapest flight from Guinea to the US is via Air Maroc. It will be about $4000 for all four of you. I am going to do a little fundraising with a few other professors, that is if you don't mind me telling them about your ordeal. I want to get your permission first," Professor Nambuya explained.

"Professor, please do whatever you can. No, I don't mind you telling them. Also, there is a really good friend of mine at the university named Keza Mugisha. He is African as well, originally from Rwanda. He would likely help if he knew what was going on. So, please locate him and let him know. You can ask Professor West about him. We were in her Intro to Psychology class together and she liked him very much. She will know how to reach him."

"Excellent! I will ask Prof West as soon as I get off the phone with you. It will be better to speak to Keza first and see what we come up with before I tell the other professors, you know, I'm trying to contain this as much as possible. You and your boys deserve privacy," Professor Nambuya said.

"Thank you so much, Prof!" I said with relief and gratitude. "Also, you have my permission to give Keza my number should he ask for it. Please make it quick, Prof. I trust you will. I don't know how I got myself into this mess. I cannot believe I am in Guinea, I cannot believe I am in the middle of nowhere, I cannot believe I am a fugitive."

"Zhuri, life happens fast! And you're doing the best you can to make the best of what life has turned out to be. It has not stopped you in your tracks. You are not paralyzed with fear, even though you're afraid. Being afraid is natural, but you're doing everything you need to do while still afraid. That is so badass of you! You were afraid but you fought back, you were afraid but you went to the embassy, you were afraid but you fled to Guinea, and you're still afraid while trying to get out of Guinea. You are a brave woman, a strong woman, a smart woman, a beautiful woman and very soon, a free woman." I could hear the pride in her voice as she tried to encourage me.

"Pheeeeeewwww! Thanks Prof! I hate the word strong, but I'll take it."

"Why do you hate it? Why do you hate being called strong," she asked.

"I hate it because agony, suffering, trauma, heartbreak all precede it. It's almost like you have to earn being called strong by actually enduring and coming out of distress to get that badge. It's just a Zhuri thing. Maybe it doesn't make sense, but it's just how I feel."

"And your feelings are valid! What a smart thing to say! What a perspective to have! I've never heard it expressed this way. But it makes perfect sense. Unfortunately, we do have to earn being called strong. But what's the alternative? The alternative will be falling apart or giving up. Your children are going to be proud that you were strong not only for yourself but also for them. So, don't hate the word too much. Use it to your advantage. It's serving you well right now. Use the hell out of it!" she told me with so much resolve in her voice.

"Thanks Prof. I am still in shock. I don't know if I did everything in my power to help my husband not be this way. He wasn't raised by his father, so he doesn't know how to be a husband or a father. It wasn't modeled for him, you know. I thought if only I loved him right, loved him harder, I thought my love was going to-"

"Zhuri, it is not your job or any other woman's job to fix a broken man. It is his job to want to be the very best version of himself that he can ever be. It is his job to fix himself, so that he can show up well-equipped for the roles he chooses, a husband, a father. It is his job not to spill his brokenness unto other people, especially those closest to him. The right woman encourages and supports a man doing the work of bettering himself, but a woman's love is not a substitute for the counselling and therapy that a broken man needs. Your love, no matter how powerful you think it is or how potent you give it, will not fill the hole in his soul. He has to want to do the inner work. A therapist can try to help him do the work for his own restoration, but he has to participate fully in the process. There is just so much anyone can do for him; you, a therapist, his friends, support only works when he recognizes he has to do the work of seeking answers for the things in his life that trouble him. So, do not spend one more minute blaming yourself for issues he should have dealt with before he met you or should have been working through while he had your support."

"All those times I tried to love him and he rejected me time after time. It affected my self-esteem. It made me cry, it-"

"Zhuri, what you must learn, and this is also something I had to learn the hard way. What you must learn is, nobody has your worth and value in their hands unless you make it so. He can toss you aside like he just recklessly did, but it is on you to know that you're valuable. He can call you ugly, but you have to know you're beautiful. He thought you were dumb and naive and you've now outsmarted him, you have proven your astuteness. He minimizes your abilities, but you know of your own strength and capabilities. So, it doesn't matter what he thinks as long as you do not think that way about yourself. His rejection does not mean you are ugly, undesirable, undeserving. It meant he was cheating on you, it meant he didn't value what he had at home, it put his marriage in jeopardy. That has nothing to do with your looks. It's a flaw in his character," Professor Nambuya explained.

"He was supposed to love me, he owed me his love and devotion, his commitment. He made a vow to forsake everyone else. I felt entitled to that love because I was promised just that, before God and man." I said matter of factly.

"Zhuri, I see we will have lots to talk about when you come back here. I used to feel that same way. I thought my ex-husband owed me love, fidelity and commitment, after all that's what the marriage vows entail. However, as much as it would be nice if he had honored his vows, I started thinking about it this way: I am not entitled to anything someone can easily take away. Love is a gift and a privilege. It is not an entitlement. Just as much as he chooses to love me, he can also choose not to love me. The hurt comes when I feel deeply entitled to something

I have no control over. Since then, I choose to revel in love when I get it. My current husband gives me love and I value it so much because I see it as a gift he chooses to give to me everyday. I feel privileged that he chose me to give it to. But if he were to take it away, I would not like it, but it would not diminish me because my value doesn't depreciate just because his love for me ceases."

"I guess I know what you mean, it's just that rejection can be so hurtful. In spite of your best efforts and doing everything right, you still get rejected."

"That's because acceptance is mostly not merit based. Have you ever met a couple whose partner treats them well and you think to yourself, what is she doing that I'm not doing? Sometimes you meet a man who absolutely adores his wife who absolutely does nothing. She may have multiple nannies helping with their children, staff cleaning their fabulous home, a private driver, chef and all the other luxuries and her husband worships her, yet, another woman may be struggling to take care of multiple children, work full time, come home after work tired and still do homework, laundry,cook dinner, iron and get no respect, appreciation or acknowledgement from her partner. Rejection is never about you, Zhuri. Good people are rejected all the time by people who do not appreciate, value them, or know their worth. A person who doesn't know how to love will always break your heart, and a person who doesn't value what he has will always lose it in the end. None of it will have anything to do with who you actually are as a person. People choose unhealthy, fattening, calorie-laden meals over healthy, savory meals all the time. The rejection of the healthy option doesn't make it less valuable. It is still the better option loaded with nutritious vitamins, healthy fats, high in fiber, proteins and antioxidants. Consider rejection as a matter of preference, some people just have poor taste. Your husband's taste is just woefully horrible".

"Hahaha! I wasn't going to laugh but that really is funny. What can we do about people with poor taste? It's not our responsibility to fix their palate, huh? We just go where the people with the great tastes are."

"Well, look who's getting it! Another adult is not your responsibility. What I will tell you to work on is self love. Learn to love yourself first, Zhuri. It's not selfish, it's self care. After you have learned to love yourself, you will have no patience for anyone who does not bring you peace or treats you less than you deserve. Some time back, I thought I had become impatient with everyone. But then I thought about it, I was not being impatient, I've just fallen in love with myself so much I lack patience for anything less than exquisite or magnificent. You will get there, Zhuri. Now listen, I am so happy I got to talk to you. I wanted to make a determination about your mental and psychological health. You seem to be doing fine. I am heading to Professor West's office to find out about Keza. I will call you back tomorrow and tell you how we will proceed. And no need to repeat it, sweetie, I already know how urgent it is to get you and the kids out of Guinea. I will do everything I can."

"Pheeeeeeeewwwww! Thank you so much Professor Nambuya! I really cannot thank you enough. I look forward to talking to you tomorrow. Thank you again from the bottom of my heart." As I hung up the phone, I breathed a long sigh of relief.

Professor Nambuya called Professor West's office and asked her if she knew a student by the name of Keza Mugisha. Professor West helped her locate him in the library, a tall, dark athletic built young man in his early twenties, with cropped twisted hair, blue jeans and a dashiki shirt. She asked Keza to go with her to her office where he told him everything that had happened to me. She said Keza got up from the chair he was sitting in shock and anger. She then told me all about their conversation.

"Keza, did Zhuri ever confide in you about her home life, about her marriage?"

"Yes, she told me about that loser husband of hers. I really never understood why a beautiful woman like her was ever with him or putting up with his bullshit. Sorry, I mean putting up with his crap. Zhuri has the most beautiful soul, gorgeous body, infectious laugh, incredibly brilliant, I could go on and on, but what's happened to her, I hope that her lousy husband hasn't hurt her. I will kill him with my own hands, I will-"

"Keza!" Professor Nambuya quickly interrupted him. "Zhuri is fleeing from him as we speak. He did abuse her, she has left him in Sierra Leone and has fled to Guinea with their three boys. She is in hiding and he is in hot pursuit. It is imperative that we get Zhuri and the children out of Guinea before he locates them. I have $2500 that I will send to Zhuri to help with airfare, but she has her boys too and she is not leaving without them. Airfare for all of them will be about $4000. I was hoping we could do a fundraiser with students and staff to raise the rest of the funds," Professor Nambuya explained to Keza.

"We will do no such thing," Keza stated matter of factly. "Her and her kids deserve their privacy. We will not divulge her situation to the student body and staff. Fuck all that! I mean, nah! I will give you the rest of the money. I worked last summer and saved some money. I also get a sizable monthly allowance. I will withdraw $1500 and give it to you. When do you need it? When will it be available for Zhuri? We have to act very fast. How soon can Zhuri leave? Where is she now, how is she coping, who is taking care of them?"

"Here! This is the number to reach her. She said I can give it to you." Professor Nambuya wrote my number on a piece of paper and gave it to Keza.

"Thank you! But first things first, I'm going to run to the bank now. It's just around the corner. I'll be right back with my share of the money." Keza got up to leave.

"Keza! Thank you for being a good friend to Zhuri. Thank you for showing up for her when it really matters. I'll be here for the next hour then I have a class afterwards.

"No problem, I will be back before you know it."

The next day, Mrs. Nambuya called and gave me a MTCN code for a Western Union transfer and another code for Moneygram. Apparently, it was impossible to send $4000 all at once through Western Union or Moneygram, so she sent the maximum thousand dollars per day through both of them and said she would do the same the next day. I couldn't believe my professor and my classmate, who I haven't known for too long, were helping me in such a big way. I called Umu and told her I needed her to translate to her father that I would be needing him to come with me the next day to pick up $4000 after the professor called me with the transfer pick up codes. I told Monsieur Barrie I was to pick up the money and then go straight to the Air Maroc ground office to purchase our tickets.

Monsieur Barrie smiled and said, "Je suis à votre service, Zhuri."

"Merci, Monsieur Barrie, merci pour tout," I thanked Monsieur Barrier for everything.

"Pour rien, je te vois dans la matinée," he said I didn't need to thank him and that he would see me in the morning. When we went to bed that night, I told the boys that we were very close to leaving for America.

"When are we leaving, mom, when?" Sankara asked.

"I will know by tomorrow. We will have a date tomorrow," I told them.

"Tomorrow?" Sankara asked, his eyes lighting up the room withexcitement all over his face. I had not seen him this happy since we left America. I was so relieved he was becoming the same happy, inquisitive Sankara I used to know. Shareef was laying on me, still witha slight fever. He forced a quick smile at the news and laid his head on my chest. Saami has already fallen asleep. I prayed with them, then turned out the light and slept.

KEZA

At about 4am in the morning, my phone rang from a US telephone number, but different from the one Professor Nambuya used the day before. I picked it up very fast so it wouldn't wake up the boys. I tiptoed to the bathroom and said under my breath, "Hello?"

"Hello! Zhuri?! Fuck! Did I call at the wrong time? The time difference! This is Keza!"

I smiled a bit. "Of course it's Keza! Who else would call me and say fuck?"

"Ha! Zhuri! Are you okay? What about the boys, are they okay? Please tell me that dude hasn't done too much damage to you. I want to fly to Sierra Leone to kick his ass. Fucking coward! Why didn't he pull all that bullshit right here? Why pull it when you are with a woman and little boys. That's some premeditated, cowardly shit! Someone needs to burst a cap in his ass-"

"Keza! No time for that now. We need to get away from him first. Thank you so much, the professor told me about your contribution. I do not know how to thank you, Keza. I honestly cannot thank you enough."

"No need for thank yous. I told Professor Nambuya I would send the remaining funds this morning. She has lectures this morning. I have some money transfer pick up codes for you to get the money from Western Union and MoneyGram. But if it's too early and you cannot find a pen, I can call back when you're up properly."

"Hold on, Keza! Time is of the essence here. I cannot let you get off this phone without getting those codes. I will quietly walk to the living room. I saw some pens on one of the tables in the living room yesterday". I tiptoed quietly into the living room, turned the light on and grabbed one of the pens on the table in the corner.

"I have a pen right here, Keza! Please give me the numbers."

Keza gave me the money transfer codes and repeated them three times. Then he asked me to read them back to him. After we confirmed every detail, he assured me, "Zhuri. This money is a gift from me to you.

You do not have to pay it back. I just want you and your boys to be safe. How soon do you think you can get back here?"

"The very first flight we can get. Air Maroc only flies out of Guinea a couple of times a week or so. The next flight out of here will have me and my boys in it. Thank you very much, Keza, for your kindness and generosity. Words really fail me. I cannot begin to tell you what this gift means to me and my boys. You have given us so much! You have given us hope, escape, a second chance and new opportunities. I didn't know how I was going to get to America with three children in tow after having been stripped of everything. But, I knew I wanted better for me and my boys. I knew I wasn't going to settle for the life he thought I had no choice but to resort to and settle for. I knew I was better than that. I knew my boys deserved better. They needed to be happy and not be stressed out by a traumatic change of life from how they once knew it. They did not deserve quarrelling parents, a medling, vicious grandmother, strange relatives coming to threaten their mother, running after their father so he wouldn't hurt their mother, fearing for their mother's life and safety. I just want them to be carefree, Keza. Happy and carefree, with no worries of the adult world to think about. I want them to be free, to have opportunities, but most of all, for them to be happy."

"Zhuri, I read somewhere that whenever you have the courage to take one step towards your goal, the universe takes 150 steps towards you. The universe arises and aligns with you. It becomes your ally. You could've felt sorry for yourself, you could've lived your entire life saying 'my professor warned me,' you could've tried to accept your new normal, no matter how miserable it made you feel. But you rose up! Your spirit said fight! And even though the odds were stacked against you, you never stopped believing. I was thinking about how revolutionarily badass you are! This was your reasoning, Zhuri: 'No passports? Can't stop me. No money? Can't stop me. No belongings? Can't stop me. No house to return to? Can't stop me. No car? Can't stop me.' Do you know how badass that is? Do you know how much chutzpah that took? You had the temerity, the absolute gall to defy that chauvinistic pig and the nerve to say, fuck all this deeply ingrained societal misogyny and patriarchial marlarkey. I'm getting out! I have seen better, I know better and I will settle for no less than I deserve and neither will I want my boys anywhere near it. You deserve a Nobel prize, Zhuri! That's some queen shit right there! You nubian queen, you! Remind me to bow when I see you! This right here, is what queens are made of," Keza said with satisfaction.

"Oh wow, Keza! You never cease to amaze me! Your encouraging words. Now I actually believe I can fly. Truth is, I never thought of it like you, just so perfectly articulated. I was just a desperate woman and mother who refused to be beat down and subdued by a man, society, or a system. My whole being became strong and rebellious. Anything less than would have been a defeat of my soul, my spirit, my being, my essence. I couldn't settle for that. It's ironic that instead of running towards my husband for protection, I am literally running from him for protection. He should have been our protector, our rock, instead he is the predator."

"Zhuri, have you ever heard of the term femicide? I was blown away when I heard that term. There is actually a term for the brutal murder of women because they dare want agency over their own lives. How dare they want to choose who they can fall in love with or who they can marry or what they can wear, whether or not they want to leave their relationships, carry a baby, or choose not to carry one. Women are killed every day by the fucking men who are supposed to protect them in the first place. Honor killings are the rage in some countries because women dare choose who they can have sex with and when they can have sex. Fathers and brothers kill their own daughters and sisters, husbands kill their wives. I am really just grateful that you are alive and fighting back. The boys are going to need a mentor, they're going to need a strong male role model in their lives. I volunteer at the boys and girls club. I will be available to take your boys to soccer practices, wrestling matches, boxing..."

I gasped. "Keza! Stop it! Those sports are so violent, I couldn't..."

"And that's exactly why you're going to need a male mentor, because you're not allowed to baby them. It was Michelle Rosenthall who said, 'Trauma creates change you don't choose. Healing is about creating change you do choose.' Those boys have been traumatized. You must be very intentional about their healing. Those Princes hail from a fiery queen who has nothing but is a few days away from gaining freedom for herself and them. Say no more your royal highness.".

"Keza! What am I ever going to do with you? You and your quotes. You're a walking encyclopedia. Thank you so much for everything. I have to tiptoes back to the bedroom now. You just made my morning by the way. You just made my whole day! Tell Prof I will let you both know about our travel plans as soon as I find out today. Thank you, Keza, thank you so, so much!"

"Don't mention it and please do not use any of that money to call us. We'll call you! I will call back in about eight hours. Stay safe, Queen Nzinga!"

"Queen Nzinga?" I asked, chuckling under my breath.

"Yes, Queen Nzinga. She was an Angolan warrior queen! She was ruthless, powerful and fearless. She fought for freedom and the stature of her kingdoms against the Portugese! This queen shit didn't start with you, Zhuri. It's in your bloodline. It just lays dormant in some women but for some like you, the blood of Queen Nzinga is alive and pulseasting. That's how you know who the queens are from the rest of them. Hahaha! I will call you in eight hours, queen!"

"Keza, you never cease to fascinate me with your stories. Now I have to read all about the original queen badass extraordinaire, Nzinga!"

"Hahaha, indeed! That's what I'm talking about. Talk to you soon, Zhu!"

I hung up the phone relieved that we now had the means to return to the US. Professor Nambuya and Keza came through! I went back to the bed with the biggest grin on my face and held my boys closer. We were just a few hours away from finding out when we would be back in America, back to Tennessee!

ESCAPE

I tried to sleep after I made my way back to the bed with the boys, but the excitement was overwhelming! I actually wasn't dreaming. I really had enough money to buy our airfares back to America, something that had seemed so far-fetched a few weeks ago. I wasn't certain about reclaiming the children's passports, let alone affording flights back. And now, just a few hours away, I would be in a travel agency getting four international flight tickets back to America! I looked over at my boys and smiled. I couldn't wait to tell them when they woke up.

The boys were still sleeping when I heard far in the distance, the adhan, a call to prayer in Muslim communities. The adhan is the first of five calls to prayer a day to remind Muslims to stop whatever they are doing and get ready for prayer at dawn, noon, mid afternoon, sunset and nightfall. To me, it was an indication that it was soon to be 7 a.m. I heard the Barries outside getting ready for dawn prayers. I got up and went to the bathroom to take a quick shower. I knew it would be breakfast time after they finished their prayers and then it would be time to go out and pick up the money transfers from Western Union and Moneygram.

I put on one of the dresses Madame Barrie gave to me, and it looked very beautiful. Madame Barrie was really tiny and the fact that I fitted so well in her dress made me realize how very thin I had gotten. When I walked out to the living room after their prayers in the dress, they all smiled so widely and Madame Barrie said, "Vous etes belle, tres belle." Even though Madame Barrie said I was beautiful, I did not feel beautiful. I was very self-conscious about my severe weight loss. I hardly had any breasts anymore, my butox wasn't as ample and pronounced, I could barely see my shapely curves, and I felt more like a famine victim. However, I was grateful for my keep and of course for my dress. "Merci, beaucoup. Vous etes gentil, tres gentil. Merci."

Monsieur Barrie told me that Umu was going to come with us, so that she could translate. But just then, my phone rang witha call from

Freetown. My heart skipped, but it was my cousin, Saana on the other line.

"Zhuri! How are you? How is Sankara and Saami and Shareef? Is Shareef feeling any better?" He asked.

"Shareef is not completely fever-free but otherwise, we're safe and doing as best as we can under this circumstance."

"Any word yet about your departure from Conakry?"

"I will know in just a couple of hours. We are about to leave for the day to get that accomplished."

I heard him sigh on the other line. "Look, I am trying to play it cool, but you have got to leave as soon as you can. Your husband is over here putting a lot of pressure. He has had several people arrested who he thinks might know where you are. I was just at the police station with your friend, Sadia. We had to turn ourselves in or be arrested. Both Sadia and I told them we know nothing about your whereabouts, but the sooner you leave, the better. He is in hot pursuit, whatever you are doing, do it fast."

My gut twisted. "I am so sorry, Saana."

"Don't worry about us, Zhu-Zhu! This is our stomping ground. We will handle things accordingly. You and the boys, however, do not know a thing about what these so-called law enforcement officers are capable of. Just get out soon!"

"I will. I will call you back as soon as I find out. I promise we will take the next flight out."

After I hung up, I explained to the Barries in broken French that my husband was putting pressure and looking around for us.

"Allons-y! Allons-y!!!" Monsieur Barrie said, let us go, let us go, as he led the way outside. I pointed to my bedroom indicating to Madame Barrie that the boys were still inside sleeping. She waved me away, "Aller! Aller! Je vais m'occuper d'eux." She told me to just go and she would take care of them. We got into the white Toyota SUV and the driver started talking to Mr. Barrie. I assumed he was asking him where we were going. We picked up the money in two different locations. It was the first time I ever had $4000 in cash. Our next destination was the Air Maroc ground office at the airport. Mr. Barrie told the agent that we needed to get on the next available flight to the U.S. Umu translated that the next flight was the next day at 11 p.m. The total came to $4050. Mr Barrie paid the difference and we hurried back into the car. I breathed a long sigh of relief as I held the tickets in my hand. Umu smiled at me and held my hand. "It is going to be alright, Zhuri. You are strong. You are going to be alright, you and the boys."

I started to thank Monsieur Barrie for his kindness and hospitality, but he didn't want to hear any of it. As far as he was concerned, he was taking care of one of his own. He said my dad would have done the same for one of his own children. I told him I would need to get some phone cards to call a few people in America and Sierra Leone before we left the next day. I needed to tell my dad, Professor Nambuya, and Keza about our travel itinerary. I also had to call Sadia and Saana in Freetown to let them know we were going to be leaving Conakry the next day, so they could stop worrying. Monsieur Barrie insisted he take me home safely first and then he'll send the driver to go get some phone cards for my international calls. "Vous ne pouvez jamais être trop prudent," he said one can never be too careful. I agreed with him. I wanted to get home as soon as possible so I could be with the boys who must be missing me as everyone around them were strangers.

Once the gateman opened and let the car in, Sankara came running towards the car. The driver stopped and let me out.

"Mom! Mom! Where have you been?" he asked as he hugged me.

"Just went out briefly, baby! Where are your brothers? How is Shareef?

"They are inside."

Once I got inside, I saw Shareef laying on the couch watching T.V and Saami was still in the dining room eating cornflakes.

"Reef! My Shareef, how are you feeling, my baby?" I rushed to the couch.

"I'm fine."

"No, baby, you're not fine. Your fever is back. My poor baby. Did you manage to eat something?"

"I ate some cornflakes."

"Okay, I'm going to give you some more of that children's motrin. I suspect you have malaria. You might need some chloroquine tablets."

"No, mommy! I am fine. I don't want any medicine."

"I know you don't want any medicine but you need some medicine, baby. I will make sure you do not taste the chloroquine. I have my tricks."

I asked Umu if they had some chloroquine tabs in the house, and she assuredme they did. Malaria was so common in West Africa that every household had malaria tabs just like people in America keep tylenol at home. I went to the refrigerator and got some fruit juice. I got the motrin from the bedroom and asked Shareef to just swallow the dosage I had on the measuring cup quickly. After he did, I gave him some juice. "Now Shareef, keep the juice in your mouth okay, do not swallow it yet. I am going to put one chloroquine tablet in your mouth, then swallow it with the juice and you won't taste it at all." Shareef was too weak to argue. I put one pill in his mouth and with one gulp, he swallowed it.

"Good boy! That's my baby! Now, drink some more juice, Shareef. Drink some more for mommy, okay? You are going to feel better soon."

I called Saami and Sankara as I took Shareef back to the bedroom. He needed to rest. As we all got in the door, I couldn't hold it any longer. "Guess what?"

"What? What? What?" Sankara asked, jumping up and down with a mischievous glee in his eyes.

"We are all going back to America tomorrow!"

"Yaaaaaaaaaaaaaaaay!!!" Sankara yelled loudly. Shareef broke out a weak smile, his eyes lighting up as he mouth. "What time?"

"What time? Little man, all you need to know is that we are going back tomorrow. What time? Do you have somewhere else to be?" I asked Shareef as I tickled him.

"Yes! The airport!" Sankara yelled.

"Ain't nobody asked you nothing, Sany! This is between me and Reef!"

Saami came and grabbed my leg. "I'm going to see my BFF tomorrow?" Saami asked me, referring to his grandpa who always called him his BFF.

"Yes, my baby! Pretty soon you will see your BFF and Tennessee and your friends at the Kingdom hall, just like it was before."

"Yaaaaaaaaaay!!! Sankara and Saami yelled in unison. It was the first time I had seen them be so carefree and happy since we left Tennessee.

Yes! My boys are back to their old selves, I thought to myself. *This is what I want for them, happiness, sheer, unadulterated happiness and freedom.* But as quickly as I was happy to see them be free and happy, I became saddened. I knew our family was no longer going to be the same anymore. And in some kind of twisted, bizarre way, I started missing their father. I still had a lot of love in my heart for him, and I started feeling sorry for him. He must've been so traumatized finding out his whole family had left him. We were all he ever had for almost twelve years. If only he hadn't been so calculating and abusive, then we all would've beentogether. Then as I had that thought, my phone rang. It was Professor Nambuya's number. I answered it very quickly. "Hello Prof."

"Hello Zhuri! How are you and the boys? How is the sick one? Getting better I hope?"

"We are fine, Prof! I just gave Shareef his medicine. I was going to tell you, I just bought our tickets. Our flight leaves at 11pm tomorrow night. Thank you so-"

"Oh stop with the thank yous, Zhuri! I am finally relieved! I have been so worried about you guys. I cannot wait to see you over this end. You're such a brave one, Zhuri. So brave, I'm trying hard not to say strong. I know how you hate that word."

"It's okay, Prof. I am going to step outside and speak to you, hold on." I told the boys to stay in the house while I went out to the compound. "Prof, are you there? I want to ask you something. Please do not judge me, not that you will, but please...something doesn't make sense to me."

"You are missing him already?" Professor Nambuya asked.

I tried to explain my conflicting feelings to Professor Nambuya. "How did you know? So, you're psychic too? I'm sorry, I am embarrassed to say so, but after I got our tickets and everything was all set, I was happy for a bit , but then this sunken feeling set in. I felt sad for him, for us, for our family. If only…"

"Your feelings are perfectly normal, Zhuri. No need to be embarrassed. They are by no means strange or wrong or humiliating. Why do you think so many abused victims keep going back to their abusers? It is more common than you can imagine. That which is familiar feels comfortable. Zhuri, how long were you with this man?"

"It would have been our 12th anniversary in five months."

"Zhuri, you know this man more than anybody else, which means, you also know his good qualities. He did not just become abusive overnight, which means you know his charming side, his tender side, his sensitive side and so many other virtues. What you felt for him was real and deep-seeded. You built a family with him for God's sake. The love you have for him is not going to go away just like that. There has been so much investment in your marriage, literal blood, sweat and tears. It is not easy to let go of all the ideas and plans you had for your family or of growing old together. It is a lot to let go of at once. It is also not wrong for loving a person for who you thought they could be. But most times, what you're missing is not really your ex but the internalized image you have created of them in your mind. It's how you wish things would have turned out if only they had chosen not to abuse. You have very high hopes for them. The Author Elizabeth Gilbert, in her book *Eat, Pray, Love* wrote so candidly about this. This is a quote from her that I love because I identify with it so much. '…I have the tendency not only to see the best in everyone but to assume that everyone is emotionally capable of reaching his highest potential. I have fallen in love more times than I care to count with the highest potential of a man, rather than the man himself. I have hung on to the relationship for a long time (sometimes far too long) waiting for the man to ascend to his own greatness. Many times in romance I have been a victim of my own optimism.' Can you relate to that?"

"Oh wow! Wow, wow, wow! That's exactly how I feel. I know he can be romantic if he tried, I know he can be faithful if he wanted to, I know he can be fiercely protective if only he wanted to. This doesn't make any sense. He has a good life, a beautiful, young wife who adores him, three incredible boys all healthy and happy, a thriving medical practice, patients who adore him, and is making good money. Why throw all of that away?"

"Zhuri, that is not your problem. You cannot love the abuse away! You cannot make him make your marriage and the children's happiness a priority. You cannot make him value all those things you just mentioned. He wants happiness on his own terms, not what is best for the whole family. Even if he wasn't physically abusing you, he didn't care about those countless nights you cried yourself to sleep at night, he didn't care about his children seeing him being violent to their mother. Think about it, does he feel bad about what he did to you or do you think he is feeling bad because of your reaction to what he did? Zhuri, the man is in a society now which enables and normalizes his behavior. His attitude towards abuse is going to be cavalier at best. There is no more 911 for you to call. There is no more losing his medical license if he lays his hands on you. There is no prospect of him going to jail or getting in any trouble whatsoever. Remember one time when you commented in my sociology class that there is a fable about the women of the temne tribe from your country, who think their husbands do not love them unless they beat them? There is some truth to that. Patriarchy has embedded in some women's psyche that a man beating you or hurting you in any way proves passion and care, that he really must love you, or else he wouldn't care. What he did was very calculated and intentional. It's not the actions of a man who wants to stop his behavior or wants to be accountable. It's the actions of a man who took his wife to an environment where this behavior is normalized, a man who wants to get away with his abusive and chauvinistic ways. It is not the actions of a man who has seen the light."

"I do not know why this is happening to me. I did nothing to deserve this. I was a great daughter. I did everything my parents told me to do, everything! I was a good wife, Prof. I swear I was! I did everything I could. My whole heart was in this marriage. So, why should this happen to me?" I asked frustrated and let out a long sigh.

"Zhuri, life isn't happening to you, baby girl, it's happening for you. Trust that life is happening for you. It's all about your perspective, sweet girl. You could say, I have such a long way to go, I have to start all over again. Or you can say I've come so far, all of which are true. But, whichever one you choose to emphasize is what's going to determine whether you're positive in life or negative. You could say life is happening to me or life is happening for me. The same thing is happening, but your perspective is what changes it to make it happy in the happening or sad in the happening. It's all how you look at it. Be intentional about your outlook and about becoming happy in this season of your life, Zhuri."

"I guess you're right, Prof. Do not get me wrong though, I may be unsure about my deep feelings for him, but what I am very sure about is knowing that I will no longer tolerate any abuse from him. I am also sure about not wanting my boys to be around any form of abuse. I do not want them to witness it or learn it actively or passively. I want the internalized Ollie I see in my mind, but since I cannot have him. I must learn to make peace with that. It's going to be really hard, but I can do this."

"Zhuri, sometimes the heart and the head are on different speeds. Usually the heart is slower to catch up with the head but it will get there eventually. There is going to be a lot that comes with this, a complete change of lifestyle. It's going to be a shock to your system but you're made for this. You have made the hardest decision by leaving. No one needs to endure or put up with abuse."

"I am so ready to leave tomorrow. I know if I were to return to Ollie tomorrow, nothing would change. He would be even worse than he already is. He would blame me for all his problems and treat me even worse for trying to leave. I am my own woman. I have agency over myself and my decisions. I am ready to start over."

"There you go! And if imagining how he would react petrifies you, it is a sure sign of an abusive relationship. In a healthy relationship, you think about having difficult conversations in times of conflict. But there is never any fear about a backlash, threats to harm, silent treatment or a beating. It will be just two adults figuring things out or going to therapy if the need arises. But there is never the fear of getting hurt physically or verbally. Conflicts become an opportunity to grow with your partner in a healthy relationship. It is not detrimental to it, rather it reveals things you both have to work on, it develops character. Zhuri, there will be times when you will miss him again and second guess yourself. That would be perfectly normal as well. But as time goes on, you will miss him less and less and then one day you will wake up and not miss him anymore. You can't imagine that possibility now, but the day will come when you will be blissfully happy and oblivious about his existence."

"Thank you so much, Prof. You have been more than a professor to me. You have been my mentor, my friend, my life-coach, my way to freedom. You are everything to me. Thank you for having the foresight to warn me, thank you for keeping your promise to help when it mattered most. You are my hero!"

"Are you kidding me?" Professor Nambuya chuckled on the other end. "You're mine! All I'm doing is sending money. That is the easy part. You have done the impossible. Your boys will thank you for it one day, my brave girl. Let me know when you make it back stateside. Have a great flight tomorrow."

Professor Nambuya always knew what to say and just what I needed. It was the perk that made me go back in the house and started packing the very little clothes we had. Madame Barrie gave me six dresses, my handbag, two panties, and the boys' clothes.

I called my dad and told him the happy news, and he started crying on the phone. I couldn't take it. I needed strength at this time. I told him I would call on our way to the airport the next day. Sadia and Saana were ecstatic that I was leaving the next day. They were afraid to talk to me for long for fear their phones may have been bugged by the phone company. They were not taking any chances about the length Ollie was capable of going.

I decided to spend time with the children telling them what to expect the next day and when we got to America. Sankara was too distracted with joy to sit still. He had already told everyone in the house he was going back to America. Madame Barrie then asked him if he would take her with him. "Yes! Everyone can come. You and you and you and you!"

Everyone laughed. They all wished they could say more to Sankara, but the language barrier kept the conversations short. The body language and sweet gestures were on full display. They could tell that we were more relieved than we were the day before. I could tell that they knew how grateful we were by the peaceful look on our faces, and how often I put my hands together in a praying stance and a bow of my head in their direction. Sometimes one doesn't need words to convey what can be easily seen by our body language.

Late in the evening when we were all gathered together watching TV to pass the time, my phone rang withKeza's number. I picked up and walked to our guest room.

"Hello Keza!"

"Tell me something good, Queen Nzinga!"

"Ha! Well, I'll have you know that this queen here is about to leave for the U.S with her princes tomorrow evening.".

"Yes! Oh my god, Zhuri! You fucking did it! You did the damn thing! You're so dope! You's a bad, bad chick!"

"Well, I'm nothing without my sidekicks. There is you and prof and Sadia and Saana and Olu and Steven to say the least. No one can do it alone, Keza. I am so blessed to have you guys, all of you."

"My part in this is so minimal, I can't dare to take any credit whatsoever! This is all you, Zhuri! Own that shit."

"Keza, your part may have been minimal but very necessary. No good deed was too little. They all culminated in what's about to happen tomorrow for me and my children. I cannot thank you enough. I hope you know how grateful I am."

"Well, I am grateful to know a queen in real life, a queen in flesh and blood, not the ones I read about in books. You are the real deal. I know you won't hardly sleep tonight, but please continue to stay safe until I see you again in Tennessee in the flesh," he said with emphasis and excitement in his voice.

"I cannot wait to see you soon, Keza!"

After we hung up, I got the boys ready for bed. By the time we wake up tomorrow, it will be only a few hours before we head to Gbessia International airport to get checked in and wait for our flight at 11pm.

The next day, I woke up but felt like I was floating in the sky. It was a surreal feeling. All my efforts had led to this moment. I got on my knees and thanked Jehovah in quiet tones. My boys were still asleep. The chloroquine had helped Shareef and his fever had all but gone. I went outside after the Barries were done with their morning prayers, and joined them for breakfast after Madame Barrie gestured for me to sit with them at the table.

"Merci, merci, merci beaucoup pour tout tout le monde," I thanked everyone for their kindness and hospitality. They all smiled widely and nodded their heads in acknowledgement. After breakfast, I hugged every single one of them.

Towards evening, Steven came to bid us goodbye. The boys were ecstatic to see him and jumped all over him. As for me, I pulled him away to talk, except I couldn't say a word. I just held him tightly, my head on his shoulder. He kept rubbing my back telling me it was his honor and obligation to help us. He told me he was proud of me and asked me to look after the boys. I continued to hold on to him, so tightly he could feel my heart beating. "Zhuri, I can feel your heart, I know your heart, but you have to get these boys ready for the airport. C'mon let me help you get them ready for the airport," Steven said as he pulled me back into the house. I got the boys dressed up in the jeans and t-shirt Madame Barrie had gotten them and Steven put their shoes on. We only had one bag to carry. Monsieur Barrie was coming with us to the airport. He said he would not leave until our plane ascended into the sky. I wore jeans and a red T-shirt and kept all the dresses Madame Barrie gave to me.

Once we made it to the airport and checked in, we still had about an hour and half before our flight was to leave. My boys became bored, then very sleepy. It was their bedtime even though we were waiting to board the plane. Monsieur Barrie and Steven weren't allowed where we were waiting, but they could still see us. All three of the boys were clinging to me, looking for any comfortable spot to lay their sleepy heads. I had Saami on my lap, Shareef's head on my chest and Sankara had his head on my shoulders. This was how it was going to be from now on. We were all we've got and we held on to each other for dear life.

When they called us to board, I woke up the boys and told them it was time to get on the plane. They were still very sleepy, so I carried Saami and asked Sankara to hold Shareef's hand and come with me. I sat in the middle seat once we were in the plane so Saami and Shareef could have access to each side of me. Sankara was seated in the seat in front of me, so that I could see him at all times. Saami and Shareef both leaned their heads on my body and continued sleeping. Sankara was fascinated by the little television screen in front of him. He kept fidgeting until he found a children's show he liked. I asked the flight attendant for headphones for him. He put it on and got completely lost in his own world. He was very aware that we were on our way back to America and nothing else mattered.

The flight attendant announced that we were about to start our journey to Casablanca and would have a three hour layover before we left for New York afterwards. Then, the plane ran through the tarmac and propelled up into the air.

I let out a long sigh of relief. I looked outside the window and noticed the buildings and trees getting smaller as we continued our ascent. "Thank you, Jehovah." I whispered to myself. I tried to fall asleep, but my mind was very full. Just as I had thought getting our passports back from Ollie was near impossible, so it was now that we were sitting on a plane flying back to America. Six weeks ago, I hadn't envisioned any of this. I was hoping the boys would be making new friends and trying to adjust to life in Freetown. I was supposed to be adjusting too, visiting extended family members and friends, notifying them about my return with my new family in tow, not being the main character in an elaborate, impromptu escape operation. I had escaped from my husband. I had refused to accept the life he had planned for me in Freetown. I had refused to be subjugated. I achieved my freedom, my life now was mine, my family would no longer be the same, but most importantly my boys were free. They would now grow up without ever seeing their dad put his hands on me ever again. They were going back to their own country, with their mother who wanted them to have all the opportunities they could possibly have. When our plane started descending into John F. Kennedy International airport, I noticed the same brilliant lights on the skyscrapers I saw the first time I arrived with Ollie after our wedding. I heard the flight attendant's voice on the speaker asking us to put on our seatbelts and prepare for landing.

Sankara heard the announcement as well. He turned to the back, looked me straight in the eye and said, "Mom, you are a strong woman. Thank you for bringing us back to America."

I choked up. It took everything in me not to cry. I rubbed his head, took one of his hands and kissed it. "I told you if anything were to go wrong and if you boys were not happy, I would do everything in my power to change that. All three of you are my world, Sany. I love you guys so much. Thank you for trusting me," I said to him with so much content.

I became anxious about going through customs. The embassy had told me that I might be detained for questioning if Ollie filed a police report that his children had been kidnapped. He said I would be cleared of all wrongdoing eventually, but there was no telling how long I would be detained until the investigation was done. As we exited the plane, we held on to each other. My heart was beating fast, pounding in my chest because of my stress and anxiety. I was nervous and very much afraid, even though the boys were excited and asking me to buy them happy meals from McDonalds.

As I stepped up to the customs officer, I greeted him with a wide grin and handed him all our passports. He asked the boys to each tell him their names. Then he gave each of them a high-five. "Welcome home. It must have been a long journey from Africa even though these three lil guys don't look tired at all," he said as he let us through. I couldn't reply. I couldn't believe he had just let us through, no questions asked. I gathered the boys around me and we all embraced in a small circle and just breathed. We had returned to the life we knew. I had returned to having agency over my own self. I love my beautiful country, Sierra Leone, land of some of the most beautiful beaches, home of the tastiest jollof rice and rosbeef, home of the most beautiful and hospitable people. It's the land of my birth, it molded me, it gave me my essence, my beauty, my identity, but I wanted to return on my own terms. I want to return because I love and miss it dearly, because I want to contribute to its development. I didn't want to be deceived and hoodwinked into returning. I didn't want to be made to stay quiet and stay put by force or by appeasement with my own menial employees tending to my house or my front gate. I didn't want Ollie to decide how and where I was supposed to be happy.

I wanted to be free of him and his control. I wasn't ready to be in an environment entrenched by staunch patriarchy, cultural and institutional long-held beliefs which he was there to take every advantage of. When I decide to return, I want to be able to be part of the solution to dismantle centuries long beliefs of the oppression and subjugation of women be it physical, religious, economic, systemic, social or psychological. I wasn't going to stay back and endure unconscionable maltreatment from my own husband and become part of the statistics of women who are so often and casually told, "na for biya." Those three words are told to women in abusive marriages, 'na for biya' which means endure it, put up with it, without any consideration for the mental and psychological damage to the women. Men aren't told to stop their abuse or shamed for being abusers. They do not bend their heads down in shame and refuse to make eye contact because they abuse women. There is no stigma for them whatsoever! But women are constantly told to endure their abuse. They are told to be careful not to stress their husbands or offend them in any way.

I remember one time when I told a woman on the street just outside our house about my black eye. She replied, "You're lucky, at least your husband only just beats you. Mine hurls abuses at me in front of the whole neighborhood. He tears my clothes off my body to disgrace me, and on top of that he doesn't provide for me and my children. You're lucky my sister, trust me. That's your house over there with the big gate and security, right? Sister, just try not to talk when he talks, act like you don't see or know anything. Even if he has girlfriends, just act like you don't know. You will enjoy your life more that way, sister." I looked at the woman, no more than 31 or 32 years old, already settling for the life of amoral imposition by another and so accepting of her own unfulfilled life. There was no mention of her own desire for her husband to meet her needs and she didn't even think that was something to look forward to.

I didn't respond to her because words failed me. I learned that engaging with people who are close-minded or limited in their thinking only makes one frustrated. If someone had deliberately chosen to follow the status quo and go with the flow of the world around them, their choice should be respected. I didn't have the energy to invest to start reasoning with her to change her perspective. I didn't have the time to tell her that she had the right to want to feel secure, one of a woman's greatest needs. She needed to know she was safe, secure and well provided for. She needed to be engaged in respectful communication, she needed his affection and reassurances. The fact that she didn't think her needs mattered was a turn off for me. All I knew was I did not want to be one of these women. I wanted to return when I could empower women to love and value themselves, boost their psychophysical stability, and with educational empowerment afinancial independence for them.

Until then, I needed to come back to heal myself, to learn to love myself well. Not just learn to love myself, but to learn how to love myself *well*. I needed to teach myself that I mattered too. I needed to not only learn about self-worth, but to understand how it pertains to me and how I let people treat me. I needed my education to put myself in a position of power to make and influence decisions and policies pertaining to women and to have a high earning power, so I would not ever be at the mercy of another person. I needed to return to become more of me, so much more of me that I could choose to give of myself to others in the future without feeling depleted or taken advantage of. And when I return, full of love for myself, I would look back at my journey and be proud of the woman I have become.

www.ingramcontent.com/pod-product-compliance
Lightning Source LLC
Chambersburg PA
CBHW071309110426
42743CB00042B/1228